EDUCATION AND THE CRISIS
OF THE FIRST REPUBLIC

BY MICHAEL J. ZEPS

EAST EUROPEAN MONOGRAPHS, BOULDER
DISTRIBUTED BY COLUMBIA UNIVERSITY PRESS, NEW YORK

1987

EAST EUROPEAN MONOGRAPHS, NO. CCXXI

CONTENTS

Chapter 1

THE BACKGROUND

When Maria Theresa declared in 1770 that the schools were a "politic-um" and that the state had an interest in reviewing hiring policies in the primary schools, she was extending claims she had begun to make for the schools almost two decades earlier. The case in question involved a teacher who was also the church sexton. When the offices were combined, de-clared the Empress, the pastor could not fire a person on his authority alone, and if the offices were separate the hiring and firing of the teacher fell to secular authorities alone.[1] The clergy could be forgiven for sup-pressing a smile despite Maria Theresa's brave beginnings in 1752 when she began state supervision of secondary schools and in 1759 when she set up the Court Commission for Studies as the supreme supervisory body for education because elementary schools, where they existed at all, were merely an adjunct of the parish ministry. Schools existed to teach the catechism and to train children's choirs, for which an ability to read was needed. Writing and arithmetic were added. The teacher was a factotum, combining the officers of sexton, sacristan, organist and acolyte with his teaching duties, and school was often held in his house. Parental interest was minimal because school took children away from work on the farm.

Attendance at these rude schools, called Trivialschulen, lasted a merci-fully short time. After two or three years, at the age of ten or so, a division took place based on future employment. Most children went into ap-prenticeships or returned to the farm. A few girls might go on to secondary school at a convent, but not beyond, for higher education was almost exclusively the preserve of the male aristocracy and the commercial middle class.

Secondary education, being more exclusive, was considerably better off, but far from highly developed. Boys entered boarding schools called Gymnasia or Latin Schools where they lived from four to six years. They followed a curriculum in Latin, German, natural science, history, religion, mathematics and sometimes Greek and French. Practically without exception one teacher, oftentimes a priest, taught all subjects to a single class. Religious orders ran most secondary schools, particularly the Piarists and the Jesuits until their suppression in 1773. Even afterwards, many Jesuits stayed on to teach as diocesan priests. The Jesuits trained their teachers according to a classical course of studies called the Ratio Studorium, which was generally better than the training of the Piarists. The Jesuits also had an advantage over the Piarists in larger endowments which allowed them to admit poorer students, but in the course of the 18th century tuition came to be charged in most places making the schools more elite than before.

Graduation from a gymnasium did not automatically entitle a person to enter the university as it does now. Another two-year course of broadly philosophical studies which included mathematics and natural science was required before taking an entrance examination.

The University consisted of only four schools: Philosophy, Theology, Medicine and Law. The "faculties," as they were called, of Theology and Philosophy were under church control while Medicine and Law had won a measure of independence over the centuries despite the prominence of Canon Law in the Faculty of Law. Involving the issue of academic freedom more than in primary and secondary schools, the development of universities and technical colleges forms an area of study that goes beyond the interest of this work.

For a number of reasons there was little alarm among churchmen when Maria Theresa declared the schools a politicum. The Empress had proven her loyalty to the Catholic Church many times over, and the symbiotic relationship between church and state inherited from the Counterreformation still possessed vitality. The church was heavily represented at court and clerics sat on all educational committees. The schools, moreover, were not so highly developed that leading churchmen had any great interest in a particular set of policies. Finally, the bishops were loyal nominees of the Crown. The Habsburg ruler down to the end of the monarchy had the ancient personal right to name bishops to vacant sees for confirmation by Rome.[2]

Conditions changed dramatically in 1780 when Joseph II succeeded his mother. Fifteen years earlier, when he was named co-ruler with his mother he began to argue that the church was a stagnant, hypertrophied institution that prevented modernization of Austria and had become untrue to its own ideals of service. Centrally located monasteries of sedentary contemplatives were filled while the scattered peasantry lacked parish churches and schools to meet their needs. On his own authority Joseph closed many monasteries to provide priests and nuns for directly ministerial work. Their extensive lands were sold, often at unfavorable prices, to form a Religion Fund for the support of apostolic activities while the remaining great monasteries were forced to support a number of new parishes with money and manpower. Every parish was to have a school.

Education underwent intense reform activity in administration, curriculum and pedagogy. Joseph joined his mother in exerting fuller control over education with the General School Code of 1774 and added some innovations of his own. Perhaps the most imaginative was the Hauptschule. Perceiving a need for centralized academic training in disciplines related to the economic and cultural life of the population at large, he transformed many of the four-year Gymnasia into schools that stressed vocational training and German culture rather than the humanities and Latin. Another new school was the Realschule, an advanced technical school roughly parallel to the Gymnasium that offered theoretical preparation for successful performance in a trade. Dreamer that Joseph was, his reach exceeded his grasp when he ordered compulsory education for all children between the ages of six and twelve. The government simply did not have the resources available in money or manpower to enforce the law. Efforts that were made encountered resistence from parents and eastern magnates who resented the loss of help around the farm or the estate and failed entirely when the government was forced to charge tuition.

The Political Consitution of the Schools passed in 1806 after Joseph's death restored church supervision. In addition it accommodated opponents of Joseph's policy by setting extremely low minimum standards for success in school. Metternich went along with the reaction throughout his long tenure in office. Still, the work of Joseph II was not entirely undone.

The Hauptschule and Realschule remained in existence, and the law on compulsory education stayed on the books to inspire an increase from around 4,000 schools in the crown lands when Joseph died to 18,000 in 1847, a number unsurpassed as late as 1936.[3] The increase in quantity provided at least the raw materials for later improvement in quality.

The year 1848 is memorable for developments in church-state relations and eduation as well as for revolution. The bishops early on caught the liberal spirit and used it to dismantle Josephinism still further, but when the revolutionaries began to whittle away at both absolutism and the hierarchical values cherished by the church, the bishops rallied to the ruling house against the new heresies of republicanism, nationalism and liberalism. They were faced with a coalition of Josephinists and liberals united not by religion—the liberals in their extreme moments advocated complete separation of church and state—but by a common concern for the absolute sovereignty of the state apparently being conceded to the bishops by the Habsburgs.

For the moment the bishops held the high cards. They met for nearly two months in 1849 to present their ideas to the government knowing that the Habsburgs were desperate. Their demands that the state recognize church independence in matters of religious practice were met, but beyond that, the paucity of ideas was shocking. They could only reformulate the principles of 1806 despite the crying need to reform education, and a government accounting on administering the religion funds so confused them that they agreed to let the state continue handling church finances.[4]

It was especially lamentable that the church could not cooperate with liberals to reform education. The reformers were well-known both for their model views on state sponsorship of education and for their moderation on religion. The document they came up with in 1848 while the liberals were in power called the Fundamentals of Public Education in Austria gave the church ample representation on local school boards, but the bishops wanted control, not reform. Overall control of education by the state was anathema; it was a reversion to the Josephinism they had escaped in 1806. They were not moved at all by the pathetic quality of the schools. The aristocratic bishops thereby betrayed a preoccupation with power rather than a concern for the intellectual and social developments of the time. When the revolution was put down by force they found it unnecessary to make any concessions, particularly in the primary schools where their control was strongest.

But the need for reform was so patent that even in defeat the liberal reform commission was allowed to continue its work of adapting secondary education to modern needs. The document it produced, An Outline for the Organization of Gymnasia and Realschulen published in July 1849, remains the basis for the organization of the secondary schools in Austria after nearly a century and a half. The gymnasia became eight-year schools rather than six by incorporating the two-year preparatory course for the entrance into the university. Successful completion of the final comprehensive examination called the Reifeprüfung or Matura entitled the graduate to enter the University without an entrance examination. This created an integrated system of gymnasia and universities that gave the higher institutions a significant interest in the quality of secondary education. The Realschule became a six-year school without Latin that prepared students for the technical colleges that were beginning to appear.

The government was anxious to include religious education in efforts at reform, but the bishops were reluctant partners. The Education Ministry repeatedly criticized the content of religion courses and the emphasis on memorization, but their pleas were met with hostility and accusations of interfering in church affairs. The bishops were content with a preamble to the *Outline* stating that the goal of secondary education was the moral and religious development of the student without updating their views on what that involved.[5]

The Concordat of 1855 confirmed the triumph of the Church in all particulars. The School Constitution of 1806 with its minimal tests for competency on the primary level was reaffirmed as were customary church control over the doctrinal content of religion courses and a veto over selection of teachers for Catholic religious doctrine. All teachers in Catholic gymnasia had to be Catholic, and all teachers in Catholic primary schools were subject to church supervision. Protestant and Jewish schools begun by Joseph II survived intact.[6]

The specifics of the Concordat were less important than the issue of sovereignty. As a state treaty between the Holy See and the Austrian Crown, the Concordat regulated a series of contractual arrangements between Catholic Austrians and the Austrian government. It tied the hands of the government in important internal dealings with Austrian citizens by forcing it to go through church authorities when the issue involved something covered in the terms. Church authorities in turn were responsible to Rome which implied a loss of sovereignty for Austria. The Concordat was part of the Austrian constitution broadly speaking which could not be altered in sovereign fashion by the Austrians themselves. No wonder that liberals and Josephinists were united in opposition; sovereignty was of highest importance to both. Luckily for them, the Concordat appeared in Austria as an imperial edict which enabled them to use the doctrine of popular sovereignty to force the Emperor to rescind it unilaterally without consulting the pope. The Austrian state, taking on a life of its own, was slowly rousing itself to oppose both church and monarch.

First to crack was the monarchy. The system of neo-absolutist centralism suffered a severe blow when Austria lost to France in 1859 at Magenta and Solferino. The church for the moment lost none of its control over the schools, but the Education Ministry was demoted to a department in the Ministry of State, and a new Educational Council (Unterrichtsrat) had only consultative duties as federalists won more autonomy for the provinces. The schools were most affected when the financial burden devolved upon provincial and local governments. There were some improvements as a result.[7]

The federalism of 1860 was reversed in 1867 at the same time Austria and Hungary became the Dual Monarchy, but not to the advantage of either monarchy or church. Hungary henceforth regulated domestic affairs by itself, which enabled the German liberals in the Austrian Reichsrat to create a Constitution. (Staatsgrundgesetz) more to their own liking. The principle of popular sovereignty formed the basis of their efforts, while other ideas rooted in faith in science, progress and a value-free approach to the problems of human life also influenced their work. Education was all-important to the success of their endeavors, and they resolved to regain control of primary education from the church. The liberals, however, found themselves divided into two major camps on the question of religion in the schools which required a compromise in order to assert the doctrine of popular sovereignty successfully against the Concordat of 1855. The Liberals in the Chamber of Deputies, many of whom were agnostics or even atheists, needed the support of the Josephinists in the House of Lords who thought religious education was a necessary part of forming responsible citizens. They came together in opposition to church and monarchy with a plan for centralized control of education and reduction of church influence in the schools.

During the summer and fall of 1867, it became clear that the liberals intended to reject the Concordat and that Franz Joseph had no choice but to acquiesce. The Minister of Justice Edouard Herbst declared that the state could not give up its power over education to an "independent power" and shrugged off violations of the Concordat by saying that conditions had made the Concordat obsolete.[8] Herbst found himself on shakier ground when he articulated the principle of equality before the law regardless of religion because most liberals had no intention of separating church and state or of unilaterally restricting the authority of the state to regulate religious organizations as it would any other body of Austrian citizens. They much preferred the evil that they knew to the imponderables of complete religious freedom, and they agreed to favor some religions with recognition by the state together with paying the salaries of clerics. They made a nod in the direction of freedom of conscience by saying anyone could worship in private as he wished but a religious organization had to be legally recognized to conduct public services or proselytize. Even irreligious liberals did not want Muslims or Baptists disturbing the serenity of Austria or making claims on the state for financial support.

Another reason the liberals did not want to separate church and state was that they now had a say in naming Catholic bishops through their control of the Emperor. The government could make sure that bishops were not nationalists, federalists or sympathetic to social revolutionary causes. Within a few years the value of retaining the right was shown when Rome wanted archbishops in Vienna who would have fought the government on the school issue. The appointments were blocked, and opposition ended up coming from the provinces while Vienna remained calm. Two archbishops of Vienna later voted with the liberal Constitution Party in the House of Lords on most occasions.

The wrangling in the summer and fall of 1867 included four major participants; most directly involved were the liberals and the bishops while the Emperor and the Holy See in Rome added what they could. As a bellwether to test sentiment in the Chamber of Deputies on the Concordat, Edouard Herbst submitted a proposal to separate church and school. It provoked a sharp letter from Cardinal Joseph Rauscher, the former tutor of Franz Joseph, to the Emperor equating the attack with opposition to religion itself. The government then tried to slip around behind the bishops by approaching Rome on the possibility of concessions in the areas of mixed marriages, divorce, and marriage of former clerics in return for saving the school provisions of the Concordat. There were hopes that the Holy See would prove conciliatory, but when the bishops assembled to defend the Concordat by suggesting a separation of church-state relations from the basic rights of citizens in the Constitution they polarized both sides. The liberals reacted vehemently, refusing utterly to delete articles from the Constitution on individual rights in religious matters and drafting new legislation on the schools even before the Constitution had passed the House of Lords. Pius IX congratulated the bishops on their defense of the Concordat, but when the Austrian government replaced its ambassador with a hardliner whose job it was to inform the Curia that the Concordat could be saved only by making concessions, the pope wavered and eventually expressed a willingness to conduct negotiations.[9]

By that time it was too late because the Emperor had joined the liberals. First he reproved the bishops by pointing out the duties of a constitutional monarch which the liberals interpreted correctly as withdrawal of support for the Concordat. Then he answered Pius IX by saying that he remained a true son of the church though he was no longer able to legislate as he wished. The church might consider dropping impossible claims, he added, in order to save what was possible.[10] The bishops and pope together then turned to defending the particular interests of the church in the schools and in marriage laws not touched directly by the Constitution.

The first of two constitutional documents affecting the church and the schools was the Imperial Representation Law (Reichsvertretungsgesetz) which asserted the right of the Reichsrat to legislate in matters dealing with church and state.[11] It granted the Reichsrat authority to establish the fundamental principles governing gymnasia and elementary schools.[12] This meant that the imperial legislature would not usually take up the details of school legislation and reflected the liberals' desire for subsidiarity even at the risk of encouraging nationalism.[13] The central government could legislate in greater detail if the provincial Diets agreed individually to implement the laws. This legislation became known as "paktiert" because it took effect under a pact between the imperial government and each individual province.

With its competence delineated, the Reichsrat proceeded to publish the principal constitutional law on December 21, 1867 known as the

Fundamental Law of the State (Staatsgrundgesetz). Four articles referred
to the church and education. Article 3 stated that all public offices,
including teaching positions, were open to all citizens; this implied that
Catholic children could be taught by non-Catholics. Article 15 stated
that legally recognized religions had the right to conduct public services,
regulate their own internal affairs and hold endowments. This seemed
to imply that the Catholic Church would eventually manage the Religion
Funds formed earlier by sale of church properties. When it did not happen,
Catholics became bitter at being deprived of the means to establish an
independent, church-supported educational system. Article 17 granted
anyone the right to open a private school as long as it met state requirements, said that the different churches were responsible for religious
instruction in the schools, and that the state possessed the right to direct
and supervise education as a whole.[14] The article that led to the most
debate in the 1920's was Article 14. It stated that no one could be forced
to particpate in a religous service unless he or she was under the legal
power of another.[15]

Though none of the provisions directly violated the Concordat, it was
just a matter of time before legislation derived from the Constitution
broke with it. The Chamber of Deputies had already passed a package
of three laws one of which dealt with church and school, by December,
1867, but passage in the House of Lords involved the old debate about
the merits of Josephinist patronage of the church. Cardinal Rauscher
tried to have the education bill tabled in committee without success.[16]
The Lords agreed only to drop the phrase "without regard to creed"
from the regulations on hiring teachers to accommodate church objections
that Catholic children might by taught by unbelieving teachers.[17] Then,
in a compromise with the Chamber on the matter, one word was added
so that the final text read, "The teaching positions in the schools and
education institutions designated in Paragraph 3 are open *equally* to
all citizens who have proven their competence according to the law.[18]
Seeing that the law was a violation of the Concordat, the bishops withdrew from the House of Lords when it became apparent that the bill
would pass. It was published anyway on May 25, 1868 along with two
others on relations among religious denominations and on civil marriage.
Together they became known as the May Laws and began a Kulturkampf
not unlike that of Germany which broke out three years later.

Much of the law on church and school dealt with the mechanics of returning once again to state supervision of primary and secondary education. It set up provincial, district and local school boards to replace the cumbersome double system that had the church supervising teaching while the state handled the finances. The law put bishops in a bind by providing for representation from religious bodies concerned with the religious education taking place in the schools. The bishops named the representatives, but the nominees had to swear an oath to uphold the law. To do so meant acquiescence in the unilaterial rejection of the Concordat; not to appoint Catholic representatives to the school boards meant that the church was failing to supervise religious eduction.

The bishops were split on the matter. Cardinal Rauscher protested but took the lead in cooperating with the government.[19] The opposition was led by the powerful Cardinal Friedrich Schwarzenberg of Prague and the fiery Franz Rudigier of Linz. Intervention from Rome did not make matters easier for the Austrian bishops because there was enough residual Josephinism among the bishops that they resented the interference of Pius IX.[20] It served rather to split the bishops further by providing a court of appeal for the side that opposed the government.[21] The split became public in September 1868 with an exchange between Rauscher and Schwarzenberg, leading Pius IX to withdraw from the fray. He issued a rescript in February, 1869 leaving the final decision up to the bishops; he conceded that it was admissible to join the school boards to protect religious and moral education, but above all he appealed for unity.[22] Rudigier in Upper Austria persisted in his defiance despite threats to cut his salary,[23] finding support in the Tyrol where efforts to enforce the May Laws were frustrated by both church and provincial authorities until a compromise was worked out in 1892.[24] The situation was bad enough for the bishops to meet in conference between March 2 and 9, 1869. Thirty four bishops agreed that church representation on local school boards was needed to protect local religious eduction, but membership on district and provincial school boards was left open for further discussion.[25]

While the Constitution established principles of state sovereignty and rights of individuals, and the May Laws determined the outlines of relations between church and state in education, many aspects of education still needed attention. Reorganization of the gymnasia in 1849 was adequate for secondary education, but primary education showed the effects of neglect. To remedy these conditions the Education Minister Leopold Hasner and a committee of professional schoolmen prepared a bill to improve the elementary schools.

The liberals, again wary of the reception the bill would receive in the House of Lords, emphasized moderation in questions of religion. Paragraph One set down the goals of primary education, the first of which was moral and religious education. Another paragraph provided for religious instruction should the churches fail to nominate teachers. The liberals were finally able to get the phrase "without regard for religious confession" into a law on hiring teachers for the public schools. Finally, if there was a private school in a locality that was accredited by the state and adequate for the town, the community did not have to erect a new school. This enabled religious orders to maintain their schools without competition from public schools and freed many towns from the burden of financing new schools.[26]

The law, known as the Imperial Primary School Law (Reichsvolksschulgesetz) passed the House of Lords on May 14, 1869 without changes, so well had Hasner and his colleagues done their homework. Opposition came mostly from federalists and nationalists who objected to the central government regulating local schools. Less immediate but more deeply rooted opposition came from the peasantry which saw no reason for extending the period of compulsory schooling from six to eight years. With the backing of the church the farmers continued their agitation for shortening the time until provision was made in 1883 for withdrawing from school after six years.[27]

The improvement in education was quickly noticeable. While 57 per cent of school age children attended school in 1869, the figure stood at 83 per cent in 1883. Army recruits who could read and write their names rose from 45 per cent in 1870 to 67 per cent in 1883.[28] Hiring of teachers proceeded with a view to religious sympathies in most places, which irked the liberals, but Catholics objected that their children were exposed to agnostic teachers in Vienna and Bohemia where liberals were in the ascendant.

Bold though the liberals were in enacting the May Laws and the Primary School Law, they hardly represented a political consensus in Austria. Their vulnerability showed in 1871 when they lost control of the government for more than eight months in a wave of reaction to the unification of Germany. The monarchy, the church, the federalists and the Slavic nationalists all gained at the expense of the liberal German nationalists. Franz Joseph in particular won renewed sympathy among the masses as a counterweight to the German colossus. He improved his standing with the Josephinists by formally repudiating the Concordat at the out-set of the Franco-Prussian War to drive a wedge between them and the liberals. Furthermore, the liberals, by identifying German nationalism with liberalism and state centralism, had alienated the Tyroleans and others who took more pride in their religion and their home province than in their nationality. This prevented the Germans from forming a single voting block.[29]

The period of open reaction to liberal policies lasted only a short time, but when the liberals returned to power under Adolph Auersperg they were chastened by the experience. They could hardly take on all opponents at once, and decided to concentrate on keeping the Empire together by preserving the German character of imperial administration. Auersperg conciliated the church by replacing Leopold Hasner as Education Minister with Josef Stremayr who spent the next four years until Cardinal Rauscher's death trying to reassure him that the government was not hostile to the church. Rauscher bombarded the Education Ministry with letters complaining about the schools and called another ad hoc meeting of the bishops to formulate another appeal to the government, but there was little Stremayr could do considering the amount of local control provided for in the law. Finally in desperation Rauscher began a futile call for a Catholic confessional school system.[30] The faithful saw no reason for it with religion and religious exercises still sponsored by the public schools, and the liberals were absolutely opposed to having the state finance a competing school system when they felt that the existing public schools were dominated by the clergy. For his part, Stremayr had a list of complaints Rauscher found hard to remedy. Tyrol was re-sisting the May Laws, and the church was unwilling to reform religious education. Badly trained religion teachers used poor teaching methods, and the project of revising the catechism had languished since 1860.[31]

One important meeting of minds occured in 1873, however, to clarify the authority of the school to enforce attendance at religious exercises. The state was interested in setting limits on the rights of parents with respect to the authority of the state in the schools, and the church was interested in using the power of the state to require attendance at religious exercises sponsored by the school. Together they approved of a decree by Stremayr that stated, "Schoolmen should not doubt that, when it comes to following the school laws, school children are subject to the authority of the school in this matter."[32] The decree cited the intention of the constitutional lawmakers when they excepted persons under the legal authority of another—school children and convicts were mentioned in the debates—from the constitutional guarantee of freedom of religion.

The government quickly followed this concession with a package of four laws in 1874 to reveal its underlying Josephinist statism. Stremayr said as he introduced the bills dealing with outstanding questions of church and state,

> It is a matter of establishing state influence in church affairs. Contemporary political theory recognizes no other sovereignty in the state than that of the state itself. It counts the church as well only among circles of individuals. The view that the church is as sovereign in its affairs as the state can today be agreed with less than ever.[33]

The protests of Cardinal Schwarzenberg, Count Leo Thun and the pope succeeded in blocking only one of the four laws. The Emperor covered his complicity by saying he had made the last of his concessions to the liberals, but in the next year when Rauscher died and the government nominated Johann Kutschker over the preferences of Pius IX, Franz Joseph promptly made him his personal choice. A functionary in the Education Ministry suspected of Josephinist sympathies, Kutschker was approved by the Vatican without much delay and joined the liberals in the House of Lords to prove that the government's trust had not been misplaced.

With the government's man in Vienna, the impossible task of uniting the bishops fell to Schwarzenberg of Prague. The bishops of Salzburg, Styria and Carinthia were ready to pull their religion teachers out of of the public schools and provide instructions elsewhere, but other bishops were not inclined to follow their lead. Schwarzenberg took up where Rauscher left off, sending complaints to the Education Ministry and finally demanding publicly supported confessional schools. Stremayr delayed and then replied that he was in no position to initiate changes in the school laws.[34]

It was time for the laymen to step in. Speeches by Rauscher to the Archbrotherhood of St. Michael before his death led to the decision to call a general meeting of Catholics from all over the Empire to discuss questions of religious and political interest.[35] This, the first of many Catholic Congresses (Katholikentag), met on May 1-3, 1877. Leo Thun worked closely with the bishops to provide an agenda based on guidelines the bishops had drawn up in the last of their ad hoc meetings on the school question.[36] The Congress was a conference of delegates rather than a mass meeting, despite the presence of 2,300 participants, which met in sections to work out resolutions on six areas of concern passed by the whole assembly at the end. The resolution on the schools concluded that Catholics felt bound in conscience to change the whole system and to oppose efforts to make the schools the responsibility of the state alone. Practical suggestions included restoration of the school funds to the church and freedom to erect publicly supported Catholic schools. Though parts of the resolution dealt with the middle schools, the universities and teacher training, the attack was directed mainly against the public elementary school.

Professions of religious motivation did not conceal other agendas. Conservatives, federalists and nationalists all had parts of their programs included. One item in the resolution on the schools, for example, stated that there should be no attempts to suppress a particular language in a Catholic school. The Congress avoided setting up centralized structures to implement its resolutions. No Catholic school organization was set up for the Empire nor was any publication dedicated to the school struggle. Leo Thun revealed his political motives in a letter to Schwarzenberg in December 1877 when he wrote bluntly that help in preventing the dechristianization of the schools was absolutely out of reach under the Constitution; he proposed a boycott of sessions in the House of Lords as a means of destroying the Constitution.[37] Schwarzenberg wisely demurred.[38]

When the legislative period of the first directly elected Reichsrat ended in 1879, the liberal domination, built as much on divisions within the opposition as on its own strength, ended along with it. The Czechs, who had boycotted parliament in hopes of wrecking the Constitution, gave up some federalistic demands and joined the Reichsrat, and when the

elections of early summer eroded support for the liberals, Franz Joseph
called on Edouard Taafe to form a coalition government of Slavs and
German Catholic-Conservatives. While the cabinet was being formed,
the Bohemian bishops under Schwarzenberg stirred the waters with a
letter asking for changes in the Elementary School Law and threatening
to withdraw their communicants from the public schools.[39] The result
was the opposite the bishops intended when the liberals found out. Instead of a Catholic-Conservative, Taafe appointed an Education Minister
who seemed to be neutral on the question of confessional schools.[40]

With the appointment of Sigismund Conrad von Eybesfeld, Taafe
began a period of compromise involving church and school. The Catholic-
Conservatives tried at first to bluff Taafe with a demand for formal repeal of the school legislation as the price of their support, but when he
refused they concentrated on amending the law to favor the church
and their peasant constituents. The liberals wanted no change but could
not prevent it. The result was frustration on both sides, perhaps worse
among the Catholic-Conservatives and their supporters because the structure
of liberal school legislation remained in place. This led to charges of
hypocrisy and opportunism as the Catholic-Conservatives remained in
the coalition for fourteen years without noticeable changes in the school
system. Taafe accomplished this feat by making it clear that the liberals
were welcome in the coalition should the Catholics defect.[41]

The best Taafe would do for the Catholics was to encourage Conrad
to prepare a bill amending twenty-five paragraphs of the Elementary
School Law. Most reforms dealt with curriculum, organization, rural
school districts, hiring policies and supervision of teachers that had little
to do with religion, and on the whole they show increased a commitment
to education by the government. Money was still a problem, but rather
than saddle the local community with the bills, as in the Elementary
School Law, the law now said that the province was to decide where
financial responsibility lay. Another amendment met criticisms from
peasants that eight years of compulsory school was too much by allowing
exceptions in cases where a child could prove he or she had acquired the
essentials of reading, writing and arithmetic. Though the bishops were
most active in supporting the peasants here, the liberals were not especially opposed; they were even willing to sacrifice the eight year period
if they could keep education from falling into the hands of the Slavic

nationalities and the church. Two liberal deputies introduced bills of their own to reduce the term of compulsory education.[42]

The most controversial amendment was to the paragraph that said teaching positions were open to all without regard for religion. The change provided that the principal should be qualified to teach the religion of the majority of children averaged over the last five years. In practice it meant that the church named candidates for the job of principal and was tantamount to church control over hiring in most places because most schools had only one teacher. The liberals objected with cause that the amendment violated the Constitution, which said that all public offices were open to citizens without regard for religious affiliation, because it put legal restrictions on the promotion of teachers within the civil service system. The Catholics were unmoved. Not having the requisite two-thirds majority to change the Constitution, they relied on the weakness of procedures for judicial review of legislation. A Constitutional Court strengthened by the Constitution of 1920 finally struck down the amendment, but in the meantime it proved to be a convenient compromise which prevented effective agitation for publicly-supported confessional schools while it met the objections of Catholics who could not trust non-Catholics to respect their beliefs. Rudgier responded immediately by calling off his boycot of the school boards.[43]

Before the amendments to the Elementary School Law were passed in 1883, the see of Vienna became vacant once again. Kutschker had played his role well and avoided conflict with the government over the schools. Franz Joseph could blame the liberals for forcing his hand in that appointment, but he could not use the same excuse for the appointment of Cölestin Ganglbauer over Leo XIII's candidate since the conservative victory in the elections of 1879. Ganglbauer, an abbot with a seat in the House of Lords, regularly voted with the Constitution Party and was as determined as Franz Joseph to avoid confrontation with the liberals in Vienna. It was becoming apparent that when the Emperor had to balance political forces in the country including some that were hostile to the church, his right to name bishops no longer served the best interests of the church.

The vacuum of leadership in the church began to be filled by laymen and lower clergy. Kaspar Schwarz, a Viennese physician, founded the Catholic School Association together with a group of laymen to lobby for publicly-supported confessional schools. Until that goal could be reached, it opened private Catholic schools and became a watchdog to defend Paragraph One of the Elementary School Law with its stress on moral-religious education as the goal of the primary schools. The lower clergy became active in the Christian Social movement which attacked the Catholic Conservatives for their failure to represent the church within the government. The issue of Catholic schools became a political football in the process. The goal of a Catholic school system remained nominally one of the top priorities of the Catholic Conservatives leaving them open to the charge of opportunism when the government refused to support the demand, but the Christian Socials used the issue only to woo voters away from the other party. They were realistic enough to know that most Catholics were content with the place of religion in the public schools and would not support a separate Catholic system, publicly-financed or not. Their real position did not become clear until they were in power. Even then they were able to conceal for a time their unwillingness to change the status quo with statements of principle and accusations that the bishops were not united on the subject.

The intramural Catholic struggle over the schools was closely associated with the personal odyssey of Prince Alois Liechtenstein who was chairman of the Catholic Conservative parliamentarians. An abortive proposal in 1880 to change the liberal school laws gave him solid credentials as the leading Catholic Conservative school politician. In 1888 he decided to press the issue of concessions to the church in the schools before the rising tide of nationalism cut into Catholic strength at the polls. He proposed a law that amounted to the re-establishment of the confessional school system with supervisory control exercised jointly by church and state. The bill was calculated to wring concessions from the Taafe government or to force the Catholic Conservatives out of the coalition. Cardinal Franz Schönborn of the Catholic Conservatives came to the rescue of Taafe by going Liechtenstein one further. He insisted on nothing short of complete church control of the publicly-supported confessional school system.[44] This brought any realistic negotiations between the government and Liechtenstein to a standstill, stalling Liechtenstein's bill and another sponsored by the Education Ministry that was probably designed to fail in order to save face for the Catholic Conservatives.[45] Liechtenstein resigned, laid down his mandate from a Catholic

Conservative district of Styria and in 1891 won a seat representing a Christian Social district of suburban Vienna. It was ironic that the party to which he defected was no more interested in Catholic schools than the Catholic Conservatives, but the new party at least provided an outlet for his interest in social questions.

Another forum for the development of Catholic opinion was the Catholic Congress. The Second General Catholic Congress took place in 1888 as a carefully orchestrated attempt to maintain the alliance between the church and the Catholic Conservatives. The only thing new on the schools was to recommend centralized political agitation in favor of confessional schools and endorse the Catholic School Association. It was a meaningless show when Catholic lawmakers refused to support the Liechtenstein bill before the Reichsrat. The Christian Socials were not taken in and resolved to turn the next Catholic Congress into a confrontation with the Catholic Conservatives by adopting a "sharper manner of speaking."[46] The rousing reception given Kaspar Schwarz of the Catholic School Association at the next Congress in 1892 disguised the hesitancy of delegates to make substantial changes in previous demands.[47] The real confrontation came in the meeting over the press. After heated discussion, the assembly passed a resolution calling for a new "independent daily for the Christian people of Austria" to be published daily in Vienna. *Das Vaterland,* owned by aristocrats, now had competition in the *Reichspost* to serve the Catholic cause.

The Christian Socials planned to embarrass the Catholic Conservatives again in the next Catholic Congress scheduled for 1894, but the bishops cancelled the meeting. The Christian Socials then called one for Lower Austria alone, and though the new archbishop of Vienna Anton Grusha did not forbid the congress he boycotted it as a sign of his displeasure.[48] So discomfitted were the bishops and the Catholic Conservatives that they sent a delgation under Cardinal Schönborn to Rome where they complained about disrespect for hierarchical authority among the Christian Socials. The party even welcomed Protestants. Cardinal Rampolla, Papal Secretary of State, heard them out but refused to condemn the movement. This may have been a reason Franz Joseph exercised another ancient Habsburg prerogative and vetoed the election of Rampolla as the successor of Leo XIII.[49]

Franz Joseph and the Catholic Conservatives tried other last ditch efforts to stop the Christian Socials as the democratic movement rolled on. When the Christian Socials in 1895 wrested control of the City Council from the liberals in Vienna the Emperor refused to sanction the election of their flashy and mildly demogogic leader Karl Lueger as mayor. Supported by the Catholic Conservatives, he called for new elections which produced the same result. Franz Joseph survived the setback well enough, but the Catholic Conservatives were devastated. Baron Joseph Dipauli left the Hohenwart Club of conservative parties with nineteen Tyrolean delegates and formed the Catholic People's Party. They were deceived by Christian Social rhetoric into thinking that the new party represented a possible ally in the struggle for confessional schools.[50] Eventually the Emperor was forced to relent and approve the election of Lueger who then remained mayor of Vienna until his death in 1910.

The job of the Christian Socials was to prove that a democratic party could be "kaisertreu" and that a religiously pluralistic political conservatism was possible within the framework of Catholic principles. They accomplished the former without much difficulty with their loyalty to the Constitution, their rejection of the treasonous agitations of Georg von Schoenerer and most significantly with their purge of the feared Social Democrats from city payrolls. Two young teachers among the victims, Karl Seitz and Otto Glöckel, became the mayor of Vienna and the chief socialist school politician respectively in the coming decades.[51] Proving their Catholicity was no more difficult. The Catholic Men's Movement of Heinrich Abel was already a great success in bringing men back to the sacraments, and the party participated actively in the Fourth Catholic Congress held in 1896. It sponsored a resolution that repeated the old shibboleth of a Catholic confessional school system, but this time on the basis of Paragraph One of the Elementary School Law. In deferring to the law, the resolution was merely a face-saving appeal for an unlikely return to co-supervision by church and state.[52] The social program rather than education was at the heart of Christian Social politics.

First to be disappointed by the revelation were the Tyroleans when the Christian Socials faced a major decision as a newly minted national party. It had to do with the language decrees issued by Minister President Casimir Badeni early in 1897. He ordered that in areas of mixed speech in Bohemia all government officials had to conduct business in both German and Czech. Because few Germans bothered to learn Czech while the Czechs had been forced all along to learn German, the decrees meant that most jobs would fall to Czechs. The Germans reacted with fury, German students went on a rampage at the university and the Reichsrat was in turmoil. Badeni needed support badly and offered the Germans of the Alpine provinces a decentralized system of school administration in return for their support. The Christian Socials found themselves in the middle. Baron Dipauli informed Ambros Opitz of the *Reichspost* who huddled with Lueger and Joseph Scheicher, editor of the *Korrespondenzblatt* which served the lower clergy. They decided not to disappoint the Sudeten Germans or the Germans of Vienna for the sake of the schools.[53] This dramatic refusal to subordinate political and national concerns to confessional interests rang the death knell of a Catholic school system. Whether Badeni could have delivered on his promise is moot, but it became evident that the place of religion in education created by the compromises of 1867 and 1869 would endure.

The hesitation of the Christian Socials to identify the party with a confessional issue probably did the church a service in the end. The German liberals and radical nationalists attacked the church vehemently because the Catholic Conservatives supported Badeni, but the position of the Christian Socials weakened their argument. Schoenerer's *Los von Rom* movement had little success in persuading people to leave the church despite the fear it aroused in the church.[54] The party cut itself off from the Slavic nationalities, but given the inroads the nationalistic Young Czechs had already made on the loyalties of Catholic voters in Bohemia, the Christian Socials were losing little while gaining the sympathies of Germans.

As it turned out, the split in the Catholic camp was only temporary. A common attachment to the principle of private property confirmed by Leo XIII in *Rerum Novarum* made possible the ultimate unification of landowning aristocrats with middle class artisans and shopkeepers. At the Catholic Congress of 1905 the Jesuit Viktor Kolb made a plea for unity in the face of the *Los von Rom* movement. He made it clear that the church could embrace both political programs. The union took place two years later after Christian Socials and Catholic Conservatives found they could work together in a press club set up by the Congress. The resulting block of 95 German Catholic delegates made the Christian Social Party the largest unit in the Chamber of Deputies.

The second largest party in the Chamber with 87 votes was the Social
Democratic Party which had experienced a meteoric rise since 1889
when Viktor Adler led a group in writing the Hainfeld Program. Drawing
on the accumulated wisdom of the German Social Democratic Party,
the Hainfeld Program echoed the Gotha Program of 1875 in saying that
religion was a person's private concern. This downplayed the official
atheism of marxist doctrine and enabled people with religious beliefs
to vote Social Democratic. Education was so important to the party
that the question of church-state relations was subordinated to a discussion of the schools in the Hainfeld Program.

> In the interest of the future of the working class, obligatory, free
> and secular instruction in the elementary and continuation schools,
> as well as tuition-free accessibility to all institutes of higher learning,
> is absolutely necessary. The necessary precondition for it is the
> separation of church and state and the declaration that religion
> is a private matter.[55]

Values in education were to be the secular ones of tolerance, democracy
and social consciousness. The Hainfeld Program by no means ended
discussion among socialists on the place of religion in the platform, and
the statement was rewritten with more anti-clerical emphasis in 1898,
but in 1901 doubts were expressed about the wisdom of antagonizing the
indifferent with an anti-clerical program.[56]

Despite immense differences on the question of private property,
the Social Democrats and liberals were united on more than just having
Jews as leaders of both. The socialist school program of 1898, which
called for separation of church and school, state control over certifica-
tion of teachers and development of a secular course in morality and
justice, appealed enough to the Freemasons that they joined the socialists in 1905 to form the *Freie Schule,* an organization dedicated to secular-
izing education in the public schools. Compromises were necessary in several areas, and the program contained fewer socialist elements than the
party platform, but total unanimity was found in opposing mandatory
religious exercises in the schools.[57] A key figure in forming the *Freie
Schule* and keeping social liberal values uppermost in socialist school
politics was Otto Glöckel who consistently avoided the inflammatory

rhetoric of the class struggle despite his total loyalty to the Social Democratic Party.

Glöckel and other school reformers had enough enemies without creating more by using marxist categories. The Catholics were just as united in opposing further concessions as socialists and liberals were in wanting them. It was the socialists' turn to be as frustrated trying to secularize the schools as the Catholics had been trying to rechristianize them. Then there were significant elements in the liberal camp that opposed change, not because they felt threatened by the socialist economic program but because they feared a decline in the quality of education offered at Austrian schools if the socialist program should go through. These men were concentrated in the professoriate at Gymnasia and the universities. Greater numbers would inevitably mean lowering the standards for successful work in the Gymnasia and for entrance into the university. The socialists had trouble answering these charges because they were having trouble persuading working class parents that their children would benefit from more education. All too often parents resented the prospect that their children's achievements might exceed their own, or they simply did not entertain hopes that their children's lives could be better than their own. The socialists therefore faced a three-front war, against the church, the elitist liberals and the inertia of their own supporters.

A critique of the existing system and a solution to the problems was summed up in the plan for the Einheitsschule or unified school.[58] The chief defect of the system was that it forced an irrevocable decision about a state of life upon children of ten years. Either a person entered a Gymnasium or Realschule at that time or finished up elementary education in schools from which one could not transfer to secondary schools. The Hauptschule or advanced elementary school established by Joseph II in urban areas had been renamed Bürgerschule by the liberals, but it was still the dead end it was before. In rural areas all eight, or since 1883 oftentimes only six, years were together in a one-room schoolhouse. Since the talents of children were frequently not apparent at the age of ten the socialists suggested strongly that all children should be kept in a unified school for all eight years of compulsory schooling, that is, until the age of 14 or so, and only then should be directed into different tracks. The plan also increased the likelihood of rich and poor children sharing the same schools where democratic values could be taught and social distinctions worn away.

The socialists found few people willing to accept the plan. Liberals and conservatives alike opposed the Einheitsschule, and since the proposal was endorsed by socialists, the Catholics opposed it for fear that the socialists would use whatever influence they gained to advance the cause of secularism.

Instead of reform in root and branch, the government modified the system. Increased need for training in science and modern languages led the liberal Education Minister Gustav Marchet in 1908 to introduce the Realgymnasium and the Reformrealgymnasium, both of which ended with the comprehensive examination that entitled graduates to enter the university. Latin, the all-important prerequisite for acceptance into the university, was taught from the third and the fifth classes respectively. All gymnasia were restricted to boys; a few girls entered girls' Lycees which were parallel and allowed girls to matriculate at the university, but these schools reflected new attitudes among the well-to-do rather than a mass movement to educate women. All the new schools were housed in separate facilities to give the impression of proliferating school types rather than flexibility in education.

The types of schools available after 1908, therefore, were the following. All of them included religious education while the elementary schools also made religious exercises mandatory. These included attendance at Mass, processions and confessions. The *Volksschulen* were elementary schools with from one to eight classes depending on local circumstances. All eight grades might be together in one class in the countryside. The *Bürgerschulen* were elementary schools with three classes taught according to subjects with specialization by teachers. Located in the cities, these schools contained only 5% of the students in 1913.[59] *Teacher training academies* were four year schools predominantly run by the church which trained children from the age of 15 in pedagogical techniques to be used in elementary schools. They provided more general education but without the academic emphasis of the gymnasia. The *Realschulen* were seven year schools which stressed science and technology. Another year had been added since 1849. Closing with a Matura, they trained graduates to enter technical colleges but did not enable them to enter the university because Latin was lacking. The three kinds of gymnasia, *Classical, Real-,* and *Reformreal-,* all provided preparatory work for entrance into the university. *Lycees* were six year schools ending with the Matura, but few graduates went on to study at the University. After 1908 little changed until after World War I. Obstructive nationalists so paralyzed the Reichsrat that essential legislation had to be decreed under Article 14 of the Constitution.

Changes in the episcopacy echoed those of Catholic political parties as aristocrats gave way to administrators. In 1901 the aging archbishop of Vienna Anton Grusha announced the appointment of a coadjutor bishop with the right of succession. Franz Nagl would take office on his death. His successor was Friedrich Piffl, one of the earliest members of the Christian Social movement. Unfortunately for Piffl, the lines between Christian Social and Social Democrat had already hardened to the point where he could do little during his twenty year reign to mediate. Furthermore, the conservative Pius X had replaced the progressive Leo XIII as pope. Piffl's rather rotund appearance did little to dispel an impression of weakness that came more from the circumstances than from personal deficiencies.

The Empire and the monarchy did not survive the First World War. No longer could the church rely on more staunchly Catholic parts of the Empire to form a counterweight to the liberals, nor could the church count on the Habsburgs to support it as best they could. The alliance between the church and the Christian Socials became more important as a consequence. But the Christian Socials, with a new conservative cast that followed amalgamation with the Catholic Conservatives in 1907, needed the church as well to oppose the threat of revolution at the close of the war. In the uneasy times that formed the decade and a half of the First Republic, church and party were thrown together, each clutching the other against the onslaught of the Social Democrats.

Chapter 2

SCHOOL POLITICS AND THE
CONSTITUTION OF 1920

Austria in 1918, though defeated, starving and freezing, stripped of its chief agricultural and industrial areas, and reduced to a rump state of 6 1/2 million people nonetheless found considerable reservoirs of energy to invest in the cultural struggle while attempting to define its constitutional life. The major tasks of the provisional governments were to make peace with the Allies and to write a constitution. As it turned out, the first was out of their hands when the Austrian delegation at Paris was left in its hotel while the Allies drew up a peace treaty. While the Treaty of St. Germain determined the broad outlines of Austrian politics in the postwar era, it gave the Austrians considerable freedom to arrange their domestic affairs so that the Constitution of 1920 was by and large a product of Austrian tradition and the political forces operative at the time. The tensions that accompanied writing a constitution and governing in the meantime were traceable less to revolutionary activities on the left or right as in other countries than to the legacies of nationalism and religious strife inherited from the Empire. The enmity between socialism and capitalism especially proved illusory when starvation forced Austrians of every economic persuasion to unite; Social Democrats and Christian Socials differed on many issues, but they united to approve agreements with Czechoslovakia to obtain sugar and coal and agreed that expropriation would only make the economic situation worse.

The Renner-Beneš agreement of January 1920 and the Treaty of Lana were signed at the expense of agreeing to abide by the Treaty of St. Germain with particular reference to the article against seeking political union with Germany. It was painful for the majority of Austrians who were obsessed with the apocalyptic notion that economic survival was possible only if Austria became part of the German Reich. The dream of Anschluss faded when Austrians realized that the Allies had no intention of allowing the principle of self-determination to apply to their case, but Anschluss remained the chief ingredient in the despairing sentiment for revising the Treaty of St. Germain.

Effects of the Treaty and the agreements with the Czechs were especially devastating on German nationalists. Opinion favoring Anschluss was strongest between 1918 and 1920 when despair was the greatest, but economic realities, the attitude of the Allies and the paradoxical need to form a strong parliamentary Pan-German Party with ineluctable responsibilities for building a state to go with achieving Anschluss left nationalists confused and incapable of taking a united stand on much of anything during the period. Nationalism was without doubt the most widely shared set of ideological principles in Austria, but its chief influence on writing the constitution came with attempts to keep Austrian legislation compatible with that of Germany to facilitate smooth incorporation into the Reich when the time came. The nationalists for the time being left the cultural struggle to the socialists and Catholics.

The conflict that endured essentially unchanged from the Empire to leave a major scar on the Constitution of 1920 was the controversy over the role of religion and the Catholic Church in Austrian marriage legislation and the schools. Divorce, civil remarriage and religious education were extremely volatile issues that resisted the unifying effects of the economic crisis even as they were almost free from Allied interference. This curious combination of circumstances therefore provided a forum for emphasizing political differences even as it offered prospects for partisan political victories. Anticlericals could compensate for national or economic disappointments by pushing the church farther out of public life as had happened in 1867. Catholics, too, could still hope to defeat liberalism and socialism in a replay of the Counterreformation.

The church-state controversy divided Austria more than any other issue in the crucial years of writing the constitution. Greater issues of nationalism and reconstruction were too closely regulated by international forces to allow advocates of one system or other to exert a preponderant influence in writing the constitution, but the battle between Catholics and secularizers continued with vehemence. The Constitution of 1920 became a monument to the struggle when it was adopted without articles regulating church-state relations and with an especially prominent gap on the distribution of authority in the schools between the federal government and the provinces which did little to disguise the fact that the basic conflict was over religious education.

The work of 1920 was never completed. After much wrangling, and in the sober aftermath of the riots in 1927, two school laws were passed with the two-thirds majority needed for a constitutional amendment. The laws formed the basis for school legislation in the Second Republic, but the controversy refused to die. Another bill regulating the schools was passed in 1962, again with a two-thirds majority because no constitutional provision allowed legislation by simple majority. Indeed, the parties have become so jealous of the issue that at the time of this writing any law dealing with primary or secondary schools requires the same two-thirds majority needed for a constitutional amendment. Since 1920 all attempts to reform primary or secondary education have been constitutional questions not in the broad sense that a law might or might not be constitutional, but in the narrow sense that every law itself, unless passed in identical form by each individual provincial legislature, is the equivalent of a constitutional law.

II

When it became evident that the Austro-Hungarian Empire would dissolve in 1918, the three political camps in German-Austria were in varying states of readiness for a republic. The nationalists were an array of more than a dozen splinter parties which did not unite to form the Pan-German Party until work on the Constitution was finished. Even then a Peasants Party maintained its independence despite sharing many of the Pan-German attitudes. The Social Democrats were the foremost republicans if independence were forced on Austria. The Christian

Socials found themselves free to choose between the monarchy and a republic because they had consistently endorsed the compatibility of monarchy and democracy. Shortly before Emperor Karl stepped down, the Christian Social spokesman in the Provisional National Assembly declared, "While maintaining their fundamental loyalty to the monarchial form of government, the Christian Social deputies will work for the democratization of German-Austria."[1] This opened them to charges that they were lukewarm toward the Republic. The Austrian bishops did not help matters much by taking a stand as recently as August 1918 against "that false body of ideas such as 'popular sovereignty, majority rule [and] self-determination of nations'."[2] They retreated to support the Christian Social position in early November, but as late as the day before Emperor Karl left the country, Cardinal Piffl of Vienna along with Dr. Ignaz Seipel, the prominent priest-deputy, was soliciting support for the monarchy from the Christian Socials. Within hours they were persuaded that the dynasty could not be saved, and Piffl hurriedly tried to redeem himself by addressing a letter to the clergy of his archdiocese on November 12 ordering them to support the new government.[3] Collectively the bishops tried to make up for their hesitancy with a pastoral letter in January 1919 justifying the republic with citations from St. Thomas Aquinas.[4]

The Provisional Government before the elections of February 1919 for a National Constituent Assembly was a coalition of sorts between the Social Democrats and Christian Socials. Karl Renner of the Social Democrats took the title of Chancellor. The parties agreed not to attack each other publicly and to resolve important issues in a bipartisan committee. Both had reason to fear a bolshevik revolution, especially when Hungary to the east and Bavaria to the north set up short-lived soviet republics. A Communist party came into existence in Austria, but Freidrich Adler and the left wing of the Social Democrats refused to collaborate with it.

Both major parties were careful to avoid overt confrontations during the campaign of early 1919. With reference to cultural and religious issues neither party hinted that the schools would soon be a major object of contention. The Christian Socials restricted themselves to their customary emphasis on Paragraph 1 of the Elementary School Law which defined the goal of the schools as "moral-religious education." The Social Democrats were somewhat bolder in calling for freedom of conscience and "free" schools, but did not suggest a practical program. The party was following the outline contained in Otto Glöckel's pamphlet of 1917 entitled *The Portal of the Future* which defined the free school as at very least independent of church influence. Glöckel's ultimate goal was a secular, unified school of eight grades in which all children regardless of social background would study together during the eight years of compulsory education without being broken up into groups after five grades when the gymnasia skimmed off various social and academic elites. For the time being, however, problems of food and fuel pushed such questions into the background.

In other matters there was enough agreement that the business of state-building could proceed. Both parties and the loose association of Pan-Germans agreed on a republican form of government based on democratic principles, the right of the people to decide civil, social and cultural issues, the right of women to vote, and the need to reorganize the ministries of state. The Social Democrats in addition called for legislation to protect workers, a social security system, and political union with Germany without meeting opposition from the Christian Socials. Though the Social Democrats wanted to nationalize large industries and break up the great landed estates, they were realistic enough not to oppose the Christian Socials on retaining a capitalist economic system. As Karl Renner said, "One cannot socialize debts."[5] The socialists vigorously opposed many provincial Christian Socials who wanted a high degree of federalism in the new Austria, but the Christian Socials were themselves divided on the issue. The Viennese Christian Socials, for example, were moderately centralist rather than federalist at all. In the balance, therefore, the Christian Socials were silent on a number of issues of interest to the Social Democrats while the socialists opposed in a general way some political goals of secondary importance to many Christian Socials.

The bishops were less restrained in the campaign than the Christian Socials. They lived in dread that a new Kulturkampf like that of the 1860's would begin after the war.[6] The same pastoral letter of January 1919 that endorsed the Republic contained the injunction, "Whoever casts his vote for agnostic or anti-church representatives shares in committing public sin. Every Catholic has a public religious duty to cast his vote in a Catholic spirit."[7] The bishops, it seemed, were relying on the Christian Socials in politics without much debate, though Piffl complained in the privacy of the Bishops Conference that much of what came under the term Christian Social was no longer Christian.[8]

Despite the warning, many Catholics voted for Social Democrats to make them the largest delegation in the Constituent Assembly with seventy-two seats. The Christian Socials were not far behind with sixty-nine while the German national parties claimed twenty-six seats.[9] Pan-German reluctance to cooperate in forming a new state originated not only in a fixation on Anschluss but also in deep misgivings about basic attitudes in both the major parties. The economics and social leveling of the Social Democrats were as distasteful to them as Catholic influence in the cultural politics of the Christian Socials. It appeared that the only alternative for Austria at the moment was a coalition of the two major parties.

Besides the main business of writing a constitution, the Constituent Assembly had the tasks of maintaining order and concluding a peace treaty with the Allies. The chaotic conditions prevented formation of a government for an entire month after the elections, but the Social Democrats found a way to use the time by formulating plans to trim the ministries of state from fourteen to nine. The Ministry of Public Worship and Instruction was one of those abolished on a provisional basis. In a peculiar move, the offices of Public Worship and Instruction were assigned to separate undersecretaries in the Ministry of the Interior which directed the national police. Chancellor Karl Renner took the Interior portfolio in a wise attempt to concentrate the meager executive power of the government which made him the superior of both undersecretaries. Wilhelm Miklas of the Christian Socials became Undersecretary for Public Worship and Otto Glöckel became Undersecretary for Instruction. Separation of religion from education in the government was an obvious move in the direction of separating church and state, but divisions among the Christian Socials prevented them from registering a strong protest. They recognized as well that the move did not represent any definitive reorganization.

More ominously, the socialists published an action program which departed from the moderation of the campaign to endorse acceptance of existing German marriage law, free education for each according to his abilities, and abolition of any state compulsion in the area of religious eduction.[10] The new program was an open challenge to the church, but there is little evidence that the bishops or the Christian Socials objected to the sharp change of direction. Cardinal Piffl merely asked for representation on the permanent council for education being planned.[11] Had the Christian Socials or the bishops protested vigorously at the time, they would have alerted the Social Democrats to the possible consequences of engaging in a Kulturkampf as part of the political revolution, and the conditions of the coalition that followed would have been clear from the start. The Christian Socials were therefore ignoring provocations in religious and cultural affairs when they agreed to join the "black-red" coalition on March 14, 1919. There was only an informal understanding that cultural questions were not to arise.

Part of the reason the party did not object was that the Christian Socials were in considerable disarray at the moment. They were united on matters of religion and the preservation of private property, but otherwise they were riddled by disagreements. Many were federalists, some particularists or even secessionists like the Vorarlbergers who voted to join Switzerland. Most were concerned about provincial or local problems rather than national ones. A monarchist wing interested in a restoration did not want to cooperate with republicans, but like the German nationalists, most Christian Social voters looked away from Vienna toward Berlin. In unauthorized plebiscites the heavily Catholic provinces of Tyrol and Salzburg voted for Anschluss by almost ten to one.[12]

The grand coalition lasted fifteen crucial months while the peace treaty and the constitution were being drafted. The government contained six Social Democrats to three Christian Socials, not because the socialists were making a grab for power but because they alone were willing to accept responsibility for the immense problems facing the country in matters of finance and nutrition. If they were not enthusiastic about the future, at least they did not have an interest in proving that Austria could not survive, so they governed more or less by default. Their willingness to hold offices that offered few prospects for partisan victories had as its corollary a tendency to consider the Social Democratic Party the sole representative of the nation. It was their misfortune along with that of Austria that they often ignored the proprieties of coalition government to alienate the Christian Socials in time.

The two great adversaries of the First Republic, the priest Ignaz Seipel and Otto Bauer, the marxist intellectual, found themselves squared off against each other from the beginning on the Committee on Socialization. The first round of their contest went to Seipel when the committee stopped far short of expropriating the capitalists in the country.

Another step towards the separation of church and state involved a decision on relinquishing the centuries-old right of the Habsburgs to name bishops for confirmation by Rome. The socialists had the courage of their convictions in March 1919 when the government unilaterally gave up the privilege.[13] It was doubtful that a republican government could have kept the privilege in any case because the church claimed it was a personal prerogative of the Habsburg emperor, but the hasty initiative of Renner and the party made clear both the timetable and the extent of separation they intended. The right to name bishops might have been useful as a bargaining chip if the socialists wanted to press the church for concessions in the context of a relationship that preserved some of the church's legal status in Austria. Though they could have negotiated for concessions on civil marriage and divorce, for example, they acted rashly and precipitously on secular principles without making a good assessment of their ability to separate church and state by themselves or with the help of anticlericals among the German nationalists.

III

Whatever energy the socialists could spare for the cultural conflict was focussed on the question of compulsory religious exercises as part of religious education. The old controversy pitted Article 14 of the Constitution of 1867 against Paragraph 1 of the Elementary School Law. Article 14 stated that no one was to be compelled to attend religious functions unless he was under the legal authority of another, but it did not distinguish between the legal authority of the school and that of the parents. Paragraph 1 had received consistent ministerial interpretation upholding the right of school authorities to require attendance at both religious instruction and religious exercises but the Social Democrats were unhappy with this exercise of state sovereignty. They believed that parents should have the right to keep their children away from religion class or religious exercises in accordance with their contention that religion was entirely a private matter. No court had sufficient authority to adjudicate the dispute, and the controversy had long since reached a bitter standoff.

The socialists took the step with the most serious consequences for church-state relations on April 10, 1919. The Kulturkampf that followed lasted throughout the First Republic. After discussion among the socialist members of the government exclusively, and with the approval of Renner and the highest members of the party, Otto Glöckel as Undersecretary for Instruction decreed that henceforth no child could be compelled to attend religious exercises at public elementary or secondary schools except where provincial law required it. Nor were teachers under any obligation to supervise children at liturgical events.[14] The order meant that school-sponsored masses, confessions and processions, not to mention classroom prayer, were no longer obligatory and that school authorities had no right to compell participation in them. It was a decree with constitutional implications because the Social Democrats, by granting to parents a right that the Christian Socials claimed for the state, were adjudicating the old dispute over whether the school authority possessed a legal right under Article 14 of the old Constitution to require attendance at religious exercises. That it violated Paragraph 1 of the Elementary School Law was clear to the Christian Socials and to Catholics in general, but in the eyes of the socialists, Paragraph 1 was merely a vague preamble inserted in 1869 to assuage fears that the liberals were antireligious.

The Social Democrats expected little protest because no one had raised a voice against their decisions of the last two months. Renner politely notified Piffl before the news became public so that he would not have to read it first in the newspaper.[15] But the Glöckel Decree, as it soon came to be called, caused an immediate reaction and remained a source of bitter contention for fourteen years to the day until Anton Rintelen, the Minister of Instruction in the Dollfuss government, repealed it in a gesture of angry triumphalism. Catholics close to the government were alarmed, and Wilhelm Miklas resigned as Undersecretary for Public Worship. He agreed, however, to delay the announcement for the sake of the coalition.[16]

The decree set off a flurry of activity in the Christian Social parliamentary club. Some deputies from Catholic rural areas objected strongly that the Socialists were violating the understanding that cultural questions were not to arise.[17] Miklas tried to act as mediator by proposing that the Principal Committee (Hauptausschuss) of the Constituent Assembly decide on the legality of the decree, but the socialists recognized that no good could come of a debate under the circumstances and declined the invitation.

It is uncertain exactly what informal assurances Miklas received, but the immediate crisis was over almost as soon as it arose. Both parties knew that it was a bad time for a crisis. On April 17, a demonstration before Parliament turned into a riot in which two persons were killed and thirty-six wounded. Soviet-style governments were in power in Bavaria and Hungary. Even a group of teachers had demonstrated recently after a part-time teacher died of starvation.[18] On the same day Miklas' resignation was made public the *Neue Freie Presse* wrote that the move would not endanger the coalition. Subsequently the Principal Committee refused to accept the resignation and Miklas stayed on.[19]

Not fettered by immediate political concerns, Cardinal Piffl pressed Renner to revoke the decree. He answered Renner's note on April 22 in the name of all the bishops, saying that Catholics regretted the decree deeply, especially the bishops who had a mandate to protect the legal rights of Catholics. He said that the state was exceeding its authority, reminded him that the bishops had caused no trouble when the new state was being erected and warned him that such decrees were not designed to further the interests of the state. He feared worse because the Pan-Germans had recently introduced a motion in the Constituent Assembly to nationalize all the schools, including Catholic private schools, and warned him about the consequences of such a law.[20]

Weaker rumblings continued to come from the Christian Socials. The parliamentary club issued a statement that there was no legal basis for the decree under the Constitution of 1867, that church authorities had not been consulted under the terms of the Elementary School Law, and that the party had not been consulted within the coalition. They warned against repeating the action but stopped short of calling for actual withdrawal of the decree. They added a blanket rejection of the Pan-German motion to nationalize the schools.[21]

Renner took responsibility for the decree, but the inspiration came mostly from Otto Glöckel. Glöckel was a fiery anticlerical who found his way into the Social Democratic Party as a poorly paid young teacher. A social liberal rather than a marxist throughout his life, he avoided the terminology of the class struggle and contributed perhaps more than he knew to making the party moderate and reformist rather than revolutionary. He became the party spokesman for education by 1905, and by the end of World War I he had a comprehensive blueprint for government-sponsored educational reform in which religion had no place. During the heady days of the revolution he proved that the decree was his favorite tool for implementing the program, oblivious to the contrast between his authoritarian methods and his democratic ideals. He never resolved the tension between the purity of his prophetic vision for Austrian education and his status as a national politician called upon to make compromises in a parliamentary system. He served democracy by going into opposition with the rest of the party in 1920 and concentrating on modernizing the schools of Vienna in a democratic spirit, but when the reforms met opposition from national leaders who claimed Glöckel was violating national laws, he fell back on his base of power to defy the government. His record is therefore mixed; while he was one of the best influences on school reform, he was one of the worst influences on polarizing Austrian political life between the wars. He participated as a full contributor to the tragedy of the First Republic, tainted as so many others by the degree of ideological emphasis he brought to the struggle.[22]

Glöckel was somewhat chastened by the storm of opposition he had loosed, although he did not issue any explanation that might have mitigated the force of the decree. Miklas later said that Glöckel and the Cardinal had patched up the matter behind the scenes and that Glöckel was under pressure from radical teachers.[23] Glöckel indeed passed over the issue of religion in response to a commendation from the anticlerical school organization Freie Schule by emphasizing other aspects of the reform.[24] Three days later he named Ignaz Seipel an honorary professor at the University of Vienna with the right to teach moral theology and social science.[25] He quietly presented an outline for school reform on April 24 which the Social Democrats and Christian Socials together used as an excuse to kill the Pan-German motion to nationalize the schools. For the time being, Glöckel found himself in an embarrassing position, unable either to implement or rescind the decree while Catholics took it as proof that school reform was exclusively a socialist project. Piffl and high ranking Christian Socials joined a mass meeting of Catholics on April 27 to hear attacks on Glöckel and school reform.[26]

Renner replied to Piffl's letter in early May with weak legal arguments. He tried to blur the distinction between compulsory schools and compulsory school age by saying that children at gymnasia and similar secondary schools could not be compelled to attend religious exercises because the schools were not compulsory schools even though the children attending them might be under 14 years of age. He also argued that Tyrol had passed a special law regulating religious exercises which implied that the stipulations of the Elementary School Law were not enough to insure that religious exercises were compulsory.[27] The arguments were pettifoggery, but without a constitution to form the basis for a review or a court system to conduct it, there was no way to judge the merits of Renner's contentions. It was clear that a settlement on the place of religion in the public schools would involve a complicated process of redefining religious relations between church and state.

Piffl saw that the matter could not be pursued further and turned his attention to the proposed school reform. Through a representative he negotiated with Glöckel who promised to respect church sensibilities and not to initiate action against Catholic private or convent schools. He reserved only the customary right of the state to review the credentials of the schools for accreditation.[28] Piffl sent copies of Renner's letter to the other bishops with comments and a warning that the Glöckel Decree might be implemented in some areas. He added with satisfaction that the Christian Social deputies were beginning to defend the church more energetically than before.[29]

The episode concluded so tentatively was one example among several of the way the socialists arrogated to themselves the representation of German-Austrians. Their decision to proceed by fiat assumed a groundswell of support for unilateral actions. It was true that neither the Christian Socials nor the bishops had confronted them earlier, but the socialists presumed on the combination of goodwill and weakness among political Catholics to ignore the danger of alienating them and provoking a reaction. The combination of doctrinaire anticlericalism and political naivete led them to forget that the Christian Socials were fully their equals at using the apparatus of state for different ends. The Social Democrats perceived only the opportunity to initiate secular changes in the schools taking advantage of the chaos without recognizing that the plan involved constitutional relations between church and state rather than a few minor adjustments to an established educational system. The fact that only the socialists were privy to the discussions before the decrees were published smacks of conspiracy, but the openness with which Renner admitted the fact reveals a healthy concern for a modicum of trust among political rivals. It was not disdain for the power of the church but rather an unrealistic view of their capacity to implement the decree that led the socialists to change the customary practice without a fresh legislative basis.

IV

As summer approached in 1919 one set of uncertainties vanished with the arrival of peace terms from Paris. The job of the Austrians was simple—accept them without modification. The conditions, of course, determined the general outlines of the Austrian Constitution: nothing could violate the peace treaty without risking Allied sanctions or even military invasion.

The Treaty of St. Germain contained an article which recognized the right of all inhabitants to practice their religion privately or in public as long as it did not threaten the public order or good morals. This effort by the Allies to protect religious minorities had the effect of undermining the old distinction between legally recognized and unrecognized religions under which the Catholic church had maintained its religious supremacy in Austria. Baptists and Moslems, for example, were now free to worship in public and to win converts.

The article established the foundation for complete freedom of religion but did not itself impose separation of church and state on Austria. There was nothing to prevent the state from paying the salaries of some clergymen and not others, for example. Furthermore, it did not seem to affect the preamble to the Elementary School Law nor did it appear to touch the interpretation of 1873 that said school authorities were legally entitled to require children to attend religious exercises.[30] As a result, the treaty did not put an end to the argument whether parents or the state had a prior right over the religious education of children or form a clear basis on which a Constitutional Court could decide the issue one way or the other.[31]

V

The first government of Austria felt its duties were finished when the peace treaty was ratified on October 17, 1919. When it resigned, the task of writing a constitution remained and another hard winter loomed ahead, which led the parties to renew the grand coalition. This time, the Christian Socials demanded that the conditions be spelled out. The formal agreement stated that relations between church and state would be regulated within the framework of the constitution, disallowing earlier decrees and interpretations.[32] The pointed reference to the Glöckel Decree meant that implementation was now suspended by mutual agreement and that church-state questions would pass to the committee for drafting the constitution led by Michael Mayr of the Christian Socials and Hans Kelsen, an eminent jurist who represented the Social Democratic point of view. The parties then set about formulating proposals.

The Bishops Conference likewise set up a committee in November to discuss constitutional articles. It met only a few times, with the major meeting held on January 27, 1920 at which two sets of articles written by Seipel and Max Hussarek-Heinlein, former Minister President of the Imperial government, were discussed. Seipel was cautious in dealing with relations between church and state because the socialists were almost certain to oppose any paragraphs acceptable to Catholics. Hussarek dealt with relations between church and school as well as church and state in two articles, one which contained ambiguous language on religious exercises in the schools while the other revealed a profound misconception about the Social Democratic Weltanschauung by discussing it in language derived from religion rather than in economic or scientific terms as the socialists preferred.[33] The deliberations apparently had little influence on the final form of the constitution, but the leaders of the Christian Socials continued to meet with Cardinal Piffl every month on other matters.[34] Seipel was also invited to brief the Bishops Conference on the political situation every year until 1926.

The scientific ideal of constitutional thought on the socialist side was best expressed by Hans Kelsen based on his theory of legal positivism. Skepticism about ultimate norms led him to conclude that a constitution could not be "justified" by reference to extralegal norms or metaphysical principles. Only the political process could explain the genesis and binding power of laws, so his ideas did not allow for theories of state sovereignty which rested on anything other than coercive power. The natural law philosophy of the Enlightenment, the Catholic theory of authority delegated by God, and Marxist economics were all equally inadmissable as bases for constitutional rights. It was difficult for him to escape the accusation that ultimately might makes right.[35] He was at his rigorous best when he set out to put commonly accepted rights and duties into the most consistent and correct legal terminology, and when he criticized the vague formulations of 1867.[36]

Kelsen was a lucky find for the Social Democrats because they were far from united on the foundations of civil liberties. Certain fundamentals of liberal belief like the nature of man and the sovereignty of the state were so widespread in society that some aspects of marxism disturbed party unity rather than provide an ideological focal point for a mass movement. Otto Bauer, the chief Austro-Marxist theoretician, drew elements from Kantian philosophy to modify the materialistic determinism of Marx but succeeded only in providing a theoretical basis for courses of action already decided upon. He concurred with Kelsen in rejecting natural law, but had difficulty finding more than limited acceptance by 1920. Austrian socialists, like all others in Europe, faced the complicated decision of whether to follow the lead of Lenin whose successful revolution spawned Communist cadres throughout the continent hopeful of repeating the Russian phenomenon. The doctrinal uncertainty among thinking Social Democrats that resulted forced them to fall back on the list of rights and duties inherited from the liberals of 1867. Their leaders were sure only that they rejected God as a source of authority in the state and that they stood for democracy. They were quite unprepared for a thorough discussion of civil liberties that went beyond this. Furthermore, they could expect opposition from the Christian Socials if they tried to restrict the role of religion more than the Constitution of 1867.

The Christian Socials had less difficulty deciding that civil rights and duties could not be reviewed. The drift from Josephinism and religious indifference among the liberals to active hostility among the socialists was obvious. The prospects for fanatical resistance from Social Democrats to any revision of the Constitution of 1867 inspired by religion was also clear. The result was a decision as early as January 1920 to "hold all bastions" in relations between church and state and in cultural politics. By tacit consent, therefore, both the Social Democrats and the Christian Socials agreed not to include a new bill of rights in the Constitution or to engage in a fundamental discussion of church and state. The Christian Socials found encouragement to hold the line on religion when they detected a swing away from the Social Democrats among the voters in early 1920. Seipel openly looked forward to gains in the next elections though they were not scheduled for another year.[37]

A combination of growing anger at the highhandedness of the Social Democrats and hopes for more seats should elections be held earlier than scheduled led the Christian Socials into more active opposition even at the risk of destroying the coalition. The threat made the task of writing a constitution more urgent lest the constitution be unfinished when the final break with the socialists came. Accordingly Seipel goaded the Constituent Assembly to hasten its work. He was prompted also by jealousy over the status of the central government since the provinces began meeting to discuss the constitution without inviting the government to send representatives.[38] Seipel's fear took form in June 1920 when the coalition collapsed well before the constitution was finished. The occasion involved another unilateral move by the socialists, this one dealing with military organization, which the Christian Socials claimed violated the terms of the coalition. Austria suddenly found itself in the precarious position of having no governing majority in the Constituent Assembly while it lacked constitutional procedures to provide for orderly elections.

It was a dangerous moment, but the essential moderation of both major parties made the crisis pass. They agreed to oppose the forces of revolution by forming a caretaker government in which each party would take responsibility only for the actions of its own ministers. These were to be restricted to administrative functions as much as possible. The parties moved up the date for new elections to October 17, which meant that work on the constitution had to be finished or fresh problems would arise because it was unlikely that the Christian Socials could win enough seats to rule by themselves. Middle-level government officials, among them Otto Glöckel, remained at their posts. Evidence of the dampening effect on school reform is provided by the fact that only five of sixty-seven major decrees were issued after the coalition collapsed, none of them containing innovations.[39]

The political parties presented drafts of a constitution to the Constituent Assembly within a month. Despite federalism in the party, the Christian Socials went a long way to accommodate socialist wishes for a strong central government based on an omnicompetent parliament. Indeed, the price leaders like Seipel and Mayr paid to prevent excessive diffusion of political power stopped little short of parliamentary absolutism. The Federal President became a figurehead. The upper chamber or Bundesrat drawn from the Provinces had only a suspensive veto over legislation. The lower chamber or Nationalrat, through the usual parliamentary devices of interpellation and no-confidence, could check a government or turn it out of office. The electorate did not enjoy the rights of referendum, recall or initiative. As a result, the Chancellor and the Executive proved to be weak. Seipel, who was Chancellor longer than anyone else during the following decade, became progressively disgusted with the inability of the government to enforce its interpretation of the laws and finally persuaded the Nationalrat to increase its authority by constitutional amendment in 1929.

One advance in the separation of powers came by granting the Constitutional Court considerable power to review legislation. In practice, though, the court hesitated to strike down laws or render authoritative interpretations during the First Republic. Not only were such judgements redolent of past "arbitrary" government, but the powers were something of a novelty whose lack of status implied that they could be curtailed with relative ease by the legislature. During the school controversy therefore, the Constitutional Court avoided the main issue of parents' rights versus the rights of the state at the same time the United States Supreme Court was resolving a bitter dispute in the Oregon school case by deciding that parents rather than the state have the first right to educate their children. When the Constitutional Court handed down important decisions in cases dealing with religion, it cited the Treaty of St. Germain rather than the Constitutions of 1867 and 1920.

Negotiations among the parties on the drafts took place mostly in a sub-committee of the Constitutional Committee. The subcommittee compared the outlines point for point, reached agreement on some, and decided to abide by the majority in the Constituent Assembly on others. There were, however, four series of issues on which the subcommittee found itself so divided that it had to designate special committees. When they could reach no compromise on three of these, the Constitution passed the full assembly on October 1, 1920 with three lacunae. The Constitutent Assembly tried to plug the gaps provisionally with a Transitional Law (Verfassungsübergangsgesetz) which provided that all three should be regulated later on by laws with the status of constitutional amendments. In the meantime, the laws of the monarchy would continue in force. Two of the three gaps, dealing with financial and administrative relations between the federal government and the provinces, were filled in the course of the next five years by constitutional amendments.

The area of irreconcilable differences was in relations between church and school. The technicalities of a federalistic constitution veiled the question thinly as a political problem of distributing authority over the schools between the federal and provincial governments.[40] Lack of agreement meant that all the old laws remained in force along with their unresolved conflicts. Two other provisions, one from the Constitution of 1867 and one from an earlier law of 1862, also stayed in force requiring the so-called "paktiert" legislation. Under this unworkable system, identical bills had to pass each provincial legislature as well as the Nationalrat if a law were to apply throughout Austria. Prospects for getting jealous provincial legislatures to agree to any law were extremely slim even before socialist Vienna became a separate province.[41]

By expressly identifying a gap in the Constitution, the Transitional Law had the unintended effect of politicizing the school question in a radical fashion. It rendered all previous laws and interpretations obsolete and destroyed respect for existing regulations even as it declared them still in force. The unresolved status of the issue together with the relative freedom of Austrians to settle it themselves combined to enable politicians and interest groups to exert influence otherwise lacking. Both sides could maneuver and block opposing moves in full public view, knowing that the law itself required some resolution of the conflict. Everyone recognized that education had changed since the 1860's and that the laws regarding school types and curriculum needed revision, but the rhetoric generated by the exposed legal status of the question ended by preventing a constitutional amendment from being passed. Glöckel and others railed against conservatives and Catholics. They relied on the persuasive power of their progressive views rather than acknowledge a need for Catholic cooperation in order to proceed. They did so because they insisted that any reform must include a diminution of religious influence. The Christian Socials protested in vain that they were not opposed to reform. The socialists did not believe them because they had persuaded themselves that reform was possible only in the context of an integral secular democratic program. By their rhetoric they succeeded in appropriating the term in the popular imagination, but that meant only that "school reform" came to be identified with the Social Democratic platform or more specifically with the "Glöckelschule." A person's attitude toward school reform was then determined by his attitude toward the socialist party. Despite the bleak prognosis for national cooperation, neither party wanted decentralization to the extent of Germany where education was becoming a provincial rather than a national prerogative. It was an important departure from care to keep Austrian and German legislation compatible. Catholic school politicians had been federalists in the nineteenth century when the liberals controlled the government and when the church emphasized the rights of parents over those of the state to oppose them. Now Catholics feared that socialist control of key localities like Vienna would end in the disappearance of religion from schools that served more than one-third of the population. They turned to the national government to prevent it. The socialists wanted decentralization less than the Catholics for the moment because they were confident that reforms would prove themselves in the cities and that the country schools would inevitably follow. They did not want the large number of rural schools to escape the influence of progressive reforms especially because the schools were vital to the growth of democracy.

VI

As Seipel predicted, the first elections under the Constitution went against the Social Democrats. They gave no clear majority to the Christian Socials, but the party was eventually able to persuade the Pan-Germans to enter a coalition. The socialists refused in a huff to become the junior partners in another grand coalition, preferring to wait for the Christian Socials to fail at the twin tasks of putting together a governing coalition and ruling successfully. Their sullen vindictiveness was the flip side of their former willingness to accept thankless tasks with the goal of proving that no one could govern better than they.

Glöckel followed the party into opposition and resigned as Undersecretary for Instruction. The nineteen months he was in office had witnessed great changes in education; they will be given more detailed treatment in the next chapter. During his tenure he concurred with the socialist policy of forcing the pace of change, and perhaps he contributed more than most to implementing it. His liberal use of the administrative decree for making changes, most notably the decree on religious exercises, were partially responsible for alienating the Christian Socials from the coalition. He never again held office in the Education Ministry, though he remained the chief spokesman for the socialists in the Nationalrat on school quesions. Glöckel turned instead to the city of Vienna where socialist control eliminated much opposition to reform. The city was still part of Lower Austria, though, and Glöckel's efforts would have to include winning status as a province for Vienna before the City School Board could be reorganized along democratic lines.

By far the most serious casualty of the two years between the revolution and passage of the constitution was a consensus on regulating relations between church and state. Differences between federalists and centralists over administration and finances were minor compared with differences in Weltanschauung. The differences became focussed on legislation regulating relations between church and school where it remains enshrined to this day in the constitutional practice of requiring a two-thirds majority to change any law dealing with primary or secondary education. The Concordat of 1934 regulating other aspects of church-state relations was taken over by the Second Republic after considerable infighting, but legislation on the schools could never again be passed by a normal parliamentary majority.

Chapter 3

THE CULTURAL FRONT BEGINS TO
HARDEN: 1920-1922

Mere existence of a Constitution did not guarantee that it would work according to plan. The parliamentary system rested ultimately on a willingness of the major political parties to take and share power in proportion to the number of seats in the Nationalrat. Because the Pan-Germans controlled the balance of power between the Christian Socials and Social Democrats their cooperation was needed to form a majority in the Nationalrat unless the two major parties agreed to renew the grand coalition. This the Social Democrats refused to do, expecting that they would regain power when the Christian Socials failed at the task of governing. Anyway they had enough projects of a local nature in the cities they controlled to keep them busy. The Christian Socials saw the ambush and refused to form a government without the Pan-Germans despite being the largest party, because a minority government could not hope to pass the legislation needed for reconstruction. The Pan-Germans were not interested until they had exhausted all possibilities for Anschluss, but by acting as though they believed Austria could not survive alone they were neglecting many opportunities to do what they could to provide stable government. The Allies easily saw through the scheme and refused more adamantly than ever to allow Anschluss. The year and a half that passed while the Pan-Germans played their game was a time of instability and mutual recriminations among the parties.

45

Faced with major tasks of reconstruction, the governments of Michael Mayr and Johannes Schober tried to avoid cultural skirmishes by naming a bureaucrat rather than a party politician as Undersecretary for Education. Walter Breisky turned out to be a powerless administrator who could not even control his own employees. When he tried one bold move to modify part of Glöckel's program he paid for it with open criticism from the Reform Department.

The Social Democrats were scarcely at a disadvantage being out of office under the circumstances. They had a strong base in Vienna where they concentrated on restructuring the City School Board along socialist lines. The bitterness that accompanied their failure to exclude religious representatives showed that there were dim prospects for a peaceful solution to the question of school reform.

The bishops and leading Christian Socials were not in agreement on how to approach the question on the Catholic side. Seipel tried to tell the bishops that it was unrealistic to appeal openly for state-supported confessional schools or even to ask for repeal of the suspended Glöckel Decree against compulsory religious exercises. He was not able to prevent them from entering the cultural struggle with a pastoral letter on the schools that called on parents to join the struggle over religion. Seipel's subtle mind exposed the theological ambiguities of the letter even before it was written, leading him to realize that the bishops were too confused in their thinking to present the Christian Socials with a unified plan of action. On the threshold of power in May, 1922, he knew that the Christian Socials resolution to hold all cultural bastions applied to the bishops as well as to the socialists.

II

As Seipel had foreseen in January 1920, the first elections under the Constitution brought substantial gains for the Christian Socials.[1] They took eight-two seats to sixty-six for the Social Democrats, while the emerging German national parties won twenty-six between them.[2] The Greater German People's Party (Grossdeutsche Volkspartei), commonly called the Pan-Germans, grew out of a group of seventeen splinter parties. Their goal of political unification with Germany met no opposition from either of the two major parties which made them potential partners for either side in a coalition government had they been willing to join. Instead, they were a party of subversives without revolutionary elan who wanted the extinction of the Austrian state more than anything but were unwilling to use direct methods. They were the victims of their own propaganda which held that Austria could not survive alone; they needed to do nothing more than withhold cooperation to prove their point. The twenty seats of the Pan-Germans alone would not have been enough to give the Social Democrats a majority without the six seats of the German Peasants Party (Deutsche Bauernpartei) which shared a common liberal outlook. This made the urban Social Democrats hesitant to seek a coalition with the German national parties despite their shared anticlericalism. More than differences between city and country, though, socialist and capitalist economics kept the parties apart for the duration of the First Republic.

Under the circumstances the Social Democrats decided to withdraw into opposition and demand that the Christian Socials form a government. In doing so they passed up an opportunity to cooperate with the Christian Socials in foreign policy, for the parties shared a willingness to rebuild Austria if the Allies insisted. They guessed correctly that they could cooperate with the Christian Socials on an ad hoc basis to get foreign credits for reconstruction without a comprehensive coalition agreement that included united action in domestic affairs.

Without a majority in the Nationalrat the Christian Socials did not think they had sufficient authorization to make difficult decisions about reconstruction. They were expected to form a government under the informal rules of parliamentary systems but refused to take responsibility when there was little hope for passing a legislative package. Ignoring the socialist clamoring, they arranged another caretaker government under Michael Mayr whose work on the Constitution gave him a certain acceptance among socialists despite his Christian Social leanings. Walter Breisky took Otto Glöckel's place when he left the government to take a job with the District School Board of Vienna.

The government of Mayr never got a chance to address the problem of reconstruction because Austrians were incapable of thinking about reconstruction apart from Anschluss. Mayr and responsible Christian Socials favored foreign credits for reconstruction, but they could not get them without the cooperation of the Social Democrats or without relinquishing aspirations for unification with Germany. The Pan-Germans were totally opposed to foreign help that involved reaffirming Austrian independence, an opinion so widely shared that a government risked the odium of an entire country by signing away union with Germany. When unauthorized plebiscites in Christian Social Salzburg and Tyrol showed support for Anschluss by almost ten to one, Mayr resigned. He was incapable either of starting reconstruction on realistic terms or of preventing his Catholic confreres from recklessly pursuing Anschluss.

The situation in education was more unsettled than in the rest of the government because the Constitution did not as yet regulate relations between church and state or the federal government and the provinces. Both major camps were frustrated. The secular reformers had no legislative authorization for reform or executive authority to change things by decree while the church had to rely on a hesitant and divided Christian Social Party to represent its conservative religious interests. Socialists and Catholics were willing to confront each other, but for the time being most people were preoccupied with questions of physical survival that could be solved by Anschluss. Nationalism held more promise for Austrians than religion or socialist economics; it was one passion Austrians could indulge on a national scale.

The new Undersecretary for Education Walter Breisky was a member of the Christian Social Party though not a party politician. He was from an old family of government officials and admired for his objectivity. He held various other jobs during the caretaker governments as well: he had been Minister of the Interior the summer before and was in charge of the Army for a month in the Fall of 1920; he settled down as Vice-chancellor and Undersecretary for Education throughout the governments of Mayr and Schober. With the fall of Schober he became president of the Bureau of Statistics until he retired in 1932 to spend the last twelve years of his life sadly alone and nearly blind.

Breisky's low profile as an administrator detracts from the credit he deserves for continuing school reform. The socialists were ready to pounce on anyone who tried to purge the Reform Department, but Breisky might well have risked attacks in the *Arbeiter-Zeitung* had he really been opposed to reform. Instead he allowed the Reform Department to continue its work without interference, reflecting the state of opinion among many Christian Socials that some reform was necessary.[3] Viktor Fadrus, one of Glöckel's closest associates, remained in charge of the section on elementary schools while other outspoken anticlericals like Karl Furtmüller and Hans Fischl stayed on in various capacities. Breisky also resisted a demand from the bishops for proportional representation of Catholics in the Reform Department.[4] The ideas and enthusiasm for reform belonged to the socialists, but they could not have been realized had the Catholics been as opposed as the reformers portrayed them.

The Reform Department continued its work with little interruption.[5] It proposed a curriculum for girls' middle schools, a lesson plan for the Academy of Commerce, and a day of hiking at all middle schools to complete the physical education program; it initiated a new system for describing the progress made by pupils and regulated the conditions for admitting graduates of Realschulen to the university and Agricultural College.[6] In 1922 it made changes in history teaching to match the republican form of government, made suggestions for different forms of middle schools based on a detailed poll of parents and drew up a proposal for college preparatory high schools (Oberschulen).[7]

There was growing concern for country schools. A lobbyist presented statistics to show that 75% were rural and village schools where teachers had to teach more than one grade. The phenomenon was also common in the cities so that 94% of all schools in 1919 contained some classes with two or more grades in them. Viktor Fadrus acknowledged as early as 1920 that something was needed, but it was not until 1923 that the matter became one of the main items on the agenda for the meeting of school supervisors.[8]

Had the Social Democrats been content with the progress being made in the details of educational reform the cultural struggle might never have gathered steam. But now, from the relative safety of the opposition they sharpened the war of words. Karl Renner departed from his usual moderation to call for a "battle for the school" which encouraged firebrands like Karl Leuthner to greater rhetorical extremes.[9] A new entrant into the cultural struggle was the Marxist theoretician Otto Bauer who was searching for an opportunity to accomplish something after disappointments in foreign policy and economics. He published a lecture entitled *Schulreform und Klassenkampf* in Spring 1921 describing school reform as a revolutionary victory in the class struggle. Just as the reform of Comenius was associated with the Reformation and that of Pestalozzi with the French Revolution, so contemporary progress in pedagogy reflected the social revolution. With this facile use of history, he claimed that progressive education was antibourgeois by nature because a new generation of free and independently thinking teachers and pupils would eventually turn to socialism. The liberals had abandoned their principles, leaving the socialists to carry on.[10] Religion, he insisted, had no place in the schools because it was unscientific. Glöckel's pen was quiet for the time being while he was absorbed in organizing the City School Board in Vienna. It became active again in 1923 when he published *Die Österreichische Schulreform* which far outdid Bauer's modest effort, though as usual it avoided the terminology of the class struggle.

Glöckel's plan for reorganizing the City School Board rested on the larger question of separating the city of Vienna from the surrounding province of Lower Austria. The city passed from Christian Social control to the Social Democrats in May 1919 when the socialists won an absolute majority in the City Council. With little likelihood of further change the prospect of an ongoing confrontation between the socialist city and the Catholic countryside appealed to no one. A Christian Social suggestion to put the city under direct administration by the federal government like Washington D.C. was rejected out of hand by the socialists because it would have disenfranchised nearly one-third of all voters in Austria. The alternative of making Vienna a separate state meant exposing the church to the wrath of the socialists, but the Catholics thought it might be possible to control the city through the Nationalrat and the provinces. Mutually agreeable plans to separate city and country were therefore drawn up in 1920.

In school affairs, Vienna was a district run by a District School Board (Bezirksschulrat). When plans to separate Vienna and Lower Austria were well along the question arose whether to upgrade the District School Board into a Provincial School Board (Landesschulrat) with several district boards in various parts of the city or to combine the functions in a single agency. The latter plan would concentrate authority in the president of the School Board in a unique way. The socialist decision in favor of combining the boards was justified on the grounds of efficiency; there was no reason for the added expense of several school boards in view of the short distances and excellent communications. The concentration of authority would be offset by making the City School Board much larger and more democratic.

In the bill that went to the Nationalrat early in 1921 the City School Board was to be a collegial body of over 100 members, democratically organized to represent the city government, school supervisors, administrative personnel and teachers. The principle of democracy bowed to the higher imperative of professionalism on the question of including representatives from parents' organizations. They were excluded, perhaps on the assumption expressed by Glöckel in 1924 that the totality of parents and the state were identical.[11] The oversimplification did not escape Seipel's notice, but there was some justification for saying that parents could exercise control over the City School Board through the ballot box.[12]

Glöckel's plan to eliminate religious representation on the school board quickly became the most controversial aspect of the project. The Christian Socials objected that the move was contrary to the Elementary School Law but, outmanned by the Pan-Germans and the socialists in committee, they had to wait until the bill reached the floor of the Nationalrat to block it. They proposed an amendment to include representatives from the three major denominations, Catholics, Protestants, and Jews and worked out a compromise with the Peasants Party whereby religious representatives would vote only in matters dealing with religion. Mayr's threat to resign carried little weight with the Pan-Germans though it made the liberal *Neue Freie Presse* nervous. The vote was so close that the single voice of Graf Czernin, who alone represented the minuscule German Workers Party, carried the vote for the Christian Socials. The Pan-Germans had not been untrue to their liberal ideals, as Bauer claimed, but the socialists could not overcome their own myth of monolithic bourgeois opposition to exploit the opening.

The crisis of April 1921 involved more than merely getting religious representation on the City School Board because a Social Democratic law to protect the republic from the Habsburgs came up for a vote on the same day. The Christian Socials defeated the bill by the same one vote margin, making it difficult for analysis to distinguish between political and religious affairs. The bewildered *Neue Freie Presse* did not conceal its relief by commenting, "The crisis, which suddenly became acute in the last few days for relatively insignificant reasons, is receding again for the moment."[13] Elsewhere it tried to put a purely political interpretation on the voting by saying that if the Christian Socials were provoking a government crisis over the Habsburg law it was to conceal divisions in the party.[14] The undeniable differences among Christian Socials distracted the paper from probing the sources of unity in Catholicism or the importance of cultural issues to the cohesiveness of the party. Final legislation on constituting the City School Board had to await the separation of Vienna from Lower Austria. This was necessary because the system of "paktiert" legislation under the Constitution of 1867 still applied in school affairs. After Vienna became a separate province on January 1, 1922 the City School Board came into being when identical bills passed the Nationalrat on February 23 and the Landtag of Vienna on March 3.

The City School Board was a rather unwieldy educational parliament of 108 members with the Mayor of Vienna as its titular head. The membership consisted of forty elected delegates from the City Council, twenty from the City Senate, ten representatives from the grade school teachers, eight middle school teachers, a total of twenty-three school inspectors and five others including three representatives from religious associations. The high proportion of politicians—over 59%—could indicate seriousness about democracy or the subordination of school affairs to party politics. The principle of professionalism seemed to suffer, but in the actual conduct of business power was concentrated in the hands of the awkwardly-titled Executive Second President (Geschäftsführender zweiter Präsident).[15] Glöckel was elected to this post at the first meeting on March 28, 1922 and kept it until the civil war of 1934.

III

The vote on religious representation to the City School Board gave the Mayr government only two more months of life. Weakness in the legislature was bad enough, but a direct challenge to the executive authority was intolerable. An embarrassed Mayr resigned when he was unable to prevent unauthorized plebiscites on Anschluss from taking place.

The government that took office in June 1921 was an advance over the last one in having one representative each from the Christian Socials and the Pan-Germans along with the bureaucrats to smooth out differences between the bourgeois parties. The attraction for the Pan-Germans was the leadership of Johannes Schober, the police chief of Vienna who shared many of their views. Otherwise the government remained a caretaker government with Walter Breisky as Undersecretary of Education.

The school controversy remained alive right through the cabinet crisis. After Mayr resigned, but before Schober had constituted his cabinet, Breisky issued a decree on the provisional curriculum introduced by Glöckel the year before. He said that the curriculum should be introduced only where the teachers were more experienced and prepared to teach it, and set five conditions to be met. He also reaffirmed the place of religion in the curriculum under the goals set by the Elementary School Law. Most importantly, he extended the trial period from one to five years. Breisky was deliberatly slowing down the pace of reform in response to objections that Glöckel had acted too fast. The socialists had no objection in principle to extending the experimentation; indeed, responsible school officials in Vienna itself were appealing to extend the time, but only until June 1923.[16] The decree, dated June 16, made its pokey way toward publication preceded by rumor and advance notice within the ministry, but the storm did not break until the cabinet crisis was over and Breisky had been renamed to his office. Ironically, Breisky became the center of controversy on the same day the *Neue Freie Presse* was writing, "In the other ministers Breisky, Brünberger and Paltauf the cabinet is an administrative government, which not even someone of ill will can suspect of anything other than freedom from party ties and objective conduct of business."[17]

The *Arbeiter-Zeitung* took a different view the next day. It accused him of incompetence and ingratiating himself with the Christian Socials by issuing the decree.[18] The same day, speakers at rallies hastily called in Vienna objected that the decree gave a blank check to any teacher who did not want to introduce the new curriculum. Representatives from the Reform Department revealed that they had permission from Breisky to declare publicly they had nothing to do with the decree.[19]

Schober preferred to ignore the controversy in his initial declaration of policy on June 22 rather than endanger his fragile cabinet. He mouthed the current platitudes about continuing reform in cooperation with responsible school offices, teachers and parents. The Christian Socials hid behind Breisky's status as a civil servant rather than a politician, but it was true that the content and timing of the decree suited their policy. Breisky's action improved relations between the Christian Socials and Pan-Germans who had misgivings about the pace of reform and were annoyed by the socialist tendency to use the schools for political purposes.[20] A coalition between the parties was becoming a distinct possibility as long as the Christian Socials did not pursue confessional issues too strongly. One columnist in the *Neue Freie Presse* echoed the sentiments of other liberals in expressing the fear that the socialist school reform would destroy the ideals that support man in the struggle of existence.[21]

Despite support from Schober and the *Neue Freie Presse* Breisky saw the wisdom of clarifying his decree. He wrote that there was no question about his intention to continue the reform and warned that the conditions he set for introducing the curriculum were not to be interpreted in a petty or narrow minded way. Nevertheless he did not retract the conditions or change the five-year timetable for experimentation.[22] The socialists chose to interpret Breisky's move as a retreat even though there was no demonstrable political pressure to cite. They could not believe that Breisky was sincere and used the language of victory to describe the proceedings. The shrill rhetoric left resentment among conservatives; after all, the Catholics did not take advantage of Glöckel when he bowed to pressure and did not implement the decree against compulsory religious exercises.

Taking office after three frightful winters, Schober turned out to be more of a realist than the Pan-Germans anticipated. He secretly negotiated the Treaty of Lana with Czechoslovakia for more badly needed sugar and coal in return for a pledge that Austria would not seek Anschluss.[23] The Social Democrats approved because the supplies were intended mainly for Vienna and joined the Christian Socials who wanted the aid because it protected propertied Austrians from expropriation or confiscatory taxes. The furious Pan-Germans were prevented from dumping Schober by the momentary cooperation of the major parties, but when the socialists went back into opposition in May of 1922 the Schober government fell.

Though all the parties shared the blame for the instability and misery the Pan-Germans stood to lose the most at the polls. The Social Democrats were in sullen opposition, intent on showing that the Christian Socials were holding the line on cultural and dynastic issues to precipitate crises while people were starving. But the clear contradiction of a national political party dedicated to preventing the government from improving the political and economic climate of the country made the Pan-Germans most vulnerable. Add to that the fact that all parties supported Anschluss in some form and the possibility that their liberal programs could be parcelled out between the major parties—the anticlerical vote could go to the socialists while the capitalist vote went Christian

Social—and the Pan-Germans felt acutely threatened. They would have to abandon their aloofness in order to survive.

The Pan-Germans finally made a breakthrough in their congress at Graz shortly after the fall of Schober. They expressed interest in joining a coalition government with the Christian Socials as long as they had the freedom to pursue Anschluss. Another condition was more difficult for the Christian Socials to accept. The Pan-Germans feared that they would be forced to go along with Catholic cultural policies among which the role of religion in education ranked high. They therefore demanded a formal agreement that they would be consulted on equal terms in cultural matters. The agreement tied the hands of the Christian Socials who then had to persuade the bishops that they could not follow their suggestions without jeopardizing the coalition.[24] On the other hand, if the Christian Socials violated the agreement the Pan-Germans would have to bury many differences with the socialists before they could leave the coalition. They were still the junior partners despite the pact that gave them equality in cultural questions.

IV

Schober tried with some success to downplay the importance of cultural politics during his ministry, but the bishops took up the gauntlet thrown down by the socialists early the next year. Their experiences with Glöckel were not confined to the conflict over representation on the School Board but extended to a list of harrassing actions in Vienna.[25] The evident unwillingness of the Pan-Germans to enter any coalition led them to discount Seipel's warning that any actions on religion would be answered with an immediate coalition of Pan-Germans and Social Democrats. They thought they had to do something to prevent the creeping separation of church and school especially in Vienna.

Piffl therefore decided to make the impending cultural struggle the focus of the Bishops Conference meeting in November 1921.[26] In his opening address he said that cultural questions were more important than the continuing economic emergency. The Apostolic Nunio had ducked the issue of "Weltanschauungsschulen" raised the year before by suggesting the bishops contact the pope directly. The Christian Socials were requesting guidelines and church representation on a new National School Board that would establish party policy in school affairs.[27] Clearly, something had to be done.

Johannes Gföllner presented the main paper on the schools with a nine point resolution intended as a memorandum to the Christian Socials. It was stronger than Rieder's report the year before, analyzed the Glöckel Decree in the light of canon and civil law and suggested that the bishops demand its formal repeal.[28]

In the discussion, the bishops agreed to send a memorandum to the Christian Socials, an instruction to the clergy and a pastoral letter to the faithful on the basis of Gföllner's report. They agreed that church representatives to Provincial School Boards should be approved by the local bishop contrary to suggestions from the Christian Socials that the party handle the matter. Someone suggested that the bishops direct a pastoral letter against socialism itself but Piffl advised caution on the basis of his experience. Many Social Democratic party members were churchgoers while many Christian Social farmers in Lower Austria stayed away from church. Certain practices—perhaps he meant charging extortionate prices for food—could hardly be described as Christian. This was the beginning of sentiment among the bishops that the church and the party were perhaps too closely associated.[29] The schools were important, he said, and a letter on them would amount to a statement against socialism because the Social Democrats were leading the struggle against the Christian school.[30] There was much uncertainty among the bishops on the constitutional status of the schools. Perhaps they ought to force the issue with parents, either a secular or a confessional school. Again Piffl cautioned that the effect in Vienna would be disastrous; the socialists would use terror tactics to force children into secular schools. On this indecisive note the discussion broke off to await Seipel's report the next day.

Seipel painted a gloomy picture. The Pan-Germans were letting themselves be swept along toward a Kulturkampf led by the socialists. He was less encouraging about Weltanschauungsschulen than the year before; the Social Democrats might go along with them as long as baptized children could be sent to schools with an atheistic world view. Seipel knew that several of the bishops considered it their duty to protect the faith of baptized children even from irreligious parents. He therefore asked whether current thought in the church allowed parents the right to choose a Catholic or a secular school for their baptized children. Nothing could have made the bishops more uncomfortable because they were unclear about the extent of their rights to form the consciences of children apart from their parents. Seipel could fight the socialists in the Nationalrat, but he needed cogent arguments based on a clear position about the contractual nature of infant baptism that gave the bishops delegated rights to educate children. Reliance on civil law to catechize children was not enough when the law itself was under attack. On the other hand, said Seipel, the present situation could continue; religion remained in the schools and the children were still getting something out of religion class. A good transition to confessional schools might be made through provincial aid to Catholic private schools, but he could not promise help from the national government because it was paralyzed on the issue. At any rate, if confessional schools with compulsory attendance enforced by the state could not be achieved, then religious instruction must remain in the public schools. There seemed no alternative to the present situation. He also warned against a blanket condemnation of socialism or further agitation to lift the Glöckel Decree, citing the flap over the Breisky decree as an example of socialist reaction.[31]

The bishops quietly passed over the fundamental issue of parents' rights to approach the school issue on political grounds. Repeated requests from the Christian Socials for direction led some of them to expect that if they chose one of the four alternative systems they could induce the Christian Socials to sponsor it despite Seipel's admonition that the status quo was the only realistic possibility. The alternatives were: a Catholic confessional school system with compulsory attendance enforced by the state for all baptized Catholic children; a "Weltanschauungsschule" to which Catholic parents were bound in conscience to send their children though not under civil law; state support for Catholic private schools as an interim solution; the status quo in which religion remained a compulsory subject for all baptized children whose parents were registered as Catholic at the time a child entered school. The first three required changes in the law, dependent either on a constitutional law or on ten identical statutes passed by the Nationalrat and the nine provinces. Gföllner took a hard line in favor of compulsory Catholic confessional schools, and Hefter was inclined to agree.[32]

Not all the bishops were misled by Christian Social deference in asking for guidelines. Waitz hesitated, perhaps unsure of his status as an Apostolic Vicar rather than head of a regular diocese. Piffl was closest to Seipel and urged caution. It would be all but impossible to force many baptized children in Vienna into Catholic schools, not to mention the questionable merits of identifying the church too closely with the Christian Social party. For the time being he supported the status quo in hopes that the national government could control school officials in Vienna.

Seipel now had two reasons to push the entire question into the background. The bishops were unsure about the limits of parents' rights in the education of baptized children and they were not united on a concrete program. It is easy to accuse him of cynically trying to exploit uncertainties and divisions among the bishops to maintain his control over Christian Social policy, but such was not the case. He was a dedicated priest and consummate politician who weighed carefully the possibilities for accomplishing goals that were rooted in Catholic principles. In the absence of a clear Catholic position on parents' rights or the practical possibility of persuading the Pan-Germans to support a constitutional law favoring religion in the schools Seipel applied another set of priorities among which reconstruction and a stable government ranked high. A central concern of the bishops had to be marginal for the Christian Socials because the Catholics were deficient both in theory and tactics. Seipel had a genuine concern for souls and adhered to the theology that all baptized persons were members of the church with a serious obligation to form their consciences according to the teachings of the church. But the bishops had not faced squarely the question whether the natural rights of parents to educate their children superseded the delegated rights of the church to teach faith and morals, or what happened when these rights conflicted. The bishops had made a big point in the 1860's of stressing the primary right and obligation of parents to educate their children when it was convenient for them to rely on existing dedication to the church; the situation was different in 1920 when parents no longer cared whether their children grew up Catholic. Under the circumstances Seipel favored the status quo or state support for Catholic private schools that might expand to fill the demand for them proportionate to the desire of parents for religiously sponsored education. The bishops, not Seipel, were in position to excite the necessary religious dedication.

Without it Seipel could do nothing because he lacked the votes in the ballot box.

The bishops tried to develop a Catholic response to school questions with their pastoral letter read from the pulpit in February 1922.[33] The people heard that parents had the "first right" to educate their children. An "inescapable duty" did not change the impression that parents had the primary say in educational matters. Not even the injunctions that followed modified the principle. The church as the "great teaching and educational institution of all mankind" had a task to prepare youth for a Christian life and eternal happiness; it could dispense even less with the religious-moral character of the schools than parents.[34] Since the whole of education should be permeated with religion, the bishops claimed an independent right to supervise schools. "This highest purpose of all education, however, will be reached for Catholic children only when the school has an expressly confessional character," which meant if possible separation from children of other faiths. After discussing the rights of the state briefly they criticized the school reform for its rationalism and secularism and attacked Glöckel's active involvement in the learning process. They said that just as instruction in arithmetic was unthinkable without practice, so religious instruction was unthinkable without religious exercises. They concluded further attacks on events sponsored by socialists and the socialist Kinderfreunde, an organization for preschool children, with the call, "Auf zum Schulkampf!" The rhetoric reflected Gföllner's influence and ignored Seipel's warning against mentioning the Glöckel Decree. It might have been politically wise to let a dormant issue lie, but the letter would hardly have been complete without some mention of it. Piffl could endorse it because it was a statement of principle rather than a blueprint for action.

Saying that parents had the first right to educate their children was a vague statement of principle that actually concealed the real sentiment among the bishops on the extent of parental rights over baptized children. They rather took the paternalistic attitude that their congregations were sheep to be shepherded. When in 1923 a group of laymen presented a draft of a constitutional law to them that affirmed a *natural* right of parents to decide whether their children have a religion or not, the bishops unanimously rejected it. Gföllner said simply that no such right existed.[35] This left the door open to claiming greater rights over baptized children.

The statement of principle in 1922 misled the laymen into thinking that the bishops intended to rely on their collective dedication rooted in personal responsibility for the religious education of their children, but in fact the bishops were reluctant to relinquish the right to direct the consciences of the faithful. The ecclesiology of the time left little room for freedom and initiative on the part of the laity.

Determination to battle the socialists rested on the willingness of two groups to provide the front line troops. Neither the Christian Social Party nor the parents turned out to be entirely pliant instruments, the Christian Socials by pursuing political and economic policies whose success depended on downplaying the school issue and the parents who were disinclined to follow the bishops without much consultation. The Christian Socials were active while the parents could only resist passively, but both tendencies isolated the bishops who were among the least realistic politicians in Austria at the time. The intransigence and stubbornness of the socialists were surpassed by that of Gföllner who did not have the saving feature of a solid program for reform behind him.

In the Spring of 1922, just as Seipel was about to take power for the first time, the bishops were directing the church into a Kulturkampf against his advice. He knew that his task in the future would be to hold the cultural line not only against the socialists but against episcopal attempts to have the party represent church interests with greater energy. Socialist provocations were driving Piffl into the arms of the Kulterkämpfer with the prospect of a split between Seipel and Piffl on the horizon.

Chapter 4

THE PROGRAM OF OTTO GLÖCKEL
AND THE REACTION OF THE CHURCH

I

The dominant figure in the controversy over school reform was undoubtedly Otto Glöckel. His stature as a reforming educator and nationally prominent politician from 1907 to 1934 brought together the diverse elements of the school question to make him the focus of turmoil throughout the First Republic. Because he represented both the movements toward separation of church and state and an integral democracy that sought to reconstruct the social life of Austria, he found himself in the van of bitter attacks on the church and on the conservative vestiges of an aristocratic social structure. It was his tragedy that he chose to confont too many enemies to prevent reaction from ruining much of his work during his lifetime, but many of his ideas returned after World War II to become the basis for modern Austrian education. Some key parts of his program, however, remained unrealized, due in no small measure to his deficiencies as a politician. He intended to put the schools at the service of social democratic ideals that were opposed by many as inconsistent with their religious beliefs or with national traditions. The reaction he provoked both as national Undersecretary of Education and as head of the School Board of Vienna contributed to the social strife that tore the country apart, the latter because he defied the federal government on several occasions from an untouchable position as head of the Vienna school system to point up essential weaknesses in the Constitution of 1920.

II

Otto Glöckel came from a family with close ties to the church. His father was the school teacher of a rural parish near Wiener Neustadt in Lower Austria; his mother was pious all her life, and the boy spent his summer vacations at the rectory of an uncle who was pastor of a parish in Hungary. Glöckel has some kind words for a good preacher in his autobiography, and for another priest who corresponded with him as late as 1931. He played a priest as a boy, and it was said of him often that he resembled a preacher when he spoke with righteousness and indignation about social evils.[1]

Despite these associations, his father's attitudes directed him away from the church. When he took minutes at teachers' meetings run by his father, Otto observed the bitterness felt by the teachers over poor pay, highhanded pastors who still used the teacher as organist, sexton, and acolyte and the ideals of an emerging profession thwarted by unsympathetic churchmen.

Glöckel followed his father into the teaching profession to find out soon enough for himself how poor and vulnerable teachers were. He moved to Vienna to see how bad conditions in the big cities were, receiving his teaching certificate in 1892 and teaching for five years as a teaching assistant (Unterlehrer) in a poor district of the city. In 1894 he joined the Social Democratic Party though he had a distaste for Marxist categories of thought and began together with Karl Seitz the party's association of young teachers called simply "Die Jungen"; he also joined the liberal Zentralverein der Wiener Lehrerschaft.[2] All this outspoken political involvement cost him his job in September 1897 when the newly appointed mayor of Vienna Karl Lueger fired all Social Democrats holding offices under his control. He spent the next several years teaching classes for workers in the evening while he supported himself as a clerk in various offices with party ties.

It is uncertain whether Glöckel took part in the discussions on the role of religion in the socialist movement, but he was almost certainly satisfied with the final decision that religion for a socialist was to be a private concern. The formula "Religion ist Privatsache" enabled Glöckel openly to join the socialist side while honoring in some way the sensibilities that found their expression in religion.[2] As one of the founders of the Freie Schule in 1905 he took an active part in reconciling freethinking liberals and socialists on cultural questions.

Glöckel's political career took off in 1906 when he became one of the first Social Democrats to take a seat in the Vienna City Council. In the next year he took advantage of the extended franchise to run for the Chamber of Deputies, winning a seat to represent a cluster of industrial towns in the Erzgebirge northwest of Prague. He remained in the Chamber and Nationalrat until the party was dissolved in 1934, conducted himself for a quarter century with the self-assurance of one who easily reconciled the roles of professional educator and partisan politician.

The main outlines of school reform according to Glöckel were formed in the first decade of the twentieth century. Besides abolishing religious exercises and instruction he favored the so-called Einheitsschule which would keep all children together for the full eight years of compulsory grade school before dividing them up into tracks based on vocational goals, not unlike the American system of grade and high schools. The system might have been introduced painlessly were it not for the existence of a complex system of compulsory schools, gymnasia and Realtechnical colleges after 1849 when the institutes of higher education school. The system had become integrated with the universities and techincal colleges after 1849 when the instututes of higher education were bound by law to accept students who graduated from approved preparatory schools. The professoriate in the Hochschulen, therefore, had a vested interest in the quality of the gymnasia and Realschulen without assurance that the level of academic accomplishment would remain at the current level if the Einheitsschule opened the doors of the secondary schools to more, presumably less qualified students. Glöckel had a lot to overcome in the conservatism of the university faculty as well as the professors in the gymnasia who considered themselves colleagues of the university professors rather than the equals of teachers from normal schools who taught at Volks–and Bürgerschulen. Glöckel granted that the system had accomplished much, but it served only the social elite and prevented large numbers of people from getting access to the education that would improve their social standing. The socialists did not fear the danger of an academic proletariat unable to find work that matched its expertise. They were convinced that education to the full extent of a person's talents was the best guarantee of happiness, social equality and national greatness.

The key concept of Glöckel and the school reformers was democracy. Their dedication to it as an ideal stamped their movement as social liberal rather than Marxist and left the Marxists scrambling to graft historical materialism and economic determinism onto western-style liberal democracy with its predisposition for capitalist economics. Democracy meant a total world view that made the freedom and equality of all citizens the highest goal of society. Glöckel and others modified the absolute egalitarianism of radical levelers by including the ideal that opportunities should be provided for all to find a place in society appropriate to their talents and accomplishments. In this way the social differentiation based on performance that was a trademark of bourgeois liberals found a place in the Social Democratic blueprint for society. In politics, democracy involved participation in government at all levels from the town and the federal government to the factories and schools according to the abilities of the participants.[4]

With the democratic society as an ideal, the immediate task of the schools was to educate children to become well-informed, responsible and free.[5] Democracy precluded commitment of the school to specific ideals and values with conceptual content that would restrict rather than free young minds. The goal of the socialists was to provide pupils with the personal resources to act on their own sets of moral or cultural principles discovered by themselves rather than imposed by school authorities. The implicit individualism of "value-free" education could be reconciled with the needs of society by stressing respect for the independence and inviolability of every individual and willingness to compromise by bowing to the will of the majority when an issue was important enough to be placed before the entire community for a decision.

The school reformers thought that democratic ideals required a radical reorientation of the schools; from being authoritarian institutions that formed obedient subjects they had to become more open, less rigid institutions that would develop in the child habits of work and discipline as part of individualized intellectual progress and adaptation to society.

Teaching methods would presuppose concern and even love for the child, sensitivity to its capabilities and the flexibility to fashion appropriate means to help it grow. Older schools had stressed memorization or had made the subject material rather than the pupil the center of the concern. The Drillschule and Lernschule were founded on incorrect notions about developmental psychology and had to be replaced with the Arbeitsschule or work school where the child was fully and actively engaged in learning proportionate to its ability to grasp matters at the time. In all this the methods of science were to be used. Observation, the inductive method, skepticism regarding hypotheses, criticism and acceptance of the empirically quantifiable became the proper ways of approaching subject materials once the pupil had mastered the fundamentals.

Conspicuously lacking in the discussion of democratic educational reform was the place of religious values and institutions.[6] It was difficult for the socialists to deal with the question without generating a dangerous controversy in their ranks about the place of religion in the socialist movement as a whole. Otto Bauer's view of religion as a pre-scientific atavism destined to die once the masses were enlightened was not shared widely even within the party leadership. People who voted Social Democratic continued to have their children baptized and there was a gnawing fear that they had little sympathy for an integrated materialistic world view. Strained efforts were made therefore to show that democracy grew from the scientific world view to extend the widely-presumed conflict between science and religion into a conflict between democracy and religion.[7] Still, the best way to deal with religion was to avoid discussing it.

The meaning of democracy to practicing Catholics, in contrast, varied considerably with the degree to which individuals or groups applied a hierarchical conception of religion, or of reality itself, to politics. The common Catholic belief that God delegated his authority at one time to aristocrats and at another time to the people meant that there was no contradiction between political democracy and hierarchically organized religion. It also implied that democracy should be narrowly conceived as a political system in which one man had one vote rather than as a total world view. This made the Christian Socials appear less committed to democracy than the Social Democrats. The Christian Socials had democratic origins and had always asserted the compatibility of democracy and monarchy, but when the Catholic Conservatives joined them in 1907, the party became home to people who opposed democracy. The wing was small and relatively weak, but its existence gave added ammunition to the socialists.

Glöckel expanded considerably on the theory of democracy and the Arbeitsschule in the famous *Leitsätze* (*Directives*) of 1920. There were three specific principles underlying the school reform: instruction 1) should have a basis in the life of the pupil (Bodenständigkeit), 2) should be integrated on the elementary level (Gesamtunterricht), and 3) should involve the pupil actively (Selbstätigkeit). Together they meant that the curriculum should be adapted to local circumstances in such a way that the learning environment of the child would approach as closely as possible its situation in real life. It also meant that instruction should be governed by what a child could learn at any given time.[8] Glöckel regularly used the word "Kindesgemässheit" (adaption to the child) to describe this combination of principles. One teacher was to teach all subjects to a single class to achieve the effect of building on the natural way a child learns. Even within a single class different subjects were to be integrated as, for example, in using a trip down the Danube to teach history, literature and art.[9] The principle of self-activity or active involvement of the pupil was all important. The pupil rather than the teacher was made the center of the learning process, which meant that the role of the teacher would involve more observation and testing of pupil reactions than earlier. The amount of material covered by the teacher in class was not as important as how the material was appropriated by the pupil.

The principles remained in force into the middle school years but in different form. The transition from the class system to specialized disciplines with separate teachers was to be smooth rather than abrupt. Lessons were to keep close ties with lived truth and life (Lebenswahrheit and Lebensnähe). Self-activity became self-discipline and responsibility to self after puberty when self-awareness assumed other forms. In all of these doctrines Glöckel and others like Viktor Fadrus, Hans Fishl and Ludwig Battista built on the work in developmental psychology currently being done. There was little in the psychology of men like Freud, Alfred Adler and Karl Bühler, whose influential *Geistige Entwicklung des Kindes* appeared in 1918, that they could not use to support the approaches to education Glöckel had worked out in the early years of the century.

The whole project depended on good teachers, of course, so Glöckel turned his attention to teacher training in a special way. A high percentage of the normal schools were still under church control due to the financial straits of of 1870's. As before, they took children from the ages of fifteen to eighteen and prepared them to teach in elementary schools with courses in essential disciplines and teaching methods. Normal schools were not like gymnasia or other middle schools that trained their students in analytic, scientific and critical methods; they rather tried to develop techniques for communicating "positive" knowledge like the three R's. At the age of eighteen, candidates for teaching positions were young and immature, but more seriously, their preparation was too short to give them adequate general knowledge for effective teaching in the Volkschule. Bürgerschule teachers, it may be recalled, educated themselves in their free time at their own expense to qualify as advanced elementary teachers.

The reformers proposed two years of university-level courses as a solution. They also suggested more courses in pedagogy for middle school teachers who were university-trained, prone to overspecialization and aloof from students. It was clear, though, that the church would fight to keep control of teacher training institutes since it was their last area of exclusive control in education, nor would it be easy to get middle school professors to work with slow learners when the secondary schools became less elite.

III

Implementation of the doctrine depended on good organization and attention to detail. Glöckel excelled in this aspect of education. Perhaps his most significant contributions came in developing organizations and methods for administering change in the schools. Unfortunately, when politics intruded to shorten the time he had to start the process of reform he himself was partially responsible for in no branch of government was reform pushed in a more highhanded fashion than in education. Glöckel's use of the regulatory decree was at variance with the democracy he professed and forced change at a pace even his allies conceded was too fast. His methods were at once energetic, effective and dangerously partisan at a time when reform depended not only on the strength of ideas but on the ability to persuade half the population that reforms did not threaten values they held to be important. When he encountered opposition Glöckel reacted with anger, intransigence and rhetorical appeals that lost their effectiveness outside Vienna. Here he found such support that he mistook his ability to change the rest of Austria by making Vienna a model to be imitated. The force of example was easily lost in the political passions generated by his methods so that the word "Glöckelschule" came to connote both pedagogical excellence and socialist politics.

The most fruitful period of Glöckel's activity began in March 1919 when he began his nineteen month term as Undersecretary for Education. He had been a member of the Provisional Government, but conditions were so bad he could do little more than become acquainted with procedures. One of his most important contributions was also one of the first; he established a Reform Department in the Office of Education and brought together competent educators to begin the process of adapting to the new political circumstances and to new pedagogical techniques. Most of the reformers were socialists, but he included a few Catholics like Ludwig Battista. Glöckel also divided the official publication into administrative and pedagogical parts and renamed the organ *Volkserziehung*. The Christian Socials recognized the accomplishments of the Reform Department by keeping it after the change in government in 1920 with most of its personnel intact.

Glöckel then began to reform many areas of education by decree. He issued sixty-seven major decrees and numerous minor directives on implementation in the following year and a half.[10] The vehicle of a decree was efficient but implied the backing of law that was very much in flux. It was a dangerous way of proceeding with major changes because it left the Christian Social party out of the reform by making the minister in charge responsible for changes rather than a committee. At the same time the government was becoming democratic, school reform was being imposed by government directive. While Glöckel himself may have been equal to the delicate task of reconciling potential opposition—he dispatched lecturers from the Reform Department to all parts of the country who were reportedly well-received—the more radical members of the party and the party press were not equally capable. By ignoring the proprieties of reaching a consensus on the schools or at least by spreading the responsibility to include Christian Socials, Glöckel endangered school reform from the start.

Many of the reforms were distinctly needed. Glöckel issued decrees allowing women into higher technical studies, law and political science at the universities and Hochschulen, and girls were admitted to boys' middle schools. A host of decrees concerned testing and assessment of performance by students while others dealt with supervision and working conditions for teachers. Glöckel authorized the revision of textbooks and began a centralized procedure for reviewing and approving new textbooks.[11] Another innovation was the establishment of parent-teacher organizations to advance communication between home and school. Further attempts to democratize education by setting up a national Education and Instruction Council with lay representation failed to meet expectations, however.[12]

Glöckel hoped to professionalize education and win support from teachers by setting up teachers' chambers in each of the provinces. Under his direction the Office of Education started chambers for elementary and secondary teachers, but the university professors dragged their feet over the autonomy of the university. All three chambers were in existence by February 1920 and a general congress was called to discuss school reform. Delegates from the Hochschulen were elected by their colleagues while the others were named by Glöckel from a list of suggested names. The congress was therefore packed with advocates of reform, a fact noted by the university professors who refused to be rushed into reforming teacher education. The Catholics were alert for signs of prejudice against them which they found in a proposal to forbid teachers at private, mostly Catholic, schools to vote for delegates to the chambers. After the Christian Socials took power in October 1920 the government did not call a congress again which left the working committees of elementary and secondary school teachers the only functioning organs of the chambers.

Glöckel quickly began efforts to transform evey facet of education from the Volkschulen to the university when he took office. He had an opportunity to set up model schools at six superfluous academies for cadets and daughters of military personnel. He transformed these into State, later Federal Educational Institutes (Staats- or Bundeserziehungsanstalten) open to all children on the basis of talent alone. They were full eight-year secondary schools organized into three tracks on the pattern known as the German Middle School that stressed modern languages, mathematics, science and German culture. The state paid tuition and living costs for students who were incapable of paying eventually the great majority. Eventually the schools became widely acclaimed even by political opponents as models of reform.[13]

The reformers began their systematic efforts with the Volkschulen. They invested many of their hopes in the reorganization of the first eight years of schooling along the lines of the Einheitsschule. The existing system in most places consisted of five years of Volkschule after which children went their separate ways into a complicated system of Bürgerschulen, gymnasia of various sorts and Realschulen. This system, as has been noted, made it necessary to decide on a vocation for a child at the age of ten because possibilities for transferring from one kind of school to another thereafter were almost nonexistent.[14] With little or no participation by the child in making the decision, parents often forced their children to follow the paths they had taken regardless of their inclinations or aptitudes. The reformers furthermore claimed that the schools cooperated in maintaining the system by selecting students on the basis of class rather than talent.

The master plan was to rationalize the school system by dividing the years of schooling into three equal periods of four years each for Volkschule, Mittelschule and Oberschule or Gymnasium. There was general agreement that the Oberschule should be characterized by division into tracks, differentiation of curriculum and specialization. Everyone likewise agreed that the four years of Volkschule should contain the same basic material for all pupils although the place of religion was hotly disputed, and the concept of Bodenständigkeit (instruction with a basis in lived experience) appeared to require different curricula for the cities and rural areas.

The major controversy involved the middle four years. The reformers called for a General Middle School (Allgemeine Mittelschule) that held a cross section of children from all classes of society in a single school with a curriculum divided into two tracks, one for advanced and average students, another for the less talented. The fifth year of Volkschule would become the first year of General Middle School with the three-year Bürgerschule as the remainder. No student would be forced to choose a vocation in life before the age of 14 because possibilities for transferring from one track to another were built into the system.

The reformers devised a new curriculum for the Volkschule that stressed the principles of the Arbeitsschule. Religion remained one of the subjects taught because the law required it, and the churches controlled the appointment of teachers and content of textbooks. Glöckel introduced the experimental curriculum for grades one through five by decree in September 1919 in Vienna. Ignoring complaints about hastiness, he then introduced it on a trial basis for all of Austria on September 1, 1920. He planned only a one-year trial period before making it permanent, but criticism that it was impossible to evaluate the curriculum in such a short time led Walter Breisky, his successor, to lengthen the time for experimentation to five years. Another complaint was that it was unsuited to the needs of children in the countryside. These substantial objections had little weight with the reformers who complained vociferously that the Christian Socials were trying to sabotage school reform.

Other reform plans brought the elementary schools into areas previously untouched by their activities. Glöckel's experiences with teaching poor children who came to school ragged, hungry and tired from working to help support the family showed him that education had to involve such things as health and lunch programs, physical education courses and development of plant facilities to enable the school to accept wider responsibilities. He became a tireless speaker on a wide range of issues with the goal of educating the public on the possibilities of the school system.

The concept of the General Middle School that joined the last four years of Volkschule or Bürgerschule with the first four years of Gymnasium and Realschule was the most important single element in Glöckel's plan for reform. The two tracks, he hoped, would take into account the diverse aptitudes which pupils had already demonstrated; pupils would be assigned on the basis of past performance rather than on an entrance examination. An elaborate form for describing and evaluating pupils was devised for this purpose.

At first, opposition to the General Middle School came less from the church than from social conservatives and professors at gymnasia and the universities. The idea involved a degree of academic leveling in order to achieve social equality; the ideal of democracy meant a deliberate retreat from high standards of academic excellence in higher education because the schools could not demand the same level of performance from graduates of the General Middle Schools as the gymnasia could from their students after the first four years. The proposal rested sufficiently on an analysis of class bias built into the existing system that conservatives looked for an alternative explanation. The socialist argument was based on their confidence that working-class families would appreciate better educational opportunities for their children and that talented children would be better able to resist the inertia of parents or opposition to higher schooling at the age of fourteen than at the age of ten. The reformers were trying to change the system without confronting the negative attitude of working-class parents toward higher education which more than any other factor kept working-class children from exceeding the accomplishments of their parents. The conservatives denied a necessary link between class and academic achievement. Educated parents, they claimed, communicated an interest in intellectual achievement to their children, and if their less talented children suffered from their inflated expectations it was not up to the government to protect these children from their parents. The inevitable result of universal and compulsory middle school education would be to lower the quality of graduates from the gymnasia four years later. The decline in standards would then carry over to the universities. The Pan-Germans and old liberals who were strong in the teaching profession and the government bureaucracy were especially afraid that future generations might not match the accomplishments of the past despite the reformers' stress on German culture rather than the ancient classics.

Professors at the gymnasia agreed that the quality of secondary education would decline. They acknowledged that the gymnasia were Lernschulen but defended the emphasis on academics by pointing to the achievements of their students. With the methods of the Arbeitsschule teachers would have to teach in different ways; many teachers would have to be retrained with more emphasis put on pedagogical techniques, which would involve a hardship for them. Perhaps more importantly, they feared that they would lose their identity as colleagues of the university professors with whom they shared a common training at the university. The reformers were proposing to bridge the enormous gap between graduates of the normal schools and university graduates changing the status of professors at secondary schools.

The university professors concurred with the objection that the General Middle School would bring a decline in academic achievement among students. They would be forced to deal with inferior students who had the right to enter the university without an entrance examination. At the very least they could not expect that the students coming to them would have the classical secondary education they had come to expect as the mark of all truly educated people.

The status of the classical languages as a prerequisite for university study soon became an issue of great symbolic importance in the struggle over school reform. Latin and Greek had been essential parts of a general education for their humanistic and disciplinary qualities until the introduction of the Realgymnasium by Gustav Marchet in 1908. Greek was eliminated and the hours of Latin reduced to make room for more natural science. By 1920 Latin remained important only for linguistic and theological studies at the university. It was marginal for medicine and law, and the modern languages were far more useful for modern history, natural science and advanced technology. Still, the ideal of a classical education died hard in Austria and the gymnasia were determined to keep Latin for all eight years. The issue took on religious overtones because Latin was still the official language of the church; an attack on Latin could be construed as an oblique attack on the church. The reformers gently tried to reassure the professors that a classical education was valuable but that there were more important things to study in the complex modern world. It is difficult to appreciate how emotion-laden the issue of Latin was, but the spectacle of highly-placed government officials negotiating for hours in 1927 over the amount of Latin students would study gives some indication of its symbolic importance.

With opposition to the General Middle School mounting, the prospects for the Oberschule were dim. Nevertheless Hans Fischl outlined a plan for a general Oberschule in January 1920 based on the methods of the Arbeitsschule with four tracks that represented a further refinement of the proposed two-track General Middle School or the three-track German Middle School already in effect at the State Educational Institutes. The tracks were to be in classical languages, modern languages, mathematics-science, and German culture. All four were to qualify the student to enter a university or technical college.

Another aspect of the reform was a plan to upgrade the Realschule which was still a seven-year middle school that emphasized vocational training. By adding a year and having children enter after the fourth rather than the fifth grade the Realschule could be better integrated into a unified and rationalized educational system. Progress was slow until the teachers became convinced reform was needed. Other elements of reform faced the hard realities of a poor economy. Plans for erecting more middle schools for girls and paying teachers better wages had to be shelved for the time being. Increased interest in education, on to the other hand, made it likely that money would be available when the economy improved.

The proposals to reform teacher training with a two year course of studies on the level of university work met a series of obstacles that stymied them throughout the First Republic. Opposition from the secondary school professors was brief but significant because the Social Democrats were not in office long enough to move ahead with plans once their opposition had been overcome. Socialist and nationalist teachers in the teachers' chambers were able to reconcile their differences but the university professors did not want to make room for two-year institutes at the universities. Eventually they worked out a compromise solution with the reformers. Separate two-year teachers' academies with "university character" would be built in university cities following the example of similar institutes in Germany.[15] The opposition that stopped changes in teacher training came from the Christian Socials under pressure from the Catholic church which ran five of ten academies for boys and eleven of seventeen for girls. These schools were incapable of adding pedagogical institutes with college level courses, and Glöckel's plan to transform them into Oberschulen meant the demise of Catholic control over teacher training. The need for better-trained teachers was pressing, but political Catholics could not afford another loss to the secularizers in the field of education so the Christian Socials consistently blocked legislation aimed at changing the education of teachers.

The first six months of 1920 seem to have been decisive in alienating Catholics from Glöckel's reform. The Christian Socials were not unwilling to reform education; two priests from among the Christian Social deputies complimented Glöckel on separate occasions for various aspects of reform.[16] But the decree on suspending compulsory religious exercises in the public schools left a residue of suspicion among Catholics that grew throughout the first half of 1920. Attacks on the church in the socialist press were frequent, Karl Leuthner argued in the Nationalrat that education must be purely secular and the teachers' chambers denied voting rights to teachers in Catholic schools.[17] Miklas warned the Christian Social Congress in March that Glöckel's reform envisioned the end of private Catholic teacher training.[18] No one was surprised when the coalition collapsed in June, nor did anyone think the differences could be ironed out early enough to include articles on church-state relations in the Constitution.

By comparison the opposition of the educational establishment to school reform was relatively minor. Secondary school teachers recognized the need to reform teacher education and to rationalize the school system. The objection that the General Middle School would lower the quality of secondary education had more substance—in fact it perdures to this day—but the inevitability of changes in entrance requirements to the university encouraged the professors to become more flexible. The chief fear among anticlerical opponents of the socialists in the schools was over the impact of school reform integrated into the socialist blueprint for Austrian society as a whole. Socialist economics in particular were a sufficient threat to drive many anticlericals in various branches of government service to join the Christian Socials in blocking thorough reform of the system.

IV

The goals of the church in education changed little in response to the same developments that moved the socialists toward radical reforms. It was still the main intention of the clergy to form baptized children in the Catholic faith. Beyond religious instruction and exercises, the church did not admit that the teaching of secular subjects should belong to the state alone because the Catholic faith could inform even subjects like mathematics through the Christian concern of the teacher. The church therefore continued to maintain a few private schools and insisted on keeping both religious instruction and exercises in the public schools where over 90% of the children were baptized Catholics.

The practice of baptizing children meant different things to the clergy and to a great many lax parents who had fallen away from the practice of religion in the preceding decades. The church taught that if a child died before the age of reason, about seven years, it would go straight to heaven. This led to the almost magical belief that baptism was an easy way to do a great service for a child if it were to die early. Few parents wanted to ignore a cheap form of eternal life insurance, nor could many resist the social pressure of relatives to have their children baptized. Thereafter many Catholic parents did not go to church except for Midnight Mass at Christmas or an occasional wedding or funeral and the clergy had no way of checking whether parents were fulfilling the attendant duty to raise their children Catholic during their preschool years.

Difficulties arose when the child began school. Then the example of parents often came into conflict with the demands of the church that baptized Catholics beyond the age of reason go to church every Sunday. Teachers in religion class taught that Catholics had a serious obligation to attend Mass on Sundays and holydays and receive Communion at least one a year during the Easter season under pain of mortal sin that could condemn a soul to hell. The church oftentimes found itself stepping between parents and children by trying to form children differently from the way their parents were acting. Bishops had a responsibility to insist that parents raise their baptized children in the faith and claimed that parents had delegated their rights to form children in the Catholic faith to the church by having their children baptized. Sometimes religion teachers tried to use children to pique the consciences of lapsed parents. Annoyance often turned to rage when the church used politicial means to keep religious exercises and instruction in the public schools. The church was using the police power of the state to bar them from withdrawing their children from religious influences in the schools. It was easy to have a child baptized—and the church went along with it for the sake of the child—but it was difficult to build on the original gift of faith in baptism. Parents had the option of registering with the government as having no religion, but the legality of having their baptized children follow them once they had entered school was unresolved. The church insisted that even if parents were remiss in providing religious training for their children the church had an obligation to provide religious instruction and exercises coming both from God and from the laws of the state. Likewise it had a duty to oppose changes in the laws that would make its mission to instruct baptized children more difficult.

The defensive posture of the church grew not just from the attacks of the socialists but from its own incapacity to provide innovative responses to changing times. There were no changes in the liturgy, for example, that might enable people to understand the words of the Mass and sacraments; there were no changes in traditional methods of catechesis that stressed memorization; and finally, regarding fundamental approaches to theology the revival of Thomism gave the church a powerful philosophical tool for investigating the data of Revelation so that Rome could condemn modern approaches to the Bible coming from history and literary criticism as contrary to the faith expressed in the metaphysical categories of Aristotle and Thomas Aquinas.

The church became even more beleaguered when attacks on the faith and involvement in public life turned into attacks on Christian morality as well. Broad areas of public life from marriage to censorship and public dancing became a battleground. For a variety of reasons, prominent among them the rise of psychology coming from Freud, Adler and others, the attitudes of society toward sex became more permissive. The socialists and many liberals ridiculed the uncompromising stance of the church that any use of sex outside a monogamous and indissoluble marriage was illegitimate. Church marriage legislation that allowed separation of parties involved in a difficult marriage but forbade divorce or remarriage found its way into state laws that did not permit remarriage, although for reasons dealing with property Albert Sever, the Landeshauptmann of Lower Austria, decided to challenge the law by giving great numbers of dispensations to remarry civilly in Vienna; in doing so he presented the church and the federal government with a fait accompli in civil marriage procedures. He was deaf to complaints that he was acting illegally. Freedom of expression was also being used to allow publication of material offensive to the Catholic sense of propriety in sexual matters, and the church feared that a course called *Heimatund Lebenskunde,* which the reformers wanted to use as a substitute for religion, would contain little emphasis on sexual responsibility. In this way, Catholic opposition to secular morality became part of the opposition to school reform on the socialist model.[19]

The Catholics were led by a rather heterogeneous group of bishops representing six dioceses and one temporary apostolic vicariate. Two of them were out of touch with current events; Leopold Schuster of Seckau (Graz) was seventy-six years old and Johannes Rössler of St. Pölten, though a relatively young sixty-eight, had been bishop since 1894 and was allowing Canon Michael Memelauer, who eventually succeeded him, to run the affairs of the diocese.

The five active bishops were Adam Hefter of Gurk (Klagenfurt), Ignatius Rieder of Salzburg, Sigismund Waitz of Innsbruck-Feldkirch, Johannes Gföllner of Linz and Friedrich Piffl of Vienna. The Bavarian Adam Hefter

was the youngest bishop at forty-seven, and the most nationalistic. Ignatius Rieder took office in 1918 to become the latest addition to the
Bishops Conference. He was knowledgeable on school questions and especially interested in the on-again, off-again project of a Catholic university in Salzburg. Sigismund Waitz, who succeeded Rieder in the pres-
tigious see of Salzburg, was Apostolic Administrator of Innsbruck-Feldkirch which was cut off from the bishopric of Brixen by the loss of South
Tyrol to Italy. Waitz was a declared monarchist and foe of the Republic.
He was also one of the best-informed and articulate members of the
episcopacy and took an active interest in the school question. The most
vocal of the bishops in the early years of the Republic was the fiery
Johannes Gföllner of Linz. He considered himself the heir of the Kulturkämpfer Franz Joseph Rudigier and became the expert among the bishops
on school affairs. He consistently opposed the school reformers until
a group of radical laymen drove him into closer relations with the more
moderate Seipel.

The leader of the bishops was Friedrich Cardinal Piffl of Vienna who
was fifty-four years old in 1918 and in good health. He had expressed
fears during the war that a Kulturkampf would break out after the war
and included concern for the fate of Catholic education in the pastoral
letter of January 1919.[20] He did not have long to wait before the confrontation began over the decree on religious exercises and he was at the
center of the struggle with Glöckel for the next decade and a half. His
relations with Seipel were kept close through informal monthly meetings
although he found fault with the Christian motivation and religious
observance of many who voted Christian Social.[21]

Piffl had another role that increased the likelihood of confrontation
with Glöckel; he was Apostolic Administrator of Burgenland, a slice
of German-speaking Hungary that came to Austria by way of plebiscite
after World War I with its Hungarian legislation intact.[22] Ever since the
Compromise of 1867 the internal affairs of Burgenland had been run
from Budapest rather than from Vienna, which spared the province
both the turmoil and the improvements in education that came with the
liberal legislation. The schools remained part of the parish structure
controlled ultimately by the bishop. Rome designated Cardinal Piffl
Apostolic Administrator of the territory until the diocese of Eisenstadt
was erected, which made him ex officio head of the schools. The socialists

and nationalists both wanted to extend the liberal school legislation
to Burgenland to get homogeneity in the school system, improve education and reduce the influence of the church to the level found in the
other federal states, but the Catholics blocked the move.[23] Glöckel often
claimed that Piffl wanted to use the school system of Burgenland as a
model for a Catholic solution to the school question but the truth was
that the reformers hardly felt threatened by a system everyone considered
a throwback to the Josephinist era. Yearly attempts by the socialists
to extend Austrian school legislation to Burgenland did have the effect
of driving a wedge between the Christian Socials and Pan-Germans later
in the decade, however. Their efforts resulted in only two changes before
World War II; in 1922 the Austrian system of school inspectors was introduced provisionally, and in 1923 the Austrian rules on compulsory schooling were applied to Burgenland.[24]

The sense of deja vu about the school issue evaporates when Ignaz
Seipel comes into consideration. Gföllner in Linz agitating against the
socialists with Piffl on the spot in Vienna call up the image of Rudigier
and Rauscher from the 1860's, but the big difference was that the principal
politician of the First Republic was himself a priest. Seipel had a thorough
grasp of the possibilities for solving the school question in the abstract;
the country could separate Catholic and public school with state support
for both, or if the socialists gained the upper hand and forced a separation
of church and state, Catholics interested in religious education could
support a school system entirely out of private benefactions. But Seipel
was also a realist who reported to the Bishops Conference as early as
November 1920 that neither solution was viable because the parties
were too evenly matched and too passionately involved in the question.
The old Constitution must remain in force because Catholics could not
hope for anything better. If the school question and civil rights regarding
religion came up for discussion, he predicted an immediate coalition of
Pan-Germans and Social Democrats who otherwise opposed eath other.[25]
No cooperation with the socialists could be expected unless they were
persuaded, as was Max Hussarek, that the secular world view was similar
to religion on enough points that there might be agreement on dividing
the system. This was a vain hope, as Seipel probably knew even as he
expressed it.[26] The Freie Schule ran private schools like the Catholics,
it was true, but they were secular refuges from widespread Catholic influence

in the public schools whose reason for being would end when the socialist goal of separating church and state was achieved. Since the Social Democrats were involved in a battle for the state, they had an interest in rejecting the notion of confession as applied to their world view. Seipel only confused the bishops when he applied religious categories to the Social Democrats. More to the point, he noted that while there was strong agitation for confessional schools in the Christian Social Party, differing attitudes among Catholics made it inappropriate to raise the question at the moment. He was resigned to some school reforms, he said, because the Christian Socials could not appear to be reactionary, but he conceded that there was a need for rationalizing the school system.

At the same meeting of the Bishops Conference Ignatius Rieder of Salzburg reported on the schools in more detail. He apparently agreed that social democracy was a Weltanschauung that shared much with religion and raised the old possibility of dividing the public schools according to confession. The suggestion was unrealistic not only because the Social Democrats would not agree to it; the bishops themselves could not be expected to abandon baptized children in big cities where the governments were socialist and parents lax in the practice of religion. Practically all schools would have to be Catholic according to the bishops' definition because Catholic children were technically a minority nowhere but in a few working class districts of big cities.

The Glöckel Decree still rankled the bishops. A suggestion was made at the conference that the decree be withdrawn, but the answer came that it had been decided quietly not to implement it. At least one of the bishops, unnamed in the minutes, either did not know where the matter stood or was willing to engage in a Kulturkampf by raising the question.

With at least a subtle difference of opinion among the bishops on the desirability of actively fighting the socialists, it is not surprising that there was diversity among the organizations of laymen and lower clergy that began to represent Catholic aims in education. The Catholic School Association, formed in the last century, was no longer interested in pursuing the politicial struggle. It concentrated rather on administering the Catholic private schools it supported. Another group calling itself the Christian Education Community (Christliche Erziehungsgemeinschaft) took shape under the auspices of the Catholic People's Union (Katholischer Volksbund). The motivating force came from Prof. Ludwig Rotter, a middle school teacher in Vienna, and Richard Schmitz who had been one of the speakers at the first mass rally protesting the Glöckel Decree. The articles and bylaws of the Christian Education Community went to Piffl for approval in 1920.[27]

V

At the close of 1920, though the coalition between the Christian Socials and the nascent Pan-Germans had not yet been formed and Seipel still hoped for cooperation with the Social Democrats, the main lines of the confrontation between Catholics and socialists had already taken shape. Plans for school reform were present in detail, beginnings already made, and moderate sentiment among the Christian Socials welcomed reform. But the religious stand of the Social Democrats drew such a reaction from Catholics that moderate voices soon could not be heard. Glöckel kept a low profile in political affairs for a moment, which may have encouraged Seipel to downplay the school issue, but when plans for nationalization of property and political union with Germany were frustrated in the course of 1919-1920, the Social Democrats turned to cultural issues, like the liberals in 1867, to save some part of their program.

The bishops cautiously waited along with Seipel to see what would happen. The key figure was Friedrich Piffl who was close to Seipel, in fact his religious superior with authority to curtail or even end his public life. Cautious with opponents and allies alike, Piffl was exposed to the worst attacks of the socialist press and began to waver between the moderate policies of Seipel and the hard line taken by some bishops and involved laymen.

Chapter 5

CRISIS IN THE CATHOLIC
CAMP: 1922-1924

I

Seipel set for himself the task of reconstructing the Austrian economy when he became Chancellor in May 1922. His stated priorities became the basis for a convenient economic interpretation of his first government when he resigned. He followed the path of austerity at home forced on him as the precondition for infusions of foreign capital from the League of Nations. It suited the interests of Austrian property holders because it involved strict control over the budget and suppression of inflationary tendencies such as strikes for higher wages. Seipel could point to success before the elections of 1923, but got scant recognition because the lot of the average voter improved little during the time. Christian Social losses at the polls did not change the balance of power among the parties in the Nationalrat but they convinced the socialists that their policy of opposition was working. Another year of dealing with the intractable socialists and nursing the economy was enough for Seipel; he resigned when a strike of socialist railroad workers threatened the integrity of his plan.[1]

A subtler refinement of the economic interpretation blames the Christian Social federalists whom Seipel was unable to control without jeopardizing the unity of the party.[2] The reason lay in a condition by the League of Nations that Austria eliminate wasteful parallel administrations run by the federal government and the provinces. It was such a touchy problem that the Constituent Assembly had put off regulation of administrative relations between the *Bund* and the *Länder* until a later time to create one of the three gaps in the Constitution. Seipel was not the man to put Austria's house in order on the point because his centralist sympathies had alienated federalist opinion within his own party. When the railroad union quickly called off its strike, therefore, Seipel refused to reconsider his resignation even though another government had not been formed.

Another interpretation, I will suggest, fits the data better. It turns away from economics to emphasize cultural politics and the importance of relations between the Christian Social Party and the church. Seipel had great credibility within the party as a priest and confidant of the bishops. He had enormous influence with the bishops because they looked to the party as the secular arm of the church in its battle with the socialists. Seipel used the power of his unique position to keep church and party together even as he was cultivating the Pan-Germans for the necessary parliamentary majority to pass legislation for reconstruction. The contradiction of trying to please the anticlerical nationalists and the church simultaneously became evident when the socialists engaged in an unanswered series of provocations dealing with marriages and school policy. Seipel refused to endanger the coalition by forcing the Pan-Germans to support the Catholic position against the socialists. The bishops started out with the relatively weak support of the Catholic School Organization, but when they were joined by the Viennese branch of the Christian Socials a split began to appear in the party. Seipel could not afford a split between party and church even as he insisted that he could antagonize the Pan-Germans by pursuing clerical school policies. This tension more than anything else sealed his decision to resign. He wanted to shock the bishops and the party into realizing how dependent they were on each other. It was proof of his consummate political ability that he succeeded, though he lost his position as counselor of the bishops in the process. Piffl and Gföllner were both embarrassed by the need to change their public positions and began to dream of another concordat to supercede the party politics that were leading nowhere.

II

When Seipel responded to the universal demand that he become Chancellor, it was with no illusions about the good will of the socialists. They were exasperated by his obvious control of the Christian Socials and openly wanted him to take the blame for the failure they confidently predicted. Seipel himself was inclined to agree that his chances of governing successfully were slim, not because the Pan-Germans would be difficult coalition partners in the task of reconstruction but, as he mentioned to the bishops the year before, because the church had reason to fear a full scale Kulturkampf should the Austrian currency be stabilized in the near future.[3] He therefore took the unusual step of demanding as his sole condition for accepting the Chancellorship that the Undersecretary for Education be a Christian Social party politician.[4] Perhaps he knew already that Felix Frank, a Pan-German, would become Minister of the Interior to act as the nominal superior of the Undersecretary for Education. The *Arbeiter-Zeitung* added amazement to its usual scorn for the priorities of Seipel and the Christian Socials.

> At this terrible moment, what is the greatest concern of the man who is supposed to become chancellor tomorrow? It is not only the greatest concern, it is a precondition for taking over the government. Reported exactly, it is that the Education Ministry be occupied by a Christian Social member of parliament! At this moment, this future head of the government thinks only of clericalizing the school.[5]

If members of the Catholic camp interpreted the move as a demonstration of Seipel's resolve to represent church interests actively, they were as mistaken as the *Arbeiter-Zeitung*. He needed the Education Ministry not just to prevent further secularization—undoubtedly a motive—but more importantly as a way of accommodating the church while doing nothing to change the status quo. He needed it to outmaneuver the agitators for change in the Catholic camp. A perceptive observer might have noticed that Seipel did not mention the schools in his first speech to the Nationalrat even though other speakers raised the issue.

Even more suggestive that Seipel wanted to do nothing with the office was the appointment of Emil Schneider as head. Schneider was an unprepossessing middle school professor from Vorarlberg known rather for his mild manner and lack of energy than for dynamic qualities of leadership. He was well-chosen to keep the ministry from taking vigorous steps in any direction.

The curious association of education with the national police as departments of the Interior Ministry lasted only ten more months. It was becoming clear that the Education Ministry should be revived as a separate cabinet post despite Seipel's policy of lowering the number of civil servants. This was done in April, 1923.[6]

The Reform Department continued its work as before, with less fanfare but evidently no less efficiency.[7] The Department began work in January 1923 on a separate curriculum for rural areas to answer criticism that school reform served only the cities. After consulting the teachers by questionnaire the ministry issued several alternative curricula for the Fall of 1923. A definitive curriculum introduced late in 1924 encountered little opposition after members of the Reform Department made lecture tours of rural areas to explain it and allay suspicions.[8]

The fruitful cooperation between the Catholics and the socialist reformers came to an abrupt halt over the last real attempt to reform teacher education during the First Republic. A tentative beginning was made under Breisky when the Reform Department succeeded in relaxing the entrance requirements for active teachers to take enrichment courses at the universities, but better education before entering the profession was still sorely lacking.[9] The ministry took a survey in January 1922 as the basis for framing a law, but Schneider missed the opportunity to turn it into a bill. Instead, the three major parties worked out their own bills and took them to the Nationalrat in the winter of 1922-23. It was a tactical mistake by all parties because negotiations would be exposed and vulnerable to grandstand plays by a few radical deputies.

The differences among the bills were not surprising. The Social Democrats based their proposal on the *Leitsätze* of Glöckel which added two years of college-level courses to the existing four year programs. The courses could then be taken at universities, Hochschulen or related institutions. The Christian Socials based their program on the reform of existing academies. Degrees from Pedagogical High Schools (Pädagogische

Obershulen) would entitle students to enter the university, unlike degrees from existing institutes, but their bill did not require training beyond the current four years for initial employment. The Pan-Germans called for separate Teachers Colleges (Lehrerhochschulen) based on broader general training in the secondary schools. Each province would have its own Teachers College, in association with a university if possible.

There were definite possibilities for compromise. All the parties agreed that teachers at Bürgerschulen needed training at the college level. Teachers in rural schools where all eight grades were together in the same classroom needed similar competence. The Christian Socials wanted to improve the existing course of studies to approach the quality of the gymnasia, and the Social Democrats could have agreed as the first step toward requiring more education when the Christian Socials saw the light. In addition, the Teachers Colleges of the Pan-Germans fit the category of "related institutions" proposed by the Social Democrats.

Various difficulties stopped reform in spite of the need. The socialists and many liberals would not agree to leave intact the religious affiliation of the academies as the Christian Socials wanted. The modest bill of the Christian Socials also reflected the problem of finances based on the need to balance the federal budget. The conservatism of the universities checked the reformers, but probably the biggest brake on the whole project was the momentary surplus of teachers that followed a decline in the birth rate during the war. With more pressing issues demanding attention, the Christian Socials could safely hide behind financial considerations.[10] Within a year, however, the climate for cooperation worsened so dramatically that no party even bothered to bring the bills back in the next session of the Nationalrat.[11]

III

The source of worsening relations was to be found in Vienna, where Glöckel consolidated his hold on the school system and began to challenge the church and the government. His campaign to win support from the parents was notably effective after he published directives on organizing parents' associations and delegated the *Freie Schule* to conduct the voting for officers. Its efforts were so successful that 93.6% of the 400,000 parents voted for Social Democratic candidates.[12] The *Freie Schule* was rewarded by being accepted as an official socialist organization and united with the Kinderfreunde to become eligible for financial support from the socialist labor unions.[13]

Glöckel also began testing the government on religious exercises. He signed a decree on August 1, 1922 which substituted an "edifying saying" (Erbauungsspruch) for prayer before and after classes except for religion class. He implied that he intended to enforce the decree against compulsory religious exercises by contending that unless some compulsion was involved, prayer would be impossible even if all the children had the same religion.[14] The inefficient process of publication took three weeks, a convenient duration that gave opponents only one week to register complaints with the federal government before the decree went into effect. Only one formal objection was needed under the law to prevent the decree from being implemented while the Education Ministry adjudicated the dispute. On August 23 the Christian Educational Community submitted an appeal claiming to represent 60,000 parents, and Piffl added another of his own.[15]

Glöckel then extended his campaign against the church beyond the schools. In February 1923 he announced a new movement to leave the Catholic Church by officially registering with the government as "without religion." The Social Democratic Party supported Glöckel by saying that a person could not simultaneously be a church-goer and a socialist.[16] Georg von Schoenerer had tried the same thing with his *Los von Rom* movement of the early 1900's but succeeded in persuading only 2,200 people to change their religion in eight years. Many of these became Old Catholics who objected only to the doctrine of papal infallibility. By contrast, Glöckel's movement was markedly effective; between 1918 and 1927, 120,000 Austrians left the Catholic Church, most of them after 1923 and most in Vienna.[17]

The movement was not without dangers for the Social Democrats because it removed the ambiguity hidden in the motto "Religion is a private matter" and cut the party off from large numbers of voters who remained attached to religion. When in 1926 the party tried to expand its appeal to the voters in a "struggle for the village" it had to backtrack on the issue of religion, but by then it was impossible to undo the effects of the passions aroused earlier.[18]

Complaints against the City School Board came to Piffl's attention in increasing numbers in the summer of 1923. Grievances included transfers of religion teachers, delays in naming new ones, unfair disciplinary procedures and cessation of religious exercises entirely in one district.[19] The periodicals *Sozialistische Erziehung* and the Catholic *Schulwacht* traded charges in a spirited battle in print.[20]

The socialists had grievances of their own. Half-hearted attempts by the government to enforce laws calling for compulsory religious education resulted in a few arrests of parents outside the Vienna area, trials and small fines. The infuriated socialists then turned to the courts for relief, no longer on the basis of Article 14 of the Constitution of 1867 but on the article of the Treaty of St. Germain that abolished the distinction between legally recognized and unrecognized religions in Austria. The cases slowly made their way to the Constitutional Court, but no decision came until 1926.

The socialists took greater consolation from the outcome of parliamentary elections in the Fall of 1923. They conducted their campaign on the issue of renters' protection and the municipal housing program in Vienna rather than on cultural questions and succeeded in gaining a few seats. The Christian Socials lost little compared with the Pan-Germans but they were saddened that Seipel's success in stabilizing the economy received so little recognition.[21] After Seipel restructured his cabinet he again avoided the school issue in his declaration of policy. Other speakers followed his example, knowing that the main issue at the moment was housing rather than education. Seipel's speech departed from the ordinary by containing an ominous critique of parliament for allowing the government little freedom of action. He noted that the disillusionment in Austria had parallels throughout the world as parliamentary forms of government lost ground. Still he urged the cause of democracy "in the true sense of the word."[22]

The housing program of Vienna now came to the fore as a weapon in the cultural struggle. The ambitious and generally well-administered program had been financed by loans in 1922 and 1923, but under a new plan drawn up by Hugo Breitner apartment houses would be constructed on a pay-as-you-go basis through various forms of taxation.[23] Part of the plan was to tax Catholic private schools according to the number of windows in the building. Taxes up to 30,000 crowns per window represented gigantic sums for the large monasteries with many windows. The City Senate accordingly withdrew the tax exempt status from Catholic schools which forced tuition up and made the schools completely out of reach for poorer students. The protests of the Christian Socials succeeded in having the taxes lowered. The attempt to tax the schools almost certainly contributed to Piffl's decision in August of 1924 to break with Seipel and appeal for drastic changes in the school system.

IV

The bishops were not alone among Catholics to take an active interest in the school question. Ever since the Glöckel Decree, Catholic laymen had been developing a response to the socialists that went beyond supporting Catholic private schools as the Katholischer Schulverein was doing. During Seipel's term the Catholic School Organization overcame organizational difficulties, grew strong and took an independent path with the support of the bishops. It succeeded in driving a wedge between Piffl and Seipel when harrassment by the socialists in Vienna got no response from the national leadership of the Christian Socials. This in turn had ramifications within the party as the Viennese Christian Socials began to follow their lead. The Vienna branch of the party first endorsed confessional schools as the bishops had done in 1922, unrealistic as the call was without concrete proposals on enforcing attendance of all baptized children at Catholic schools, and then threatened to disrupt the unity of the party by following Piffl when he went a step further to support separating the school systems on the model of Holland, as the School Organization had been suggesting. It took all of Seipel's politicial finesse and theological expertise to defeat the efforts of the School Organization, but once he had done so he could easily keep the bishops and Viennese Christian Socials from drifting away. Ironically, Seipel's enemies within the Catholic camp were defeated by his resignation on October 19 although it did not become apparent until the bishops met the following month. As Seipel once said, he knew when to get sick and when to resign.

Early attempts to unite the Catholic school lobby were a failure until the bishops stepped in. In Fall 1922, the Katholischer Volksbund, an umbrella organization for many Catholic *Vereine* with ties to the Christian Socials, tried to unite the efforts of the Katholischer Schulverein and the Christian Education Community which had come into existence in response to the Glöckel Decree. When they did not succeed in overcoming mutual jealousies the bishops ordered the two groups to unite under the ponderous title of School and Education Organization of Austrian Catholics (Schul–und Erziehungsorganization der Katholiken Österreichs). The group was to combine the functions of a militant organization with the customary work of supporting Catholic private schools financially. Financial support would come from collections in church and free will offerings rather than membership dues.[24] The union was proclaimed at a mass meeting in the Konzerthaus of Vienna on November 25, 1922 and bylaws were drawn up in the next six months.

The bishops recognized the potential for good and for ill in the new organization and preferred to keep it directly responsible to themselves rather than to the Katholischer Volksbund. They did so by appointing a special liaison between themselves and the School Organization, as it was soon called for short. The post went to Josef Pfeneberger, a priest and director of the diocesan seminary in Linz whose name had been suggested earlier for the post of general secretary. This turned out to be a mistake because Pfeneberger was then too far removed from making decisions within the group. His expertise in theology and church politics could have prevented the School Organization from making serious mistakes in its proposals to the bishops. Instead, the post of general secretary went to Ludwig Rotter, a zealous and energetic professor at the Pedagogical Institute in Vienna whose dedication concealed poor theological preparation and issued in bull-headed adherence to ideas and projects that the bishops would not endorse as a group. The president and chief spokesman was Alfons Johannes Ressiguier, an old nobleman from the Katholischer Schulverein who shared Rotter's enthusiasm for the task at hand though he was no more expert in dealing with matters of theory.

The resolution of the Bishops Conference to unite the efforts of Austrian Catholics on the schools wavered when the bishops went back to their own dioceses where the threat was less. Resistance to change and suspicion of Vienna among the laity forced the bishops—if they really had other inclinations—to rely on existing groups. The functions of the School Organization were handled by the Katholischer Volksbund in St. Pölten, by the Tiroler Elternbund in Innsbruck and in Styria by the Katholischer Schulverein which refused to give up its name.

A fundamental misunderstanding between the bishops and the School Organization emerged as early as June 1923 when the School Organization submitted two proposals for constitutional laws on the schools to be discussed at the upcoming Katholikentag. The second contained a passage that said parents and guardians had a natural right to determine whether their children have a religion or not. The bill said nothing about how the natural right of parents might be modified by membership in the church, but the bishops were nonetheless reluctant to acknowledge a right of parents to determine the religion of their children. The church had a missionary task to preach the Gospel that might be jeopardized by saying that parents had a right to teach something contrary to the Gospel. They recognized the ultimate inviolability of conscience, but parents had no more rights over the conscience of a child than the church, even in the natural order, to say nothing of baptized children. All four bishops that responded to Piffl's request for opinions rejected this formulation.

The School Organization quickly drew back to exclude a natural right of parents to decide the religion of their children. They substituted freedom of conscience as a civil right based on the pluralistic conditions of the modern state which could be modified by membership in a church. This was a less radical formulation of the so-called Freedom of Conscience Schools supported by the School Organization. It combined freedom of conscience in education as a civil right, that is, freedom from state insistence that a certain school be chosen for a child or that religious instruction be mandatory, with the moral obligation of Catholic parents to send their children to Catholic schools according to the directives of the bishops. Lack of state enforcement made the Freedom of Conscience School different from confessional schools. The School Organization moved so fast in the summer of 1923 that the bishops scarcely had time to prevent the Catholic Congress from following its lead. The Congress, which met from June 29 to July 2 agreed on the following formulation:

> The parents or their legal representatives have the natural and constitutionally guaranteed right, but at the same time the duty to bear the first responsibility for the moral and religious education of their children as well as for instruction in other branches of learning.[25]

When the School Organization searched for a model to follow for the Freedom of Conscience School it discovered that the school system of

Holland fit their criteria nicely. In that country there were parallel public and religiously sponsored school systems supported by the state; parents were free to send their children wherever they wished. The School Organization then brought the director of the Catholic schools in Holland, Dr. Theodor Verhoeven, to explain the system in the Fall of 1923. He spoke eloquently about Catholic reaction to the state monopoly of schools before 1848, the struggle for freedom to teach and eventual success in winning state aid after 1889. Confessional and state schools were made equal in 1920, he said, thereby ending a struggle that had dominated politics in the Netherlands for years.[26]

The bishops were less inclined to see the similarities between Austria and Holland. Austria had not been a Protestant country with a large number of dissenters like Holland, nor had the schools ever been the monopoly of a secular state. The fact that Austria was 90% Catholic changed everything as far as the bishops were concerned. Not only did they claim delegated rights over the education of children, they felt justified in having the state protect the interests of vulnerable children against the incursions of authorities inimical to religion. The School Organization, on the other hand, joined the socialists in recognizing de facto pluralism and was not interested in school authorities or lax parents. If the bishops recognized a civil right to educate children according to parental preference regardless of whether they were baptized they could be considered remiss in their duty to teach the Gospel. Consequently they opposed the definition of such a civil right because it would have abandoned thousands of baptized children to atheists. If the state had been truly pluralistic they might have agreed to the Freedom of Conscience school with the approval of Rome because the new Code of Canon Law made such accommodation, but Austria was a Catholic country by the only definition acceptable to the bishops, that is, the baptismal rolls. They could have denied baptism to the children of parents who were not likely to raise them Catholic, but they were loath to do so for the sake of the children and because it was a departure from long-accepted custom. The School Organization had the laudable motive of trying to draw Catholics into a leaner and tighter church based on free and ongoing committment rather than commanded from above, but the bishops could not lightly acquiesce to changes in a hierarchical system that had elaborate justification ranging from the theology of baptism to ecclesiology.

Both major political parties were opposed to the Freedom of Conscience School as well. Dedicated to holding all cultural bastions, the Christian Socials were not ready to concede on eliminating religion even from a portion of the public schools. Seipel agreed with the bishops that baptism made people members of the church with certain rights and duties. Rotter and Ressiguier were never able to win over the party though for reasons dealing with socialist provocations they enjoyed the confidence of Piffl. They were pained by the lack of support from the Christian Socials when they did not support efforts to organize parallel associations of Catholic parents at the public schools in Vienna despite Glöckel's obvious control.[27] Rotter commented years later, "This division between Party and School Organization was extremely unfavorable to the Catholic school movement."[28] Seipel wanted to work within the system in the hopes of recapturing it from the socialists, but the socialists had similar goals. They opposed the Freedom of Conscience School because they had hopes of imposing their ideas of reform and secularization on the entire school system. Furthermore they had reservations about the expenditures necessary to erect new schools for separate systems.[29]

V

Like the Christian Socials and Social Democrats, the bishops had not given up on the system in November 1923 when they held their annual meeting. If Seipel was serious about preserving the staus quo he might be willing to lift the Glöckel Decree and return the system to the way it was in 1918. They had evidently discussed the formal repeal of the Glöckel Decree in 1922 after Glöckel had tried to stop school prayer, but put off action for fear of adversely affecting the elections scheduled for 1923.[30] When the elections ended with no great losses for the Christian Socials the bishops decided to press the government on lifting the decree or at least for a public interpretation of it in the light of existing laws and precedents.[31] In due course they sent a letter to Schneider, but his response did not come for a full year. By that time a crisis of confidence between church and party had taken place in which Seipel pointed out the inconsistency of appealing both for a complete confessional school system and for lifting of the Glöckel Decree. The two were hardly compatible. It was becoming clear that to hold all bastions meant the party had no intention of trying to reconquer those lost as recently as 1919.

The Christian Socials found the concept of civil freedom of conscience almost as attractive as the School Organization. A few, like Richard Wollek, a school politician from Upper Austria, were adding that the bishops ought to leave the school question to loyal Catholic politicians. They may have been unaware of the bishops' decision to require episcopal approval for all church representatives on school boards—Gföllner's 9-point program was vague on the matter—so there was some confusion when a proposed law on school reorganization in Upper Austria did not include the legal protection of the bishop's right in the matter. Wollek and Josef Pfeneberger, who was in fact much closer to the Christian Socials than to the School Organization despite his position as liaison with the bishops, wrote to Piffl to quiet his fears. It was their attitude that the church ought to continue its representation in public school supervisory offices but that it ought not be overly concerned about legal protection of the rights of the church by having a clause stipulating that supervisors of religious instruction should be approved by the local bishop. In their conclusion they said that it was probably more advisable to base church claims not so much on state laws as on the convictions of believing people and their political representatives.[32] The Christian Socials and the School Organization were in agreement at least on suggesting that the bishops divest themselves of claims to have the state exercise its coercive authority on their behalf.

Piffl began to get mixed signals from Linz shortly thereafter. He got a letter from a certain Dr. J. Schwimmer, a member of the Upper Austrian Provincial School Board and delegate to the Bundesrat, who complained about the information Piffl seemed to be getting from Wollek. There were tensions between Gföllner and the party, he contended, on exactly the point where Wolleck gave the most solemn assurances. In fact, the party was not willing to accept Gföllner's nominee as their own to the Upper Austrian Provincial School Board.[33] Gföllner fancied himself a Kulturkämpfer like Rudigier, but now he began to lose confidence. He wrote to Piffl a week later saying he would wait until he knew Piffl's mind on the law in Upper Austria before he committed himself.[34] There is no evidence that he informed Piffl about the reluctance of the Christian Socials to accept his nominee. When Schwimmer wrote a second time to say that in the proposed law the church representative was named ultimately by the party rather than by the church, the usually decisive Gföllner began twisting and turning by suggesting to Piffl that another legal basis for strengthening church influence had to be found. He had written to the pope, and he suggested that Piffl contact Cardinal Merry de Val, the Papal Secretary of State.[35] Gföllner was suddenly supporting the Christian Social Party by allowing legal protection of church interests in Upper Austria to lapse despite the embarrassing coalition with the Pan-Germans that prevented broaching the subject of the confessional schools he had so staunchly advocated fourteen months earlier. Piffl's reaction to Gföllner's change of position is not recorded, but he can be pardoned for thinking that Gföllner might support him if he came out publicly in support of separating the school systems. Everyone around Piffl except Seipel seemed to be saying that the bishops ought to rely on the Catholic laity; perhaps the solution suggested by the School Organization would be the best.

Piffl drew further inspiration from a bold decision by the Viennese branch of the Christian Socials. Delegates to the local party congress in April 1924 publicized another list of socialist provocations and broke with the official stance of the party by publicly endorsing confessional schools financed by the state.[36] It was similar to the bishops' statement of 1922 in making no concrete suggestions on who would decide where baptized children were to go. Seipel was getting used to ignoring statements of principle that could not be implemented, so he took no notice until Piffl moved.

Piffl decided in the summer of 1924 that it was hopeless trying to maintain the place of religion in the public schools of Vienna. On August 24 he issued a pastoral letter calling for the separation of the schools into public and church administered systems with state support for church-related schools.[37] He directed that sermons be preached on the topic on October 5, the School Sunday of that year. Adam Hefter of Klagenfurt supported him, but Gföllner and Pfeneberger deserted him at this juncture. Piffl was forcing people to decide between the party and the church, embarrassing Seipel and threatening the coalition with the Pan-Germans.

There was a somewhat perplexing delay between Piffl's pastoral letter of August and Seipel's reply in October. Perhaps it had something to do with Seipel's recovery from the assassination attempt of June 1, 1924 or perhaps it had to do with the summer recess and the threatened railroad strike immediately thereafter. Seipel's letter of October 18 erased all illusions, however, he spoke to the national party council on the same day using practically the same words. One all-important statement was missing from the address to the party, namely a threat to resign.[38]

In his letter to Piffl, Seipel said that the party received instructions from the church on school matters but that it had the responsibility to decide what was politically possible. He gently chided the bishops for having no unified school goals—as though the weak stand of the party had no effect on the bishops—and suggested that they establish some principles before the party dealt with the issue at the next party congress. He then defended his position on the basis of Canon Law. Canon 1374 allowed Catholic children to attend "neutral" or "mixed" schools under certain circumstances if the bishop approved. Canon law could not be interpreted to mean that parents had the right to decide whether children should be considered Catholic. One ought not be an accomplice in raising children without hearing of God on the basis of such a right, he said, even in exchange for the exclusively Catholic education of part of them. By saying this he was attacking the Freedom of Conscience School using a theological argument that Piffl had been willing to overlook for the sake of salvaging some religious education in Vienna. The politician Seipel was in effect claiming to be acting from higher principle than Piffl; he was subtly accusing Piffl of being untrue to the Catholic understanding of baptism. Seipel kept the bombshell till last: ". . . in any case, my conscience would not allow me to remain in my present position if Austrian Catholics would take a position deviating from the Code of Canon Law for opportunistic reasons or, because of uncertainty about principles, would oppose each other."[39] Piffl then understood the depth of Seipel's conviction that the school question held more potential for harm than good. Seipel had sufficient backing in Catholic theology and law for doing nothing at the moment and had every political reason to avoid attaching too much importance to socialist provocations in Vienna. Piffl was suddenly a wiser and very lonely man.

The degree to which Seipel acted out of loyalty to the church rather than the party can be judged only with difficulty. His principle that baptized children had a right to be educated as Catholics implied that the bishops could determine how that education should take place. Glöckel attacked him in the Nationalrat, and Seipel had to say it was his personal position, but the statement was not calculated to win sympathizers even among many Catholic voters. It was designed to make an impression on Piffl and the bishops. On the other hand, if Seipel were truly acting on principle, he could have supported the bishops' request to repeal the Glöckel Decree. This would not have overly jeopardized the coalition since the decree was an administrative regulation that could be retracted by executive fiat. Instead Seipel covered his inaction by saying the bishops were being inconsistent on whether they wanted repeal of Glöckel's decree or confessional schools.

The main thrust of Seipel's argument was to keep the status quo with all its deficiencies. He was in a unique position to assess the impact of a Catholic initiative on political life in Austria. Its long-term effects on the undecided constitutional question of church-state relations were incalculable, but in the immediate future the bourgeois coalition would certainly suffer to some extent. The Christian Socials would be hurt if the Pan-Germans, with little parliamentary strength, insisted on being consulted as equals in cultural questions, while the Pan-Germans would be hurt if the Christian Socials dared them to leave the coalition over a cultural issue that was secondary to the economic and social goals they shared in common. The Christian Socials had the upper hand, but Seipel intended to keep faith with the Pan-Germans; to ignore the coalition agreement might plunge Austria back into political instability. The whole question was academic, however, because no changes could be made under the law without a constitutional law passed with the cooperation of the socialists.

Most importantly for Seipel, the initiative by the church was splitting the Christian Social Party into political and religious factions. Seipel could at least control if not master the federalist divisions plaguing the party, but the recent church action threatened to add the traditionally centralist Viennese Christian Socials to the squabbling subgroups on the basis of religion rather than regionalism. He had counted most on the loyalty of the Viennese but now found a revolt originating in Vienna. Piffl was allowing religious considerations to predominate over the total political context of the school issue. Furthermore he was forcing a national policy on the party and the bishops without prior consultation with either. Seipel

wanted to be sure the bishops were united before he committed the party—
if indeed he ever intended to follow a religious lead exclusively—but he
knew that now more than ever they were disunified. Piffl had just added
a third goal, the Freedom of Conscience School, to confessional schools
and the status quo modified by repeal of the Glöckel Decree. Seipel found
himself isolated too for a time, but his position at the intersection of
church and party made his the stronger position within the Catholic camp.
Unfortunately he was exposed to attacks in the press and Nationalrat
that he had to answer in a way Piffl did not.

The attacks on Seipel came from several quarters. Commentators in
the press generally missed the meaning of Seipel's speech to the party
council. The *Neue Freie Presse* called it a politically mistaken attack
against the modern educational system and then inquired, "Was it really
necessary precisely at this moment to discuss the educational program
and to propose the concordat school and determining influence of the
bishops on the educational system as the desirable ideal."[40] The *Arbeiter-
Zeitung* missed the point entirely, most likely as Seipel wanted. The paper
asked, "Has the man gone mad?" and described the two wings of the
"clericals" as the opportunistic schoolmen who wanted the Holland
solution, and the radical reactionaries who wanted Canon Law to determine how the schools were organized. Seipel was prominent in the latter
category.[41] In fact, Seipel was far less radical than the schoolmen whose
plan for retrenchment in the schools was a prelude to futher moves based
on ideology and an integralist view of Catholic politics. Rotter had to
defend himself against charges by Glöckel and Kunschak that he wanted to
start another political party. The analysis in the socialist press could hardly
have been further from the truth. Seipel was actually making concessions
to the socialists by not supporting a radical solution like separating the
school systems.

Reaction to Seipel's speech was not confined to editorials. Excited
rallies were held at several places in Vienna on October 20 to protest.
Glöckel gave an impassioned speech at a noisy meeting in Ottakring,
concentrating on Seipel's statements about Canon Law and expressing
the socialist determination to separate church and school entirely.[42]

The next day the galleries were packed in the Nationalrat to watch
the confrontation when Glöckel interpellated Seipel. Glöckel delivered
his speech as an urgent inquiry on the intention of the government to

honor the authority of the state established in 1869. Accusing him of making the confessional school a party goal, he asked several questions about state supervision, textbooks, curriculum, hiring and teacher training. He shouted that the confessional school was impossible once and for all and concluded by saying the socialists were willing to prevent it with any means.[43]

Seipel answered with more moderation than usual; it was difficult to reveal that his speech was intended to mollify the Christian Socials over the inaction of his government, and that his appeal to Canon Law was meant to hide his apprehension over the stability of the party and the coalition. He said the statement had been a personal one and did not represent a change in party policy; the coalition prevented that. Then counterattacking, he accused Glöckel of violating the Elementary School Law and politizing the schools, which made the Christian Socials in Vienna so uneasy that they felt constrained to demand confessional schools by way of change. He admitted to a split in the Christian Social Party, perhaps grateful that Glöckel had not exploited his rift with Piffl—ridicule might have been more devastating than thunderous pronouncements—but said, "the school struggle on Austrian soil is far from decided against us, and so we may not yet retreat to a second line of defense."[44] He meant the Freedom of Conscience Schools which, he noted, was rejected by the Social Democrats as well as by himself.

Karl Leuthner tried to make political capital out of the event by placing a resolution before the house reaffirming the exclusive authority of the state in school matters. The Pan-Germans were embarrassed by the possibility of a vote that would split the coalition and placed a motion of their own to proceed with the next item of business. The Christian Social president of the Nationalrat called for a vote on the Pan-German motion before that of the Social Democrats in an unusual parliamentary maneuver that raised strenuous objections from Karl Seitz, and amid racket from the galleries the socialists walked out.

Out in the street, a crowd of demonstrators formed and moved from the parliament building to City Hall a short distance away. Estimates of the size in the press varied according to the political persuasion of the newspaper, but about 6,000-7,000 persons seems to be the best estimate.[45]

Back in the Catholic camp Seipel moved quickly against the School Organization. Henceforth good relations between them were impossible.

The party issued guidelines for Catholic parents in the elections to parents' organizations in the Vienna schools that ignored the existence of separate Catholic groups run by the School Organization. It opposed the boycott called by the School Organization by recommending emphatically, "Under no conditions should parents refrain from voting."[46] When Piffl tried to bring representatives of the School Organization together with the Christian Socials, Seipel listened for a while then rose and left the room without a word.[47] Undaunted, Rotter and company continued their arguments in a long, cogently-reasoned letter to Piffl containing their interpretation of the affair. They still recommended that the school systems be separated; "schiedlich-friedlich" (separate-peaceful) was their watchword. Seipel had undercut them, though, true to his promise to shelve the issue until the bishops worked things out themselves. On November 19 he persuaded the party congress to drop resolutions supporting Piffl and the cause of confessional schools.[48] He wanted the bishops to decide at least whether they wanted him to repeal the Glöckel Decree and make religious exercises formally mandatory again or to support separating the school systems. In the process he ignored the third possibility of endorsing state aid for Catholic schools, as the party finally did in 1926.

Seipel resigned on November 11, using a threatened strike of railroad employees as the pretext. When the strike was called off on November 13 and the Pan-Germans agreed to renew the coalition agreement, he used the difficulty of getting the Christian Social federalists to dismantle the inefficient parallel administrations as another pretext to decline the invitation to form another government. Bewilderment was general even in the government. Three ambassadors wrote from Bucharest, Belgrad and London that they were at a loss for a solid interpretation of Seipel's resignation.[49] His real goal was to bring the church and the party together again which could not happen before the bishops met later in November. The timing of his resignation was perfect for the maximum impact on the party and the bishops. He had scapegoats in the socialist unions and the Christian Social federalists which kept him from suffering any loss of prestige within the party. The leadership he held in reserve was not needed until his successor, Rudolph Ramek, bungled the school issue during the summer of 1926 while Seipel was on a trip to America.

There were a number of sore, chastened and humiliated men at the Bishops Conference meeting of November 1924.[50] Seipel was disturbed by the bishops; most bishops were annoyed by the poor relations between Piffl and Seipel–they were supposed to be working closely together in Vienna. Piffl in turn had cause to be disturbed by Gföllner who, despite his rhetoric about confessional schools, was now abandoning any pretense of acting independently to side with the party in doing nothing.

Seipel argued in his political report that the school systems could not be separated without giving up claims to have the state enforce attendance at Catholic schools for all Catholics. The state in Holland did not practice such enforcement. But the fact that the bishops had asked for repeal of the Glöckel Decree the year before indicated that they wanted the state to enforce attendance not just at religious instruction but at religious exercises as well. Furthermore, Piffl had not put any noticeable distance between himself and efforts to repeal the Glöckel Decree in August when he recommended the Holland solution. To summarize, confessional schools were incompatible with the Holland solution, and both were incompatible with repealing the Glöckel Decree. Old Johannes Rössler of St. Pölten laconically recorded "differences between Cardinal and Seipel over the School Organization."[51]

The other bishops were disturbed by Piffl and Seipel. They were annoyed that Piffl had struck out on his own before the government had responded to their letter asking for repeal of the Glöckel Decree. Any law would involve the difficult task of getting the agreement of the Nationalrat and each of the provinces individually since the socialists would certainly oppose a constitutional amendment that left vestiges of Catholic influence in the schools. Even if the route of "paktiert" legislation was tried the Pan-Germans could not be relied on to support a bill. Piffl reportedly complained after the conference that no one listened to him in the Bishops Conference anymore.[52] But the bishops were also piqued by Seipel; they did not enjoy being forced to support the party. For the first time since the war they openly discussed the possibility of a new Concordat with Rome which would provide a negotiated settlement to some problems.

In the end the biggest loser was neither the party nor the bishops but rather the School Organization. The bishops issued a carefully worded rejection of the Freedom of Conscience School. They commended the School Organization for its efforts but said that as long as the Elementary

School Law remained unchanged the right of children to religious instruction and education (they meant exercises) was to be protected. The School Organization could agitate in favor of Catholic schools in areas where the rights of Catholic children were being suppressed.[54] The bishops pointedly ignored the question of civil freedom of conscience; it involved a degree of separation between church and state which they could not endorse until they had tried the intermediate step of a concordat with Rome.

The aura surrounding Seipel permitted him to escape unscathed for the moment. The bishops trusted his dedication to the church. Seipel did not intend to imply in his presentation that he had a broader view than the bishops or that religious interests were only a part of the whole political context. He was too much a priest for that. He was trying to challenge the bishops to find a solution to the school question in religious renewal rather than by relying on the power of the state to make and enforce laws favorable to the church. This attitude contained not only religious motivation but also disillusionment with the political system in Austria. He said clearly in a press conference after his resignation that his long-range goal was spiritual renewal for Austria, though the socialists dismissed it as pious hypocrisy.[55] We should have no reason to doubt this. Seipel started off his government with the coalition uppermost in his mind; nothing could be done without stable government and a parliamentary majority. He wanted to maintain the status quo on cultural questions by having Schneider as Education Minister but the party could promise only a holding action that was beginning to crumble. In the course of his government fear for the coalition turned to frustration as he discovered that the executive was severely limited by the Constitution of 1920. There was little he or Schneider could do to prevent the socialists from nibbling away at the legal status of the church. If he wanted to do something for the church as an institution he now found he had two reasons not to try, the coalition and the weakness of the executive. Seipel's inability to defend the church led not just to his resignation in an effort to keep the Catholic camp united, but also to profound alienation from the parliamentary system established in 1920. Relative success on the economic and political fronts had, after all, led nowhere. He could outmanuever Piffl, but it did not represent a victory for politics over religion in his mind. Religion was still his hope.

Seipel's turn to feel the wrath of the bishops came in early 1925. Some of the bishops, at least Gföllner and Rössler, but perhaps Hefter and Rieder as well, collaborated in submitting to Piffl a set of suggestions on re-organizing the Bishops Conference. They asked Piffl to maintain strict control over the parliamentary method of consultation, hinting that the previous meeting had been less than orderly. They also asked that minutes by reproduced and handed out to members rather than read for approval. Most significantly they had objections to the customary relationship with "political personages or state officials" because they could influence "the independence and freedom so necessary to the episcopacy."[56] In 1926 the bishops decided to work out bylaws in accord with these suggestions, and they no longer invited Seipel to address the conference.

One last issue had been hanging fire for some months. On November 21, Emil Schneider replied to Piffl on the question of repealing the Glöckel Decree. Exploring the history, law and politics of the question, he concluded that nothing should be done, and he pleaded with Piffl not to ignore the peculiar difficulties he faced.[57]

The dust settled quickly. Seipel was no longer Chancellor, though still head of the party. A potentially dangerous division between the church and the party had been averted, and the split in the Bishops Conference had been patched up. Relations between Piffl and the Christian Socials were not strained beyond saving, and Seipel was aware of the importance of education to the church. By common consent the hierarchy and party sacrificed the goals of the School Organization, but Rotter and Ressiguier would not know the extent of their defeat for another three years. They had made several errors themselves, theological in formulating the theory of freedom of conscience in an unacceptable way, church-political in blithely abandoning baptized children to the whims of lax parents and hostile socialists, and secular-political in ignoring the realities of trying to separate the school systems in the face of opposition from anti-Catholic political groups. The Christian Socials successfully resisted pressure to make the school question the issue that determined the broad outlines of their political struggle with the socialists while political stability and the economic good of Austria represented by Seipel's reconstruction plan were together more important than ill-defined religious goals.

Chapter 6

CATHOLICS AND SOCIALISTS DRIFT
TOWARD CONFRONTATION: 1924-1926

I

The eighteen months between November 1924 and May 1926 saw a
major confrontation developing between the Catholics and the socialists in Vienna over the schools. The way was paved by two sets of problems that put the Catholics in a worse position to oppose socialist initiatives. A series of court cases pitted the government against parents
who were backed by the socialists, and the decisions began to go against
the Catholics. Infighting among the Catholics weakened them as well.
Catholic organizations could not agree on distributions of power nor
could the bishops agree on united action; the School Organization tried
unsuccessfully to absorb the Catholic welfare organization called the
Frohe Kindheit and a sharp jurisdictional struggle broke out between
rival unions of Catholic teachers. The School Organization played a
central role in all the areas of agitation while Seipel and the Christian
Socials maneuvered to erode its strength as much as possible. The grating
personality of Ludwig Rotter combined with the tactical blunders to dis-
credit the School Organization in the eyes of many Catholics.

School reform in the meantime went on in some areas but was blocked
in others. There was further experimentation with the elementary school

curricula that led to satisfactory results, and there was a certain amount of agreement on the need to reorganize the secondary school system. But a law could be blocked on almost any minor pretext. Part of the pretext was furnished by differences over the reform of teacher education and part was furnished by the defiance of Glöckel, who began a campaign of disciplining religion teachers for infractions of his rules despite directives from the Education Ministry. A repeat of the confrontation between Glöckel and Seipel occurred in the Nationalrat in May 1926, after which Seipel left for America leaving the Catholics essentially leaderless as the crisis approached.

II

With the masterful stroke of his resignation Seipel achieved three goals simultaneously, concellation of the railroad strike, reunification of church and party, and agreement by the federalists to eliminate parallel administrations. The last of these was all but accomplished although his successor had to finish the job. Seipel could have forced the federalists to agree to the necessary constitutional law using the same weapon he used in 1924 when the government collected taxes and simply refused to pay the provinces a certain amount for financing their administrations. He refused to do this for the sake of party unity and deferred to Rudolph Ramek whose sole job was to make the bad medicine of austerity more palatable. Since the particularist cause was hopeless anyway, there was little resentment when Seipel remained president of the party caucus.

Ramek came with good credentials among federalists. He had received a mandate from provincial leaders the month before to frame a counterproposal to the centralistic program of the Seipel government for administrative reform. But his task as Chancellor was clear, and if the federalists really expected anything different, they were disappointed immediately when he announced his intention of eliminating parallel administrations in his declaration of policy.[1] Ramek arranged a compromise on allocation of tax monies in February 1925 and began a series of complex, tripartite negotiations among the parties, the provincial governments and the central government. With remarkable speed considering the complications, a package of laws on administration, finances and judicial structures took shape and passed the Nationalrat with the necessary two-thirds majority.[2]

The power of the federal government increased in most matters; the supervisory power of the Supreme Accounting Office, for example, was extended to the provinces. Likewise, the system of administrative and constitutional courts was developed further, which soon affected the school question as cases came up.

Mission accomplished, Ramek tendered his resignation in January 1926. Reconstruction was nearly complete with a balanced budget, a stable currency and few outstanding questions about government spending. The League of Nations followed with a program for lifting financial controls over Austria leading Ramek to think that new elections might better reflect the changes in the political situation. The Nationalrat had other ideas, though, and decided to refuse his resignation. It was satisfied with a few changes in his Cabinet. Of the constitutional issues left unresolved in 1920, only the school question remained.

III

Ramek did not replace Emil Schneider when he first took office or when he reconstituted his government. Like Seipel, he wanted to keep a lid on school reform, but unlike Seipel he had no expertise on the issues involved. That left Schneider free in a way to take steps Seipel might have blocked as, for example, when he drew up a contingency plan for lifting the Glöckel Decree in 1925. But in general, Schneider kept the Education Ministry an administrative rather than a reforming agency.

The socialists could hardly hope for changes on religion in the schools coming from the Education Ministry so they turned instead to the Administrative and Constitutional Courts. The function of the Administrative Court was to determine whether concrete decisions made by executive authorities were in keeping with the law. The courts could reverse decisions in individual cases, but these decisions did not provide precedents because the court had no power to declare illegal decrees or policies of the executive. A fortiori it had no authority to declare laws unconstitutional. The executive could ignore whatever precedent value there was in an individual case because it was difficult to bring large numbers of cases before the court. Only the Constitutional Court could declare laws or decrees unconstitutional with the authority to bind the executive and the legislature alike. This was a new power of the judiciary under the Republic, and it represented one of the few checks on parliamentary absolutism contained in the Constitution of 1920.[3]

Unfortunately, the status of neither court was sufficient to overcome the animosities that had arisen over the decades; decisions served to heighten rather than resolve political tensions over the schools. First, the courts were working with old laws whose legitimacy was tenuous under the republican constitution. It is not surprising that the courts based their decisions on the hated Treaty of St. Germain because its status in Austrian constitutional life was at least clear and definite. The courts would rather have consulted the mind of the legislator as was customary in countries with a tradition of Roman Law, but the Constituent Assembly and the Nationalrat had left them to deal with a mass of contradictory precedents based on conflicting interpretations of the Elementary School Law and Article 14 of the earlier constitution. Finally, one or two important cases that came to the Constitutional Court were not decided until the political crisis of 1927 had passed and the sides had begun resorting to unconstitutional means of resolving disputes. So despite the immense power of the Constitutional Court in theory, its decisions played only a small role in the history of the school question.

The first case to make its way through the court system dealt with the Amendment of 1883 to the Elementary School Law stipulating that the principal must be able to teach the religion of the majority of pupils in the school. The Administrative Court decided on March 25, 1925 that neither the Constitution of 1920 nor the Treaty of St. Germain had abolished the amendment. The judges maintained in their decision that the principle of equality was not absolute; certain professions could be restricted to a certain sex, occupation or religion without violating the principle. Soldiers, for example, could be drawn exclusively from the pool of single males.[4]

The Constitutional Court reversed this decision on October 19 of the same year, declaring that the amendment was contrary to the article of the Treaty of St. Germain that protected the religious rights of minorities.[5] The court refused to decide whether the amendment was contrary to the Constitution of 1867, as the complaint charged, but took exception rather to the reasoning of the Administrative Court saying that equality must be actual as well as formal. The court confirmed its decision by a similar judgment on February 29, 1928.[6] The decision did not decide the constitutionality issue unequivocally because the Treaty of St. Germain could be modified by international agreement. For the time being, though, the Treaty was an integral part of the Austrian Constitution. The bishops were not surprised by the decision. Indeed, in their meeting of 1921 they agreed to compromise should the question arise in the legislature and have the principal belong to the religion of two-thirds rather than just over one-half of the pupils.[7] Their protests over the decision of the Constitutional Court had no noticeable effect.[8]

The second series of cases was not as easy. The Constitutional Court took more than three years to reach a decision; perhaps it contributed by its slowness to the rancor that led to the riots of 1927. Because of their complicated nature it seems best to follow the cases from start to finish although they were only in mid-course when the period under consideration here came to a close.

The question dealt with compulsory religious *instruction* for children under the age of fourteen (as distinguished from religious *education* which included religious *exercises*). The key to the question was a passionate controversy over the legal meaning of a "change of religion" (Religionswechsel) and whether children could follow their parents when they changed or dropped their religion. The successful campaign led by Glöckel made the number of cases large and the problem acute.

There were disparities between the views of church and government on the question. In one respect the church was more liberal than the government; it acknowledged a certain right of parents—disputed by some theologians, it was true—to keep their children from being baptized. This kept the child from falling under the jurisdiction of canon law and the church had no right to insist that the child receive religious instruction. The government, on the other hand, interpreted Paragraph 1 of the Elementary School Law, which made moral-religious education the goal of the schools, as meaning that every child must have some religion in which it received instructions when it entered school even though it might not be a regular member of any church. Each child had to receive instruction in either the Catholic, Protestant or Jewish religions until it reached the age of fourteen.[9]

On another matter the government was more liberal. It inherited laws from the liberal era that allowed people to change religion, in contrast with the church which was unwilling to grant that a baptized Catholic could change his religion. This meant that a baptized Catholic child could take instructions in the Protestant religion if its parents changed their religion before the child entered school. The law did not allow a baptized child to drop its religion if the parents registered as having no religion.[10]

The combined positions of the church and the Christian Social government now appear unrealistically harsh. They seemed to agree that if parents dropped their religion entirely their children, baptized or unbaptized, still had to receive some religious instruction in the Catholic, Protestant or Jewish faiths. Even parents who never had a religion had no right to prevent the state from insisting on some religious instruction for their children. In this light, the Glöckel Decree relieved the state somewhat from the burdens of the *Rechtsstaat* by giving school officials a sufficient legal base to ignore pressures from local churchmen over compulsory religious exercises until the legality of the decree was decided.

Since both church and state were conspiring to force unwanted religious instructions on children, the socialists had a clear and immediate objective in appealing to the courts. They had to broaden the legal definition of religion to include any world view that provided an ultimate explanation of human life. Furthermore, they had to win agreement that any change in religious status whatsoever, including dropping religion, constituted a "change of religion" under the law. If they established both, all children, baptized or not, under the age of seven could automatically follow their parents in dropping religion and be free from the obligation to take religious instruction when they entered school. They then would fall under the provisions of the May Laws. Children from the age of seven to fourteen were in a different category because they were required under the law to take religious instruction. The socialist argument that it was abhorrent for the state to force its way between the values of parents and children in those years possessed great moral force, but its impact was weakened by the existence of laws and the inability to reach a consensus on redefining relations between church and state. It is easy to see how the bishops might interpret this thrust as though the socialists were defining their views in religious terms, and might be amenable to "Weltanschauungsschulen," but such was not the case. They were swallowing their dislike for defining scientific socialism as a religion for the sake of eventual separation of church and state. The goal of having the courts broaden the meaning of "change in religion" was more immediately attainable than putting together a two-thirds majority in the Nationalrat to separate church and school.

The trouble with the socialist argument was that only the word "change" became significant in the phrase "change of religion." The Christian Socials had a strong argument that the phrase meant a change from one conception of relations between God and man to another; a belief in God had to remain as the "terminus ad quem" as well as the "terminus a quo" to qualify as a change of religion.[11] But the category "without religion" (konfessionslos) existed on the forms for registering religion, so the government also had to argue that a declaration of religion did not constitute a change of religion.

The Administrative Court could not break the impasse by itself, but it acted boldly nonetheless by citing the Treaty of St. Germain to declare that the legal definition of religion need no longer include the concept of God. In a decision of January 18, 1924 the court said that since the Treaty had abolished the distinction between legally recognized and unrecognized religions, the concept of a belief, confession or religion had to be interpreted in its broadest sense to include the whole complex of doctrines dealing with the nature of the world and the place of mankind in nature.[12]

The government did not presume immediately that the decision of the Administrative Court would stand in the Constitutional Court.[13] Catholics condemned the decision as an imposition of American sectarianism on Austria, but they had no trouble blocking the practical results because the court could hardly prescribe in minute detail the bureaucratic procedures officials were accustomed to.[14] It was the task of the legislature to reconcile the Treaty of St. Germain with the Constitution of 1867 as it had done for the Constitution of 1920 in all but school affairs. The executive claimed, not without reason, that it could work only with the laws it had. Undoubtedly, though, the Christian Socials used the confusion as an excuse to continue the practice of requiring parents to decide on a religion of instruction when their children entered school and to disallow being "konfessionslos" as having a Konfession. The Social Democrats were probably right in complaining that the Education Ministry was dilatory in processing complaints, which prevented more cases from coming to the Administrative Court.[15]

While the battle raged between 1924 and 1927 there was little the Administrative Court could do except to reaffirm its decision. It granted wearily on March 29, 1927 that the Education Ministry might conceivably base its actions on the older laws, but said that in its opinion the Treaty of St. Germain had changed these laws.[16]

The Constitutional Court finally heard complaints on May 16, 1927 with domestic unrest increasing daily. The appeals from more than forty families dealt with the religion not only of children under the age of seven but in the seven-to-fourteen bracket as well as part of the test case. The arguments were the same; the socialists claimed that the Treaty of St. Germain made all world views equal regardless of belief in God while the government contended that it was legal to require children of parents who dropped their religion at any time after their birth to receive instructions because a declaration of confession was not identical with a change of religion. Freedom of conscience was a personal right the state could protect even against parents. The government added an attempt to intimidate the court by saying that if the future were any different the laws would have to be changed.[17] This implied that the court ought not legislate itself.

The Constitutional Court replied with a compromise.[18] It upheld the complaints in thirty-four cases and rejected fourteen others.[19] Adherence to a religion was a precondition for receiving religious instruction, so children of parents who had no religion before the child was born need not take instructions. Likewise, children under seven could follow their parents when they dropped their religion and need not take religious instructions. Here they confirmed the decision of the Administrative Court. But children between seven and fourteen could not follow their parents in dropping religion; they were required to continue religious instruction during the period of compulsory schooling. In such cases, the moral-religious education requirement of the Elementary School Law remained unchanged by the Treaty of St. Germain.

As a result of these decisions, the status of religious instruction for children was the following: unbaptized children received no instruction unless requested by their parents; baptized children under seven followed their parents if they dropped their religion and received no instruction;

baptized children over seven whose parents then dropped their religion received instructions until the age of fourteen; if parents became Catholic after the child was seven and had the child baptized, it was Catholic in the eyes of the church but without religion in the eyes of the state and the parents were free to decide whether the child would receive instructions or not.[20]

Besides the undeniably enormous amount of resentment the controversy generated in socialist circles, the social fallout was mixed. There were serious pedagogical problems for teachers when they tried to teach children whose parents did not want them to be in the class. On the other hand, parents who could not openly defy the socialists in Vienna for various reasons could have their children receive instructions without undue pressure to drop it.[21] The open tensions between religion teachers and school administrators made one thing clear; children were not protected by the schools from the political passions aroused in their elders. Leaders were becoming aware of the evil effects on the educational mission of the schools at about the same rate as they became unable to control the passions they had encouraged. Only an explosion would lead people to depoliticize the schools. Meanwhile Seipel was beginning to think that "true democracy" was not incompatible with political dictatorship.[22]

IV

Seipel was discouraged not only by the stalemate with the socialists but by disorder within the Catholic camp as well. Some of the conflicts were traceable to incompatible personalities while others occurred between organizations with overlapping interests. Against the background of the major conflict between the School Organization and the Christian Social Party several minor skirmishes took place. Prominent among these were split between the School Organization and the Frohe Kindheit with its day care centers and the jurisdictional struggle between two unions of Catholic teachers, the Katholischer Lehrerbund with ties to the School Organization and the Christliche Lehrergewerkschaft with ties to the Christian Socials.

Signs of trouble first appeared in Summer 1924 when Rotter and Ressiguier accused the Katholischer Volksbund of trying to take over the School Organization. The Volksbund had tried to absorb the School Organization earlier but the bishops prevented it by placing the schoolmen directly under themselves. The situation was different in 1924 because Gföllner and Pfeneberger, the bishops' liaison, were no longer interested in using the School Organization as a political arm of the bishops apart from the Christian Socials. The School Organization's appeal to Piffl, however, stopped the Volksbund one more time.

In 1925 it was the Frohe Kindheit that was accusing the School Organization of trying to absorb it. The unification of the two was a personal union effected when Heinrich Giese, a Divine Word priest who was Executive Vicepresident of the School Organization, became President of the Frohe Kindheit. Rotter likewise became an officer. The union had the approval of the bishops and was designed to match the Freie Schule-Kinderfreunde of the socialists. The School Organization then blundered by setting up new day care centers to which it gave the name of the School Organization rather than the Frohe Kindheit.

The conflict broke when Cyrill Fischer, a Franciscan priest, submitted his resignation from the School Organization to Piffl asking that he be allowed to concentrate on the Frohe Kindheit. He accused the School Organization of pushing the Frohe Kindheit into the background. Noting the "rather strong dislike" for the School Organization among Christian Socials he contended that it was becoming too involved in politics.[23] Rotter replied that when the bishops began a regular collection for Catholic education and welfare, the Frohe Kindheit saw an opportunity to get all the money for itself.[24] The unity of the two groups broke down completely on the Sunday after Easter in 1925 when a meeting conducted on tenuous legal grounds under the bylaws of the Frohe Kindheit was packed by supporters of the School Organization. Whatever the details, Piffl could not avoid getting involved, however reluctantly. Rotter insisted on having him decide whether the organizations should remain united while the Frohe Kindheit asked Piffl to stay out of it and let the welfare group go its own way. Apparently this is what Piffl did, for there were no more attempts to join the School Organization with the Frohe Kindheit under the same set of bylaws.[25]

Another conflict involving the School Organization grew out of attempts to make the Katholischer Lehrerbund a full-fledged bargaining agent for Catholic teachers. Founded in 1893 to protect Catholic cultural interests, the Katholischer Lehrerbund still emphasized political and cultural rather than economic and legal goals. This led Leopold Kunschak, a prominent Christian Social and leader of the Christian Unions of Austria (Christliche Gewerkschaften Österreichs) to encourage the formation of a Union of Christian teachers (Christliche Lehrergewerkschaft).[26] The goal of the new union was to represent the economic and legal interests of members' leaving the professional and pedagogical concerns to the Katholischer Lehrerbund. It was obvious to the School Organization that it would be difficult to separate economics from conditions of work so that whoever represented the teachers in contract negotiations would be representing their professional concerns as well. A confused jurisdictional struggle ensued as part of the overall conflict between the Christian Socials and the School Organization.

Kunschak moved swiftly and surely. He persuaded the largest organization of women teachers to allow his union to represent their economic interests in return for recognizing their claim to represent the cultural affairs of women teachers threatened by the male-dominated Katholischer Lehrerbund. It cost him little. Another group called the Verein der Lehrer und Schulfreunde simply dissolved itself and joined the Christian Teachers Union.[27] Kunschak also tried to have the term "union" (Gewerkschaft) restricted to organizations associated with his Zentralkommission der Christlichen Gewerkschaften, but here he failed, partly because the Lehrerbund, which began calling itself the Christliche Reichslehrergewerkschaft, could accuse Kunschak of opening his unions to Protestants and Marxists. The Christian Socials succeeded in persuading the *Reichspost* to reserve the term "union" only to Kunschak's organization, which prevented their rivals from getting needed publicity. With the bishops disunited and feeling contrained to back the party, the eventual winner was Kunschak.

The smoldering differences between the School Organization and the Christian Social Party flared up again in the Fall of 1925 when the School Organization sponsored a series of talks on the school question. A former Chancellor of Germany, Dr. Wilhelm Marx, and Theodor Verhoeven, the Dutch priest who had spoken in 1923 on the Holland solution, were the headliners. Marx visited Seipel the day before his speech and extended a personal invitation to attend. The talk contained glowing references to the unity of Catholics in Germany and to the principle of freedom of choice which encouraged parents to get involved in winning confessional schools for Catholics.[28] Next day the *Reichspost* did not mention freedom of choice or the references to confessional schools. Rotter suspected Seipel of censoring the remarks, but Friedrich Funder, the editor, needed no personal intervention to realize the value of denying the School Organization a forum for its ideas.

The series of talks by Verhoeven was delivered at several locations in Austria and drew severe criticism from the Christian Socials. The first, given in Vienna on November 8, contained historical inaccuracies and misunderstandings of Austria, they claimed. Verhoeven got a cool reception from Seipel before traveling to Graz and Linz. Whatever vague support he got evaporated quickly when an outline of his talk appeared in Graz and Linz with warnings about its content.[29] Rotter does not produce evidence for accusing Seipel of complicity, but if Verhoeven's reception by Seipel was cool, it was distinctly cold in the other major cities.

The misrepresentations were too much for Josef Pfeneberger. After a bitter exchange of letters with Ressiguier and Rotter he decided he could not keep his ties with the party and remain the bishops' liaison with the School Organization.[30] In a letter to the Bishops Conference he charged that the most serious error of the School Organization was to acquiesce in the judgment of the Administrative Court that having no religion (Konfessionslosigkeit) was the equivalent of religion (Konfession) under the Treaty of St. Germain. The socialist newspaper in Linz exploited Verhoeven's speech to embarrass Pfeneberger because he had publicly opposed the decision of the Administrative Court. When the *Schulwacht* published what he considered more untruths, Pfeneberger asked Piffl if he could resign.[31]

In an effort to clarify relations between the School Organization, the Christian Socials and the bishops one can with modifications say that the School Organization was weak on theory but strong on practice while the Christian Socials were strong on theory and weak in practice. The bishops were torn between them depending mostly on the extent of the immediate threat in their dioceses although they all had vital interests in the theological issues at stake.

The schema is true to this extent. The School Organization with its Freedom of Conscience School raised questions about freedom of conscience for baptized people that they were incapable of resolving on a theoretical level to the satisfaction of the bishops. They were strong on insisting that it was necessary to take direct political action to change an intolerable situation. This made them more radical political Catholics than the Christian Socials even though they were willing to concede on theory.

The Christian Socials, on the other hand, had impeccable theory as far as the church was concerned. They had solid arguments from theology, canon law and history to back their policies. Furthermore, the party could argue that the laws of Austria protected the interests of the hierarchical church sufficiently that it was unnecessary to concede on a civil right of freedom of conscience in a country where 95% of the people were strictly speaking Catholic. The bishops would be losing their rights by following the example of Holland and gaining nothing except the promise of more enthusiastic involvement by a smaller number of dedicated lay Catholics. But the Christian Socials did little to resolve the constitutional issue or to take initiatives to improve the status of the church in the big city schools. They did not know what to do with Glöckel or with the specter of religious pluralism rising from court interpretations based on the Treaty of St. Germain. The economy attracted them as a field of endeavor because they could accomplish something. The executive lacked authority in cultural affairs because there was no constitutional law regulating relations between church and state, because the Constitution of 1920 placed too much authority in the hands of the Nationalrat, and, because the Pan-Germans were anti-Catholic.

The bishops were caught in between. They were less than frank about their position on freedom of conscience because they could not betray a lack of consensus among them. This undoubtedly confused everyone from Seipel, who complained openly, to the School Organization, which falsely presumed unanimity on the basis of close contacts with Piffl alone. Opinion ranged from Piffl who supported a civil right of parents to choose a school, if not the principle that parents had a right to form their children's consciences as they saw fit, to Waitz who thought that the state should enforce ecclesiastical rules including compulsory religious exercises. In practical matters they were divided according to the threat in their dioceses. Piffl wanted a drastic solution while Gföllner was paralyzed into inactivity by the similarity of his views to those of the Christian Socials, a hard line on doctrine joined to an acute realization that the church could do little without the Christian Socials. Waitz could only dismiss Vienna as Piffl's problem and hope that he could prevent the same thing from happening in Tyrol.

The schema is deficient to this extent. The School Organization was supposed to be a cultural organization with a solid grasp of theory rather than a political party. When they tried to take political action they were decidedly weak. Enthusiasm and firm dedication to the church could not compensate for lack of a political base. It was the tragedy of the School Organization that they were poor in matters of doctrine, which was supposed to be their strength, while they were heavily involved in politics, for which they were unequipped. The party, meanwhile, was in fact engaged in protecting the interests of the bishops by enforcing the existing laws as best it could and by arguing the Catholic position in court cases when they arose. In the end they could claim to be doing more for the church than the School Organization, and it was relatively easy to freeze the School Organization out of contention for the sympathies of Catholics.

V

The principal attempts at school reform throughout 1925 and 1926 continued to concentrate on rationalization of the school system, teacher education and curriculum in the elementary schools. The last included a whole complex of democratic principles, progressive teaching methods and modern course content. Conservative inertia was more responsible for difficulties in the area of school reorganization while religion contributed to disputes in teacher education and curriculum. The blending of conservatism with religion to confront progressive secularism meant that every question was thoroughly politicized. The emotions involved became more charged because the legal code failed to provide an adequate framework to resolve school issues; no one needed to respect an opponent's appeal to the law because the law itself had to be changed.

While the existing system could not be described as chaotic, it was Byzantine in its complexity. By way of brief review, the elementary schools contained eight grades in the country and five grades in the cities, where the three-year Bürgerschule rounded out the years of compulsory schooling. Some pupils left Volksschule after only four years to enter gymnasia, others after five. Those left behind were in an academic dead end with practically no chance of going to college because their schools did not offer the prerequisite foreign languages. Once a child had passed the age of ten without entering a college preparatory school its opportunities in life were restricted to jobs that did not require advanced degrees because possibilities for transferring into a college prep program were minimal.

The secondary school system was more complex. Gymnasia, Realgymnasia and Reformrealgymnasia of eight years existed side by side with Realschulen of seven years whose weak academic offerings made them the stepchildren of Austrian education.

The reformers proposed the General Middle School for three reasons; it would put off until the age of 14 a decision on a life's work; it would rationalize the system by eliminating overlapping elementary schools and gymnasia; finally, it would help to democratize the country by keeping all children together without regard for social class for another four years. The two tracks at the schools, one for college-bound youths and one for those headed into apprenticeships, would be loose enough to allow transfers from one to the other as the talents of children emerged or their interests developed.

Except for the social leveling, it made good sense in the abstract, but when all interests were balanced the cumulative opposition became overwhelming. The university professors feared a decline in the quality of students entering the Hochschulen. The stratification of Austrian society died especially hard among the former elites who pointed to a long and glorious tradition of secondary education at gymnasia. But perhaps most devastating, the General Middle School could come into existence only in the context of a complete settlement of many outstanding points that involved at least religion in the elementary schools if not teacher education as well. The Catholic press insisted that legislation was necessary, and legislation was impossible without exhaustive negotiations that depended on cooperation among the parties to some degree. The politics of religion and social leveling blocked the General Middle School as much as opposition from men directly concerned with the quality of education.

It was the mix of things that stopped reform more than the reforms themselves. The *Reichspost* and the Christian Socials went along with hardly a murmur in July 1925 when Glöckel announced plans to transform nine Realschulen in Vienna into experimental schools using the curriculum of the German Middle School that was so successful at the Federal Educational Institutes.[32] This project approached the pattern of the General Middle School by having a unified curriculum for the first four years before separating into three rather than two tracks, one of which stressed foreign languages. The first foreign language—Latin, English or French—was introduced in the third year, and after four years it was possible to transfer to any of the three types of college preparatory schools. This marked an improvement by putting off a decision about a vocation until the age of twelve when a student began studying foreign languages. Special courses in Latin were also begun to enable pupils to make up that prerequisite if they missed it in the last two years of the German Middle School.

Glöckel's motives were sound from an educational standpoint, but it was becoming impossible to separate school reform from party politics. He wanted to upgrade the Realschulen and encourage the universities and Hochschulen to lower their Latin requirements by redesigning the curriculum so that students from the reformed schools could transfer after four years directly into any gymnasium in Vienna except for the Academic Gymnasium.[33] He claimed in his defense that he was not waging a war against the classics; rather, they were simply losing popularity. The muted reaction testifies to the general recognition that he was right on many points.

But Glöckel's reforms served the interests of the social revolution using the dangerous tactic of presenting the federal government with a fait accompli, much as Albert Sever did with civil marriages. School reform served social reform and was vulnerable to criticism directed at restructuring Austrian society. The socialists did not have the strength in parliament to pass legislation, so they were acting on their own with weak backing from the law.[34] The socialists were willing to risk reforming the schools by executive decree with faith that the reforms were good, that the city of Vienna could ignore or defy the interests of the federal government in a legislative solution, and that the negative effects on relations among the parties would be minimal once conservatives recognized the value of the reforms. He was right on the first two but wrong on the third, chiefly because the social revolution included secularization.

Tensions were increasing among the parties as Glöckel began changing the Realschulen. The national meeting of school supervisors begun by Glöckel in 1920 became politicized in 1924 when the Education Ministry brought in academic experts with Christian Social ties over objections from the Viennese supervisors. The meeting degenerated when the socialists complained about discrimination against representatives from Vienna and the School Reform Department during the meeting and about the method of keeping the minutes. The socialists also wanted a say in the agenda for 1925. It could not be expected that much constructive work would be accomplished in such an atmosphere.[35]

Once the reform of school types became involved with religion and the social issue it could not proceed further without resolution of more fundamental issues. The issues arose in connection with the other two areas of school reform, that of teacher education and changes in the elementary school relating to curriculum and religion.

Glöckel was as usual in the forefront of reform when he persuaded the City of Vienna to establish a model Pedagogical Institute. Set up in 1923 under Viktor Fadrus on the foundations of the liberal Pädagogium and its successor the Lower Austrian Teacher Training Academy, it was at first designed to provide enrichment courses for teachers already in service because there was a surplus of teachers for the moment. The City Council added an Institute for Experimental Psychology in 1924 under Karl and Charlotte Bühler, and in 1925 it started the Central Pedagogical Library which soon became the second largest specialty library in Europe with 200,000 volumes.[36] The list of collaborators at the Pedagogical Institute was impressive: Alfred Adler, Anna Freud, August Aichorn, Max Adler, Hans Kelsen and the philosopher Wilhelm Jerusalem added their talents. Graduates included the philosophers Ludwig Wittgenstein and Karl Popper. Teachers made use of the school in great numbers, and the *Reichspost* approved of Catholics applying even as it warned that teacher training could be fully reformed only by federal legislation.[37]

Difficulties arose when it became clear that new teachers would be needed in 1927 for the first time since the war. The City Council voted in July 1925 to set up a college-level training program at the Pedagogical Institute, and the School Board announced that it would prefer graduates of the program for vacant teaching positions. The number of students was limited to the projected need for teachers. Opposition in the City

Council was led by Karl Rummelhardt of the Christian Socials, a supporter of the School Organization who objected to "crass illegalities" because the city set up the program as a private course of studies to get around the law. He also objected to "party-political efforts" to hire only graduates of the Institute for schools in Vienna both because graduates from Catholic academies would be at a disadvantage and because it was clear that socialists would be preferred from the time they applied to the Institute. Combined with the long range plans of the reformers to transform existing Catholic teacher training academies into regular four-year high schools, the problem became so thorny that a stalemate ensued in the Nationalrat while national reform of teacher training languished.

While reorganization of the Middle Schools provided a potential meeting point and teacher education ended in a complete break, the elementary schools provided the most spectacular confrontations between the parties during Ramek's government. Agreement on the need to change the curriculum blended in by degrees to disagreement on the underlying democratic philosophy and complete polarization on the place of religion.

The end of the trial period for the urban curriculum set by Breisky was approaching in June of 1925. A favorable judgment on it would affect the rural curriculum which had only recently gone into effect because they were drawn up along the same lines. The Education Ministry began the evaluation in 1924 by publishing a set of guidelines for assessing results. The university professors were skeptical, but their opinions counted less than those of elementary and middle school teachers because they had not yet received children trained under the new curriculum.

Responses from elementary and secondary school teachers varied. The elementary school teachers in Vienna approved the curriculum overwhelmingly, as expected. Singling out the curriculum as the sole reason for their positive response can be questioned, however, because the decision of the city after the war to reduce class size rather than dismiss teachers made their jobs easier than those of teachers in the provinces. Final assessment by middle school teachers, though considered especially important, tended to fall along party lines, conservative in the provinces and progressive in Vienna where the majority of all secondary school students lived.[38] They found awakened interest in school work, frankness toward teachers, increased ability to observe, naturalness and vividness in oral and written expression, appreciable progress in drawing and hand-work, a better sense of space, and understanding of applied problems in arithmetic. On the negative side they noted less accuracy in spelling, grammar and formal arithmetic, insufficient memory training and power of concentration, inability to accomplish long tasks, and lack of discipline. It was becoming clear that the goals of the Lernschule with its "positive knowledge" were being sacrificed to the Arbeitsschule with its "adaption to the child."[39]

The process of evaluation was not finished at the end of the 1924-25 school year so the trial period was extended for another year. In the late spring and early summer of 1926, therefore, the issues of Glöckel's reorganization, the status of the Pedagogical Institute with the new policy on teacher education in Vienna, and the definitive implementation of a reformed curriculum for the elementary schools all combined to present Austria with a complex and volatile set of problems relating to education that demanded resolution in the near future.[40]

As if the negotiations between the parties would not be touchy enough on social grounds alone, Glöckel kept his secularist policy intact with an ill-advised attack on religion teachers in the Viennese grade schools. Not long after the school year started in September 1925 he started to discipline religion teachers for asking their pupils whether they had fulfilled religious duties like going to Mass on Sunday. The problem was not new; Glöckel had complained the year before in his interpellation of Seipel that religion teachers were telling children they must go to Mass even behind the backs of their parents if necessary.[41] Claiming this put undue pressure on children, he was bold enough to cite his own decree from 1919 that any compulsion was not allowed.

Schneider replied with a ministerial decree on December 23, 1925 saying that the practice was allowable as long as the teacher did not threaten the children.[42] Glöckel responded with his own decree setting conditions on such questions under the guise of "implementing" Schneider's decree.[43] The frustrated and disgusted Schneider was nearing the end of his considerable patience and commissioned Section Chief Johann Egger to prepare a contingency plan for formally withdrawing the Glöckel Decree of 1919.[44] He wrote to Glöckel saying that the School Board was undercutting the authority of the religion teacher and told him bluntly to stop contradicting the content of his decree and valid laws.[45] Not confining their protests to decrees and letters, the socialists took to the streets on January 22, 1926 with a demonstration in front of City Hall. The Catholics, not to be outdone, replied with a rally of perhaps 40,000 people arranged by the School Organization that also met at City Hall and eventually moved down the Ringstrasse to shout protests at the School Board Building.[46]

Between demonstration and counterdemonstration the Christian Social Party Congress met in Vienna. The party was being forced to give up the silence it imposed on itself in November 1924. The position that emerged had close similarities to the Freedom of Conscience School except that it recognized the political difficulties involved. Seipel and Ramek left it to Josef Pfeneberger to present the party line; he rejected the accusation that the party stood for the "concordat school" or church schools, as the socialists said, and declared instead that it wanted the "free confessional school" which would dispense with the use of police power to enroll children in one school or another. As long as this kind of school was impossible the party would defend against godless schools and support moral-religious education in the public schools. The congress adopted Pfeneberger's position as though it had been the party's position all along. In fact it was no different from the Freedom of Conscience School. They did not have to recognize the preliminary work of the School Organization because in the meantime the school lobby had moved toward the original position of the bishops by calling for repeal of the Glöckel Decree. Some party members shared their view as well, shown by Schneider's contingency plan to lift the decree, but Seipel did not. School Organization and Christian Social Party were passing in the night with little contact or understanding between them.

Glöckel continued to discipline religion teachers despite the invective directed against him at the Christian Social congress. This prompted another letter from Schneider on May 22, 1926 repeating the content of his decree and citing the law that gave directives of the Education Ministry precedence over those of provincial school boards.[47] Glöckel was unmoved and announced that he would continue to penalize teachers for abuses; his defiance fed on the emotions surrounding the court cases about whether children could follow their parents in dropping their religion.

Soon after, the complex of issues found its way into the Nationalrat where another dramatic confrontation between Seipel and Glöckel took place. It was, Seipel wrote facetiously to a friend, the price of a trip to America in June because it was really Ramek's job to answer Glöckel.[48] Glöckel addressed an urgent inquiry to the Chancellor on current topics. He accused the Education Ministry of procrastinating on complaints to prevent cases from reaching the courts. It was an "unheard of provocation" to force a child to receive instructions in a religion rejected by its parents. He declared openly that he would discipline teachers who put pressure on children even against the injunction of Schneider.

Ramek answered that federal officials were acting within the framework of existing laws. He granted that the courts would have to decide some issues and that there were problems with choosing a religion for instruction when children entered school; thereafter the law was clear, however. He was more concerned at the moment with the defiance of Glöckel; he charged him with harrassing religion teachers causing defiance on the part of pupils, and said that questions about fulfilling religious duties could be grounded in the theory of education by active involvement.[49]

Seipel added an attack on Glöckel. He accused him of making heroes of people who left the church. Granting him every right to discipline teachers who intimidated the children, he charged that Glöckel was distorting the intentions of teachers when they questioned children. He threw Glöckel's own theory of the Arbeitsschule up to him by saying he should not encroach on the exercise of religion as part of what was taught.

As one of the foremost practitioners of the "politics of the radical phrase," Glöckel replied with vehemence that he had expertise as a pedagogue when the opposition had none at all. He granted that an objection based on the methods of the Arbeitsschule was debatable, but that he acted to protect children and parents from religion instructors. He did not want children going to church when their parents did not approve. Religious feeling was "delicate and above all discussion," but for the Christian Socials it was a business.[50] By this time the session had broken down so far that even the magisterial Seipel joined in the catcalls; both sides repeatedly interrupted the opposing speaker. The fruitless and bitter session was a prelude to greater disruptions in the months to come. Unfortunately for the Christian Socials, Seipel left shortly thereafter for America leaving Ramek and Schneider to face Glöckel. Neither was a match for him, and the Catholics waited through the summer of 1926 for the return of Seipel as for a savior.

VI

Court cases and constant assaults by the socialists pointed out obvious weaknesses in the Christian Social position during the first half of 1926. Less apparent was the internal struggle within the Catholic camp that led the Christian Socials and the School Organization alike to change their positions. The party in effect took over ground occupied by the School Organization earlier by proposing the 'free confessional school' and giving up the hard doctrinal line that was, after all, intended only to cover inaction by the party. The "free confessional school" was practically identical with the Freedom of Conscience School and contradicted the earlier notion of a confessional school in which the state enforced attendance by all children at the schools of their church. The ground was not exactly vacated by the School Organization which continued to support parents' choice of a school, but the School Organization tried to get some movement into the situation by appealing for repeal of the Glöckel Decree, to make their position somewhat ambivalent. They were falling into the same trap as the bishops had earlier by calling simultaneously for freedom of choice and compulsory religious exercises.

The important thing was that the Christian Socials remained the party of stasis and were able to convince the bishops that nothing else was possible. The School Organization became more discredited by trying to convince Catholics that change was possible. It made no difference that Josef Pfeneberger contradicted himself when he accused the School Organization of subscribing to the decision that *Konfessionslosigkeit* and *Konfession* were the same in civil law as the basis for the Freedom of Conscience School and came back the next year to endorse the "free confessional school" which was the same. The Christian Social Party remained in control while the bishops followed behind. The interests of the church and the party were by no means identical, but both groups had an interest in concealing the differences from the socialists. The Christian Socials needed the church and the bishops needed the party because the alternative of a new Catholic confessional party was unthinkable. No wonder the socialists thought they were facing a monolith in the spring of 1926.

Chapter 7

THE SCHOOL CRISIS OF 1926

I

When Seipel left for the United States he was confident that he could handle any difficulties over the telephone. He was wrong. The cultural conflict developed in his absence beyond a cabinet crisis into a dangerous boycott of the Nationalrat that threatened the parliamentary system. Seipel's prediction that a Kulturkampf would break out when the economy got better came true, but fortunately, the limited extent of economic improvement served to mitigate the effects of the conflict over education when the socialists found they needed the Christian Socials to renew a law on unemployment compensation. The crisis proved all the same how dangerous the climate was when both sides could turn to open confrontation over culture despite the urgent need for cooperation on social and economic issues. Until it broke, though, few leaders took seriously the potential for disorder represented by the school issue so that the crisis crept up on an unsuspecting Austria. At one time or another as events unfolded, every major figure except Leopold Kunschak left Vienna when his presence was greatly needed. Seipel found on his return that he could have the chancellorship on his own terms, so relieved were Austrians to have someone capable of managing the affairs of state. The integral religious wing of the Christian Socials awoke to reality in the intervening chaos and were glad to have even the unsympathetic Seipel as head of the government rather than the incompetent Ramek, while the party as a whole recognized the importance of religion in the political life of Austria.

The uproar in the first half of 1926 over questioning by religion teachers concealed the fact that there were significant grounds for a compromise between the parties on education. Many Austrians would have been surprised to find that Glöckel and Schneider were working out problems connected with school reform behind the scenes. The discrepancy between public confrontation and private accommodation seriously misled the Austrian public, which presumed that the public stance of both parties accurately reflected the real situation.

In all of this Glöckel was less than frank about how he intended to use the results of negotiations. He had become the prisoner of his own rhetoric, if indeed he was sincerely trying to reach an understanding with the Christian Socials. Schneider and other Christian Socials were willing to work quietly, but the flamboyant Glöckel unveiled the compromises as though they were victory monuments to socialism. He furthermore tried to present the government with a fait accompli on two occasions in the weeks of May and June 1926, once by publishing the results of negotiations prematurely in a triumphalistic way, a second time by rapidly implementing agreements before they could be reviewed by the Chancellor. In doing so he made his negotiating partners look like dupes and destroyed their credibility within the Christian Social Party. The resulting turmoil led Ramek to reject the agreements even though he was aware of them from the beginning. When the outraged Social Democrats reacted with a partial boycott of parliament, the school question was politicized as never before. Glöckel won and lost victories in bewildering succession in June and July, emerging as a leading spokesman for the socialists, but education never again escaped the vigilance of ideological watchdogs. The net consequence was a loss of professionalism in education and a defeat for civil peace in Austria.

Emil Schneider did not fare as well as Glöckel. Whereas Glöckel acted precipitously, Schneider vacillated, delayed, retreated and then left town at a crucial moment. In favor of reform, he was unable to convince the socialists that the Christian Socials might support reform if it was not politically embarrassing. But his clumsy attempts to reach a broad consensus within his party succeeded only in embarrassing himself and those associated with him when Glöckel made him appear weak and foolish for compromising. More than anything, he made no attempt to convince the Catholic wing that religion would not be ill-served by making an agreement with the socialists. His fall did no disservice to education because he was incapable of preventing the schools from becoming a political battleground.

II

It is possible that Schneider was distracted as he was concluding the first of two agreements with Glöckel. The Middle School teachers delivered an ultimatum to the government on May 28, 1926 with a demand to be paid on a par with other academic civil servants. Ramek rejected the demands in a strongly worded note, but the teachers persisted and won the support of the Union of Academic Civil Servants. The war of nerves went on for five days until Schneider gave in on June 2, just before the deadline.

Schneider was also trying to deal with Glöckel while this was going on. With registration for the coming year due shortly, parents needed to know what kinds of upper elementary and middle schools would be available for the next year. Furthermore, the experimental curriculum of the Volksschulen had already run a year longer than planned. There were excellent grounds for agreement; Glöckel's reform of the Realschulen the year before corresponded closely to Schneider's announced intention to upgrade the Realschulen so that their graduates could enter technical colleges without entrance examinations.[1] They agreed to make the reform permanent and extend it to all boys' schools in Vienna with the exception of the humanistic gymnasia; the socialists considered this a concession on their part. Instead of thirty-nine old schools and fifteen with reformed curricula, there would be forty-nine of the new type and thirteen old.[2] Schneider tried to spread responsibility within the Christian Social Party by bringing Richard Wollek of the Nationalrat and Karl Rummelhardt of the Viennese City Council into the discussions, which concluded with an oral agreement.

The events that followed quickly became the subject of controversy. On May 31, a communique from City Hall announced that after detailed negotiations among the concerned parties orders had "already been issued" (bereits verfügt sei) changing the organization of the middle schools. The Education Ministry issued a denial so fast that both the report and the denial appeared together on the morning of June 1. There was scarcely time for reaction from the Christian Social Party, but the *Arbeiter-Zeitung* claimed nonetheless that a palace revolution of Christian Socials in Vienna had forced Schneider to rescind the agreement.[3] The note from the Education Ministry claimed that the agreement was supposed to be the basis for negotiations with the provinces for a nationwide reorganization of the middle schools. Since the *Länder* had not been consulted there was no question of a final agreement between the government and the parties, nor had there been orders given to reorganize the middle schools in Vienna. The phrase "already been issued" had been Glöckel's. He admitted in the Nationalrat on June 17 that he authorized the release and said that he told Schneider at the end of their meeting that he would have to release the information because the time for registration was approaching. He regretted only that the agreement had not been in writing.[4] Schneider got no chance to reply; by that time he was out of office and in seclusion, but subsequent agreements lent support to Glöckel's contention that the Education Ministry and high ranking Christian Socials were willing to let Vienna go its separate way without a comprehensive law reorganizing the middle schools throughout the country.

City Hall was clearly embarrassed by Glöckel's attempt to present the government with a fait accompli. In the next issue of the news bulletin it "clarified" Glöckel's statement, which it attributed to the City School Board, by saying that orders to implement the agreement had not been given. The uncomfortable *Neue Freie Presse* took the unusual step of publishing the clarification verbatim.[5]

Objections came in from the provinces as soon as the news arrived. The federalists objected not only to the method of proceeding, but also to separate treatment for Vienna that was not warranted by the law. The Nationalrat had not been consulted, even though the national government financed the schools. Furthermore the agreement disregarded entirely another experimental type of middle school in Styria. Glöckel's shortsightedness had jeopardized the negotiations and exposed Schneider to recriminations from the federalists in his own party; for the moment the religious wing was quiet. In the process Glöckel ignored the possibility that if Schneider fell his successor might not be as amenable to reform.

Shortly after this episode several leaders from both parties left town. Ramek went to Geneva to negotiate for lifting the last international financial controls over Austria; Cardinal Piffl set out to join Seipel on a trip to the Eucharistic Congress of Catholics in Chicago, and Glöckel left for Paris on business. Schneider had his own plans to leave for Cologne on June 11 as the guest of the Vienna Men's Chorus. An announcement in the *Arbeiter-Zeitung* that a mass demonstration against his decree on religion teachers was scheduled for June 10 did not alter his plans.

All the coming and going seems to indicate that neither the socialists nor the Christian Socials had a master plan to outwit the opposition. The events that unfolded over the next few days occurred in a haphazard way so that the force of personalities rather than clever maneuvering contributed more to the ensuing controversy. For one thing, Schneider had completed the definitive elementary school curriculum on May 19 but did not anticipate that when it appeared in final published form the objections would be strong enough to require his continued presence in Vienna. Likewise, contemporaries did not ascribe devious motives to Schneider when the curriculum appeared on June 7 in Glöckel's absence; the process of releasing the text of decrees was notoriously complicated and slow. This time, though, it was Glöckel's turn to be surprised, not just by the timing but by the content as well. Apparently everyone from Schneider to the printing office maintained complete secrecy for nearly three weeks and the large number of socialists in the Reform Department knew nothing about the provocations contained in the definitive curriculum. Still, Glöckel's surprise served to heighten the public impact of his outrage.

In general Schneider's curriculum confirmed the major principles of reform that had proven their worth. Learning from the environment (Bodenständigkeit) and active participation by the pupil (Selbstätigkeit) were confirmed in theory and in practice while integrated instruction (Gesamtunterricht) was modified in only a few particulars. Schneider restricted it to first and second grade, with third grade a year of transition to separate subjects as taught in the middle schools. The reformers wanted integrated instruction in all four years. Headlines in the *Arbeiter-Zeitung* like "Assassination Attempt on School Reform" typically exaggerated the changes.[7]

Objections to minor changes in the pedagogical elements of the curriculum concealed major complaints about changes in religion from the experimental curriculum. The new curriculum stressed the tradition of Austria as a Christian and Catholic country by making room for trips to local religious shrines. Popular religious songs were included from the third grade on, and the curriculum called for "moral-religious education by doing" (sittlich-religiöse Taterziehung) which was a disguised way of ordering religious exercises in the language of the Arbeitsschule.

The *Neue Freie Presse* noted laconically that a struggle could be expected.[8] It made no difference to the socialists that religion was a prominent part of Austrian tradition; they rejected that part of their history as emphatically as monarchy. Appeals to the principle of Bodenständigkeit as justifying trips to local shrines were as inadmissable as appeals to Selbstätigkeit as a reason for having school-sponsored religious exercises. Glöckel hurried back from Paris on hearing the news and huddled with Schneider a few hours after his arrival. He announced a press conference for June 9 but then postponed it because talks with Schneider were continuing. Ramek was expected back from Geneva shortly; his absence dampened the reaction for the moment because it prevented the Nationalrat from conducting business.

The talks between Schneider and Glöckel were actually a major set of negotiations. To the earlier participants, which included Richard Wollek and Karl Rummelhardt, were added Leopold Kunschak, the leader of the Viennese Christian Socials, Paul Speiser of the School Board and a representative sent by Karl Seitz, the mayor and titular head of the School Board. With the exception of Rummelhardt, the Christian Social negotiators had weak ties to the clerical wing of the party. It is otherwise hard to explain how they could pass over the major controversy about the religion teachers decrees and the inaccurate announcement by Glöckel that could easily have been attributed to bad faith. Glöckel's motives were less complex. Once he was assured that Schneider would withdraw the new curriculum he saw an opportunity to achieve in one set of negotiations a comprehensive agreement on an elementary school curriculum, middle school organization and teacher training academies.

The tactical blunder must be laid at the feet of Schneider and Kunschak, if indeed they were interested in protecting the rights of the church. No one thought it was necessary to include the Pan-Germans despite the coalition agreement to consult them on an equal basis, nor did anyone seriously consider whether various Catholic organizations might successfully resist the conclusions they reached.

On June 10 Glöckel again announced that negotiations were continuing. The clear implication was that Schneider was backtracking on the curriculum even though it had been promulgated officially. Though he postponed an official press conference, Glöckel warmed to the interview with reporters and went into so much detail that the report had to be continued the next morning in the *Neue Freie Presse.* He said negotiations were going as he hoped, which made some Catholics nervous because he remained adamant that the religious elements in the curriculum were completely unacceptable.[9]

An agreement on the middle schools was reached first on June 9 and signed by all the participants. It was contingent upon agreement on the final elementary school curriculum, which was reached on June 11; this was also signed by all the negotiators. Schneider then left for Cologne. His departure at a crucial moment was bad enough in itself, but his decision to remain for the scheduled duration was disastrous when Vienna erupted in his absence.

Glöckel presented the results of the work at the demonstration called to protest Schneider's decree on religion teachers. It was a moment of great triumph for him. He announced that the agreements confirmed those of May 29 on the middle schools, reforming all but the humanistic gymnasia along the lines of the German Middle School. The first foreign language would begin in the third class (corresponding to the seventh grade). He added, "We can now wait calmly for the old-style gymnasia to die a natural death."[10] Obsolete teacher training academies in Vienna would be transformed into the upper division of various middle schools to confirm the earlier agreement. He also claimed a victory on the elementary school curriculum; Schneider's curriculum would be used only in rural areas while Vienna would use Glöckel's curriculum of 1920. Other major cities could decide for themselves in due time. "For Vienna and the large cities, the modern school has finally been won," he told the jubilant crowd of several thousand.[11] The *Neue Freie Presse* commented, "President Glöckel has won a complete victory," describing it as cheap and criticizing Glöckel for embarrassing the Christian Socials.[12]

It was in the matter of religion that Glöckel most embarrassed the Christian Socials. Otherwise Schneider's views closely approached those of Glöckel; he was in favor of flexibility in the middle schools, opportunities to transfer from one type to another, reform of teacher training and use of modern pedagogical techniques. Nevertheless the socialists did not consider him an ally. The *Arbeiter-Zeitung* caricatured him as the hand puppet of Piffl, though the cartoon said more about the paper than about Schneider, whose clericalism was mostly a product of socialist imagination.[13]

Suddenly the Catholics discovered that the unity of the Austrian school system was important to them. Until that time unity had not been important either to the federalists who long wanted the system decentralized or to the Catholics in Vienna who recently supported the Holland solution. It was a convenient legal argument used much the same way the socialists used it earlier to oppose the Holland solution. Neither side in fact had a great stake in the unity of the system when it saw some advantage in the contrary. It became a useful argument to Catholics when they saw that Christian Social leaders were abandoning the defense of moral-religious education by allowing Glöckel to keep the secular curriculum of 1920. Catholics in Vienna especially could expect nothing good from the agreement.

The bitterly disappointed religious wing of the Christian Socials reacted sharply. The School Organization printed 500,000 flyers on Saturday, June 12 for distribution at church the next morning.[14] With Piffl gone, Friedrich Funder of the *Reichspost* took the lead with a front page editorial criticizing the agreement. The paper suggested the next day that Schneider should resign.[15] A committee of monsignori from the Cardinal's office, representatives of several Catholic organizations and a large delegation from the School Organization went immediately to Kunschak to demand that the party back Schneider's curriculum as mandatory for all schools. The Christian Social leaders met for several hours on June 12 in an effort to patch up the split in Vienna; Ramek rushed back from Geneva ahead of schedule for a meeting on June 14 and scheduled another for June 16. The amused *Arbeiter-Zeitung* predicted that Schneider would find his scalp on the belt of the monsignori when he got back.[16]

Glöckel, sensing what was about to happen, moved rapidly to implement the agreement on the middle schools. He announced officially on June 12 that certain specified middle schools would have their curricula changed, claiming thereafter that he could not rescind an officially promulgated act.

Ramek met with the cabinet as soon as he arrived in Vienna and issued a statement the same day; it said,

> The plan worked out in these negotiations endangers the unity of the Austrian school system. Moreover, on several points regarding the middle schools, and in certain conditions touching teacher training or affecting the Bürgerschule this plan anticipates legal regulation whose bases and goals are not at all clear as yet. For these reasons the Federal Chancellor is unable to approve this plan.[17]

Ramek's action can be defended on legal and political grounds. His key point, besides the unity of the system, was than an agreement on the middle schools needed legislation. It was true that the government could establish a basic curriculum on its own authority under existing laws, but types of schools were also established by law. If the Bürgerschule, for example, became a four-year rather than a three-year school, the law would need revision. Admittedly there were precedents during the Empire when innovations forbidden by the law were made, but Ramek nonetheless had solid legal grounds to repudiate the agreement. The political reasons were obvious. Besides maintaining the unity of the Christian Social Party, Ramek could claim that the school question had become so politicized that an acceptable solution would have to be found in full public view. It was beyond the capability of a committee to conclude an agreement acceptable to enough people.

Seldom had the splits in the Christian Social Party been so obvious. In the course of the subsequent crisis, dedicated party members like Kunschak and Wollek were humiliated, and politicians like the ambitious Anton Rintelen of Styria and the stolid Richard Schmitz of Vienna rose to prominence. Rintelen used the crisis to transfer his political machinations from Graz to the capital. Richard Schmitz, former Minister of Social Administration and leader of the Catholic Volksbund, had close ties to Piffl and Funder and few contacts with the radical School Organization, which made him a suitable representative of the Catholic wing within the party.

When Ramek dissolved the agreement between the major parties the Pan-Germans found some room to maneuver. Ramek was happy to have the Pan-Germans take a stance because their only sentiment could be dismay at not being consulted under the terms of the coalition. This strengthened his argument for rejecting the agreements. He met on June 15 with two leaders of the Pan-Germans who reminded him that they were to be consulted as equals on cultural matters and supported Ramek's contention that school reorganization had to be regulated by legislation rather than by ministerial decree or party agreement. One reason for their friendly attitude, aside from fear of the socialists, was their unwillingness to face new elections after the crushing defeat in the last one.[18]

Ramek met with Christian Social leaders the same day to inform them where the government stood. He said that Schneider's actions could have led to a parliamentary crisis. He named Schneider exclusively, thereby sacrificing him to the wrath of the Catholic wing, and tried to limit the damage by exonerating Kunschak and Wollek, who were in fact equally responsible. The embarrassed and angered Kunschak resigned anyway as head of the Viennese Christian Socials; he defended himself within the party during the coming week but did not join the public controversy. Glöckel claimed that he demanded public reinstatement, which Seipel provided at the unveiling of the monument to Karl Lueger later in the year.[19] Thereafter Kunschak resumed his place in the party.

The fireworks of June 15 were not yet over; the Social Democrats got their chance when the Principal Committee of the combined houses of parliament met to receive Ramek's report on the meeting in Geneva. The duties of the Principal Committee were few but important; it nominated cabinets for approval by parliament and discussed foreign policy. Since foreign affairs often contained sensitive material the rule of secrecy was part of the procedural regulations. Early in the meeting Karl Seitz made a motion to delay Ramek's report until parliament had a government that was able to negotiate and make arrangements, and another motion to make the meeting public because it dealt with internal affairs rather than with foreign policy. The committee members were able to express their sentiments before a vote. Duly noted, the motions were voted down, whereupon Otto Bauer declared that the Social Democrats would not keep the rule of secrecy because it was a misuse of the procedures to keep an internal Austrian affair from the public. The socialists then left the meeting and the discussion appeared in the *Arbeiter-Zeitung* the next day.[20]

Nor was Glöckel idle that day. He addressed a mass meeting of teachers in the Volkshalle of City Hall. His stormy speech recounting recent events and calling for separation of church and school was followed by a resolution demanding the curriculum of 1920.[21]

The Christian Social meeting across town that evening reflected the split in the party. Ressiguier declared that the School Organization would no longer tolerate such leadership; amid cries of "Pfui, Kuschak!" "Pfui, Rummelhardt!" and "Schneider is a traitor," he attacked the Pan-Germans and Ramek as well as Schneider. A simultaneous meeting in an adjacent hall of the complex came to blows between supporters and opponents of Kunschak and Rummelhardt so that the police had to be called in to break up the fights.[22]

Due back that evening, Schneider had no defenders at all. According to Fischl, he read in a newspaper bought on the platform in Linz that he had resigned:[23] Delegates from the party found him at home and asked him to attend the staff meeting that night but he refused, pleading the illness of his wife. He added that he felt hurt by Ramek's moves in his absence because he thought his actions were covered adequately by Kunschak and Wollek. The next day he resigned. Thereafter he went back to Vorarlberg and lived quietly as a member of the upper house of parliament with few duties. Glöckel later crabbed in an ungracious speech that the government was paying his as a provincial school inspector in Carinthia without asking any services of him.[24] Glöckel more than anyone was the cause of Schneider's leaving; his pyrrhic victories cost him the most sympathetic negotiating partner among the Christian Socials he ever had.

Ramek's action was noted in Rome with approval. The Austrian ambassador to the Holy See did not wait for the report of the Nuntius but himself informed Cardinal Gasparri about Ramek's suspension of the agreements. The Secretary of State reported immediately to Pius XI who directed that a telegram should be sent to Ramek through the Nuntius expressing his satisfaction over the decision.[25]

Ramek undoubtedly made a number of mistakes in the affair. He tended to ignore the importance of cultural questions and did not anticipate the hostile reaction to the curriculum Schneider was about to release but left no instructions on what to do.[26] Above all, he gave Schneider no hearing in his haste to accommodate the Catholic wing of the party.

On the other hand, people were so upset that something had to be done quickly. Glöckel had to be stopped from implementing the agreements, for one thing. Schneider's blunders were the worst, in the balance. It was unquestionably the legal right of the Education Minister to determine a curriculum for the grade schools—Glöckel had imposed one by decree himself. Schneider had at least the implicit support of Ramek and the Pan-Germans; his concessions were due to a panic reaction on his part when he should have insisted on his authority. Vacillation was bad enough, but leaving Vienna before the impact of the following agreements had become clear was worse. The highest ranking Christian Social left in Vienna was Kunschak who was far from able to take full responsibility or to break the agreements unilaterally. Schneider had reason to suspect Glöckel's good faith after the episode on revealing the middle school agreement, and he had reason to anticipate the hostile reaction of Catholics to a similar agreement. He ignored both, preferring to think that Kunschak, Wollek, and Rummelhardt represented Catholic feeling adequately in the school question.

Schneider's humiliation is traceable in large part to Glöckel. When he chose to interpret the results of negotiations as a political victory he was necessarily saddling the Christian Social negotiating committee with a political defeat. It seemed that he had tricked a small group of party leaders through a combination of defiance and bluff into treating Vienna separately. The socialists could not have gotten as much in the Nationalrat without giving up their policy of opposition. The agreement could not be used as the basis for further cooperation in the interests of school reform after one party savored the compromise as the fruits of a struggle. Glöckel more than Ramek sacrificed Schneider to the religious wing of the Christian Socials when he did not recognize his interest in protecting Schneider's reputation as an educator. He proved on this occasion once again that politics for him took precedence over professionalism in education.

The fragile unity of the Christian Socials was re-established at the meeting of June 16. The deputies from Vienna expressed their disappointment at how far events had gone before leaders had a chance to discuss matters. The caucus heard from Ramek, who reaffirmed his confidence in Kunschak, and from Kunschak and Wollek, who defended their roles in the negotiations. Kunschak even defended the agreements themselves, but the party quietly ignored his remarks in hopes that he would eventually reconsider his resignation.

The closed front of the Christian Socials and Pan-Germans forced the next move on the Social Democrats. In their anger at the perfidious government that would not respect the signature of its own minister they wanted to stop dealing with it. At this point, however, the school issue became entwined with the urgent national issue of unemployment compensation. The law providing benefits expired at the end of June; unless the Nationalrat extended the old law or passed a new one the government would be authorized to cut off benefits to thousands of socialist supporters. The prospect was not unthinkable because the government was interested in trimming expenses to meet demands from Geneva for a balanced budget. The socialists found themselves torn between outrage at the breach of faith in education and the necessity of having the government parties support unemployment compensation. The coalition parties could use the tactics either of outright refusal to extend the law or of extending it for a short period of time to use it as a hostage in other negotiations.

The first step would have been very dangerous; a mass demonstration was scheduled for Friday, June 18 to alert the government on the possible social effects of cutting benefits. The school issue was quickly tacked on to encourage more participation, but the overriding concern was with unemployment compensation. The demonstration was being organized carefully and would be policed well by the socialists themselves, so there was calm in the government despite predictions that half a million people might turn out.

Socialist politicians had a chance to show their anger over the school issue on June 17 in the Nationalrat. The agenda was purposely innocuous, but there was little chance even of awarding decorations. Glöckel reviewed events since May 29, charging the government with breaking both signed and unsigned agreements. Leuthner called Ramek a liar; the chair repeatedly called him to order as the tumult in the chamber increased. When Gürtler of the Christian Socials took the podium to reply, the noise was so deafening that the stenographer could not hear. Leaving his place, the stenographer moved closer to Gürtler. The Social Democrats objected that he was out of order; when one deputy took it upon himself to rush up and snatch the stenographic pad a general free-for-all broke out. One Christian Social tried to choke the offending deputy and was assaulted by five opponents, one of whom, on being struck from behind by a Christian Social, became enraged and began to swing wildly.[27] A recess failed to cool emotions, and when Gürtler tried to continue his remarks the noise made continuation of business impossible. With the packed gallery joining in, there was no alternative to adjourning the session.

The meeting was the most disorderly since the debates over the Badeni language decrees twenty-five years earlier. The *Arbeiter-Zeitung* wrote, "It was the most tumultuous, the most passionate session ever experienced in the Austrian Nationalrat."[29] The Social Democrats left the chamber resolving not to deal with the government except on unemployment compensation until the breach of faith had been repaired. Their boycott made a parliamentary crisis out of the school issue.

It was fortunate that the demonstration outside the next day did not match the emotions inside the Nationalrat. It was truly gigantic; no reliable estimates of the size exist, but socialist claims that several hundred thousand people marched were not exaggerated. The demonstrators assembled in various outlying districts and converged on the Ringstrasse from every direction to hear speeches about unemployment when they got there. Glöckel marched with his column from the northwestern part of the city to the University. He then walked a few blocks to the school board building, accompanied by well-wishers whom he encouraged in a short speech to keep up the struggle.[29]

Rather than one massive demonstration on the school issue, the socialists organized a series of local meetings and demonstrations throughout Austria. It was part of the recent strategy to draw more rural people into the party. In the course of the next week, protests took place in at least thirteen places with a turnout of around 30,000 people.[30] The demonstrations concentrated on Schneider's curriculum in a special way. The curriculum was enjoying a sudden and ironic rebirth after his fall because there was no one to revoke it. The *Reichspost* observed that the curriculum remained in force even though Schneider was gone. The Social Democrats countered that the agreement on the middle schools remained in force because it had been promulgated in the *Verordnungsblatt* of the School Board, and Glöckel went ahead with registration of middle school students accordingly.[31]

Under the circumstances, no one wanted the job of Education Minister. Three Christian Socials turned down the offer, and when a fourth finally agreed, it was the ambitious Anton Rintelen who was using the post merely as a stepping stone to something greater. He ostentatiously consulted the Styrian Christian Socials to demonstrate his federalism and then took office with the long distance approval of Seipel in Chicago.[32] Only Otto Bauer from the Social Democrats appeared on June 25 in the Nationalrat to register disapproval of his appointment. Rintelen could hardly do justice to the job for the first few weeks because he was under attack from the Social Democrats for a shady banking operation. In the meantime the boycott kept national business nearly at a standstill. This was not all bad; a cooling off period was probably good, and with each passing day the return of Ignaz Seipel got closer.

The government held the upper hand on the issue of unemployment. The socialists nervously warned Ramek to have no illusions about the importance of extending the law, but it was clear how much they needed a favorable vote from the government parties.[33] The coalition parties decided to weaken the boycott by extending the law for only one month; the socialists and the government would have to be on working terms by that time or the law would expire during the summer recess. The government held unemployment compensation hostage to force the socialists to negotiate on the schools.[34]

As these events transpired, a legal battle ended with a minor setback to the socialists. The Constitutional Court on June 14 agreed to review part of the Glöckel Decree that released teachers from the duty of supervising children at religious exercises sponsored by the school. The court heard the case on June 21 and delivered the judgement on June 24 that the Elementary School Law required only that teachers supervise children and not that they participate in the service. Attendance alone did not constitute participation.[35]

Once unemployment compensation was assured for however short a time the socialists resumed their boycott of the Nationalrat. Over the next three weeks the business of parliament was suspended while the socialists sought ways to soften their stance before unemployment relief again ran out. Instead of demanding that the agreements on the schools be kept in their entirety, they gradually made withdrawal of the Schneider curriculum the only condition for resuming negotiations.[36]

The confusing emulsion of economic and cultural differences left commentators certain that a parliamentary crisis more severe than a change of cabinet was taking place. The *Arbeiter-Zeitung* and the *Neue Freie Presse* concurred in rare unanimity of judgement.[37] The *Österreichische Volkswirt* commented, "The Nationalrat is paralyzed because of unemployment compensation, it is said. Or is it because of the school reform? That probably means because of the cultural struggle. But everyone argues about that!"[38] As faith in the parliamentary system declined the *Neue Freie Presse* went back to wondering openly if such a country was capable of surviving, and whether union with Germany was not the only answer.[39]

The Pan-Germans vacillated as usual between principle and reality. Of the two German national newspapers, the *Tageszeitung* was in favor, the *Nachrichten* against the school politics of the Christian Socials.[40] The socialists castigated them for abandoning their liberal principles while the Christian Socials either ignored them or criticized them for jumping in just in time to embarrass prominent members of the party. The moderate Pan-Germans found themselves surrounded by parties with radical cultural positions; demoralized by the defeat in the last elections, they were unwilling to expose themselves to further attacks for the sake of the coalition arrangement alone unless forced by the need to keep some semblance of credibility among their own voters.

It was not easy for the government to agree to suspend the Schneider curriculum in the face of Catholic insistence that it be implemented. Leaders of the Catholic and socialist teachers met at the end of June in an attempt to break the political stalemate but did not find enough common ground even to begin negotiations.[41] Rintelen used the Pan-Germans to break the impasse: they expressed their dissatisfaction with the curriculum as early as June 25, and their opposition gave the Ministry a lever to move the Christian Socials toward the "status quo ante." With this backing Rintelen contacted Seitz and then met with the socialist party presidium. Receiving their condition that the curriculum be suspended officially, he conferred with the government parties to find the Catholic wing still opposed. He then tested socialist resolve by suggesting that instead of withdrawing the whole curriculum they discuss individual points. The socialists refused, sending Rintelen back with only a threat to continue the boycott.

Cardinal Piffl was the key to disarming the Catholic wing. Until he returned on July 15 the Christian Socials were without leadership in the war of nerves. Upon his arrival the Christian Socials hurriedly sent a delegation led by Leopold Kunschak; the party needed his approval if they were to disappoint the Catholics by suspending the curriculum. The group most likely received the response it wanted because on July 17 the Education Ministry announced that the curriculum had been suspended on a technicality.[42] The probable reason was that though the party did not lack weapons in the struggle, the prospects for the church in Vienna would worsen by using them to the full extent. The same day the government again took up negotiations with the socialists.

The Social Democrats had to save face as well because they could not afford to alienate further people with religious beliefs. The *Arbeiter-Zeitung* downplayed the role of religion in the crisis, aware that the party was about to launch a "struggle for the village" at the party congress. The paper did not want to strengthen the hand of the anti-religious faction in the party when the leaders were moving for broader representation. Attacks on individual clergymen continued as usual.[43]

The vulnerability of the socialists became obvious on July 21 when the leaders of the three major parties met for the first time in a month. This time, the socialists made extension of the law on unemployment compensation the condition for cooperating on anything else. With ultimatum upon ultimatum the socialists were clearly becoming desperate in their policy of opposition. They were probably as relieved, though secretly, as the thousands of well-wishers who greeted Seipel when he returned on July 23. Never one to emphasize the school issue, Seipel could easily step in to repair the damage at little cost to the moderate wing of the Christian Socials.

Representatives of the three parties met a few days later to iron out differences on the schools. The compromise, like that of 1920, embodied the substance of socialist reforms while keeping a verbal form acceptable to religious and national conservatives. The curriculum of the elementary schools received definite form, and an agreement on the middle schools was made provisional for another year. The atmosphere was different from 1920, though; while the fact of a compromise on the Constitution could be ignored then, it had to be emphatically denied in 1926 because supporters on both sides demanded victories from their leaders. The rhetoric of Glöckel and the hard line of the *Reichspost* were taking their toll on civil peace in Austria.

The most important part of the compromise on the elementary school curriculum came in a preamble which stated that education should be conducted in a social, civil, national and moral-religious spirit. After this statement of principle agreement on pedagogical methods was relatively easy. Instead of integrated instruction in the first two grades with transition to separate subjects in the third, the new curriculum contained integrated instruction in the first three classes with the transition in the fourth. There was further compromise on the issue of the work principle (Arbeitsprinzip) versus the detailed lesson plan (Stundenausmass). Though there was no fundamental agreement that religious songs had a place in the curriculum, the negotiators agreed that religious songs customary in a district could enter the curriculum in a later class than stipulated by Schneider. The phrase "moral-religious education by doing" (sittlich-religiöse Taterziehung), which the socialists claimed was a surreptitious way of reinstating compulsory religious exercises, was dropped, as was mention of religious shrines, churches, and pilgrimage spots. With these modifications the Education Minister implemented the curriculum by decree to bring the period of experimentation to an end. The approval of the Nationalrat or the provincial Diets was not needed.

Legislation was needed to regulate the middle schools, though, so a provisional agreement was made for the school year 1926-1927. While Glöckel's reforms went through almost intact, the socialists had to concede on keeping the old names. The Realgymnasia and Realschulen received curricula on the pattern of the German Middle School, but the humanistic gymnasium was left with Latin from the first year on. Teacher training academies likewise kept the old names but received the curriculum of the German Middle School. In an article that added bitterness to the customary claims of victory, Glöckel noted that the great struggle of the clericals and Pan-Germans achieved only the disappearance of the name "German Middle School."[44] Both bitterness and triumphalism would have been unnecessary had he been able to work quietly with reform-minded Christian Socials instead of insisting that the public schools were part of an integral secular democratic socialist world view.

The matter of paying for experimental middle schools was explicitly left open in the agreements as they appeared on August 1, but after the cultural struggle the government had little taste for using the financial lever to increase its influence.[45] Glöckel moved to counter any threat to halt funding for middle schools, which were paid for by the government and administered by provincial school boards, by assuring readers that the issue would not be used to disrupt the experiment. The *Neue Freie Presse* reported that Vienna was unwilling to refund billions of schillings, but its warning that the financial question was not the least important of the school issues hinted that no one was interested in arguing about money at the moment.[46]

III

The crisis of 1926 was an inseparable part of the tragedy of Austrian politics in the First Republic. But the fact that it occurred a year before the Palace of Justice went up in flames, while it certainly contributed to the alienation leading to the rebellion, in one sense mitigated the effects of the violence, for the immensely involved question of educational reform was a step and a half closer to being resolved after the summer of 1926. The question of a modern grade school curriculum, for one thing, did not reappear, while the issues were clarified on methods of proceeding with middle school reform.

The Christian Socials finally agreed to progressive education in the Volksschule and agreed in principle with the goal of reforming the secondary schools. They had never confronted the issues in an explicit way within the party because of their potential for dividing federalists or Catholics from the centralist and opportunistic moderates that formed the leadership. Though party unity suffered briefly, the result was unified resistance to the lobbying efforts of the Catholic School Organization for dividing the public school system along confessional lines. Likewise the federalists had difficulty arguing for decentralization after the Catholics fought so hard for the unity of the school system against the Glöckel-Schneider compromise that divided the system along geographic lines. The upshot was a victory for Seipel's efforts to keep a unified inter-confessional school system; it was preferable to delivering large numbers of baptized children in the cities over to the secularists. The sobering side for churchmen was that they realized more than ever that the Christian Social Party could not be used as a tool to rechristianize Austria. The tensions between party organizations and Catholic Action groups that began to organize after 1927 originated here.

The socialists conceded on two important points. They granted that moral-religious education could be included in the curriculum as one of the goals of education. They also admitted that the reorganization of the secondary schools was not just a matter of revising the curriculum and updating teaching methods; it required legislation either in the form of a law with the status of a constitutional amendment or a law passed by a simple majority of the Nationalrat and approved by all the provincial Diets. A constitutional amendment implied that the parties would have to reach agreement ahead of time in a spirit of compromise. Such a law could not be the victorious imposition of one world view on another.

Another hopeful sign was the "struggle for the village" launched by the Social Democrats which necessitated reinterpreting the party's stand on religion. On August 6 a new party program appeared that was designed to appeal to agricultural workers. Already numerous festivals of reconciliation between the urban and rural proletariat had been organized by the Social Democrats.[47] Hitherto it had been possible to interpret the statement "religion is a private matter" either as opposing the public influence of the church or as antireligious opposition to supernatural faith itself, the latter chiefly because many prominent leaders were atheistic or agnostic. The new program explicitly restricted the interpretation to opposing the public influence of organized religion. It said, "Social Democracy therefore does not struggle against religion; but it struggles against churches and religious societies which use their power over souls to work against the struggle for liberation of the working class and support the domination of the bourgeoisie as a result."[48]

The change was a bitter pill for many socialists to swallow. The *Arbeiter-Zeitung* conceded that it disconcerted many freethinkers. It said, ". . . many party comrades have serious reservations about the statements that declare religion to be the private concern of the individual."[49] The article, possibly from the pen of Otto Bauer himself, praised freethinkers as among the "intellectually most advanced sections of the working class" but called them a narrower community within the party, similar to the abstinent who would not think of including a plank against drinking alcohol in the party platform.[50] Opportunistic or not, the "struggle for the village"meant that the socialists were willing to break the integration of ideological Marxism and daily politics in the realm of culture to loosen the hardening voting fronts. It was a gamble that involved restraining the strong Marxist wing; unfortunately it was too late to reverse the trend represented by the school crisis. Mutual suspicions had already issued in formation of increasingly active paramilitary groups.

Despite the best efforts of the leaders and party press, the limits of cooperation between Christian Socials and Social Democrats were reached over the issue of religious education in the grade schools. The Constitutional Court had not yet delivered its decision in the case of children whose parents registered as having no confession (*konfessionslos*) after they were born.[51] Religious education was still obligatory for such children, and the government felt it had to enforce its interpretation of the law. In late August Rintelen issued a decree stating that children who did not take religion were not to pass to the next grade. A number of children who had passed other subjects in the previous semester but had not taken religion were to advance contingent on passing a test in the coming semester on the material missed. The order created the absurd possibility of children being returned to a previous grade after they had passed the first semester of the grade they were beginning.

The reaction of school politicians and people in Vienna, delayed by the summer recess until September 16, was no less vehement than before. A meeting at City Hall overflowed into the square in front where clashes between police and freethinkers took place.[52] Another demonstration of teachers on September 25 gave notice that a great cultural chasm still existed between socialists and Catholics.

Chapter 8

THE COMPROMISE OF 1927

I

A year and a day after the definitive elementary school curriculum appeared, two laws for reorganizing the Bürgerschule and all forms of college preparatory schools were passed. The government spent the first few months of the intervening time formulating and assessing a set of guidelines for reform that the Christian Socials tardily developed in response to the *Directives* (*Leitsätze*) Glöckel had presented in 1920. After opinions came in from various quarters, the government worked up two bills and presented them to the Nationalrat. The exhausting work of negotiating with the socialists only then began. The question of reforming the education of teachers did not arise except in passing, tied as it was to the insoluble problem of the religious affiliation of many teacher training academies. Another question left for later, despite the momentary defection of the Pan-Germans on the matter, was the extension of Austrian school legislation to the province of Burgenland which still had the Hungarian system of church-run elementary schools. With two issues directly involving the church on the back burner, the parties were able to arrive at a painfully worked out compromise in which differences were based less on religion than on attitudes toward progressive education and the distinction between practical and academic training.

Though partisan rancor over religion was less than the year before, it had by no means died. The Catholics kept the issue alive by insisting that the law in force demanded religious training for all pupils up to the age of fourteen regardless of the school they attended. The Education Minister tried to insert a preamble providing for moral-religious education similar to that contained in the VS curriculum into the law reorganizing college preparatory schools that accepted children from the age of 10. The socialists opposed the move on the historical grounds that no such statement had been part of regulations regarding the middle schools since 1849. Eventually the preamble found its way into the law when it was broadened to include social and national as well as religious principles to demonstrate again that religion was not nearly as divisive an issue in the secondary schools as in the elementary schools.

What the controversy over reform lost in religious antagonism it gained in differences between progressive and traditional education. A purer form of conservatism became evident in discussions about reform due to the weight of opinion from conservative and nonreligious university professors who were relatively aloof from the elementary school education. Their opposition to socialist plans for reform confirms the judgement that conservatism rather than religion motivated the bulk of the opposition to the socialists in discussions leading to the reform of the middle schools.

Just as the political parties were beginning to agree on ways of reforming the schools the country as a whole began to feel the effects of the discord in high places. Brawls and armed clashes between socialists and assorted right wing groups occurred more frequently as the months of 1927 wore on until the Viennese workers rioted and burned the Palace of Justice in July. Glöckel joined in the sober reappraisal of the socialist "policy of the radical phrase" that was meant to be a substitute for revolution and became more moderate in his public statements. He admitted in the Nationalrat that the rule of law had been ill-served by the lack of legislation to reorganize the middle schools. This statement can be construed as an admission that his attempts of the previous summer had been misguided. The damage done in the previous six years that culminated in the events of the summer before would take much longer to repair, but the laws of 1927 that refashioned the Bürgerschule into the Haupstschule and reformed the secondary schools were at least a start.

II

Anton Rintelen's tenure as Education Minister did not prove to be the stepping stone he had hoped it would be. In fact he did not even get his job as Landeshauptmann of Styria back when troubles over his financial deals brought his fall.[1] The scandal was enough to bring Ramek down along with him, if his poor handling of the situation in June and July had not been cause enough. By the end of September there was open discussion about a new cabinet with Seipel as Chancellor.

Finding in the post of Education Minister nothing but a headache for the party, Seipel no longer thought it necessary to have the portfolio held by a Christian Social. He dangled it in front of the Pan-Germans who were tempted for a time to take the bait as a way of getting representation in school questions, in response to having their sensibilities ignored during the crisis, but since there was little chance of implementing part of their program regarding extension of Austrian school laws to Burgenland they had second thoughts. Seipel then offered the job to the smaller Peasants Party (*Landbund*) as an incentive to join a solid bourgeois bloc against the Social Democrats. The agrarian party preferred the Ministry of Agriculture, which Seipel had not offered them, so they declined to enter the government. The Education Ministry was insufficient recompense for their support on other issues.[2]

Reluctantly Seipel turned back to his own party and persuaded Richard Schmitz, head of the Catholic Volksbund, to accept the post even though he had originally offered him his old job as Minister of Social Administration. The bigboned Schmitz was not afraid of controversy. He was shrewd enough to avoid becoming involved either with the School Organization or with the group around Schneider who were willing to make concessions to Glöckel. A patient man, moderate in negotiations, not given to extremes of rhetoric or weak self-effacement, Schmitz was a good choice to take over the clearly defined task of seeing reform laws through the Nationalrat. For the next ten months as the civil situation deteriorated he was in charge of the increasingly difficult negotiations with the socialists. The Haupt- and Mittelschule laws of 1927 owe much to his solicitude and quiet persistence.

Late in December Schmitz published a set of *Guidelines* (*Richtlinien*) for restructuring the middle schools. Conservatives at last had a coherent set of proposals to support as an alternative to the *Directives* (*Leitsätze*) of Glöckel which had been the focus of attention since 1920. Schmitz submitted them to individuals and various groups for evaluation and solicited comments from German educators in the interests of eventual Anschluss.

Revision of the legal structure of the middle schools involved three major sets of topics. There was essential agreement, first of all, that the school system should be rationalized to have three segments of four years each prior to the university rather than the current chaos. There was less agreement on variations in the curricula of different schools that would leave open the possibility of transferring from one type of school to another and put off an irrevocable decision on a vocation until the age of fourteen rather than the current ten. Finally, there was total disagreement on the place of religion in the revised schema. The dispute centered on whether all pupils up to the age of fourteen must receive religious instruction once he entered a Gymnasium or Realschule at the age of compulsory schools, that is, Volksschulen and Bürgerschulen. A decision favoring the socialists would exempt anyone from compulsory religious instruction once he entered a Gymnasium or Realschule at the age of ten.

All parties agreed that the urban Volksschule and Bürgerschule should become four-year schools instead of five years and three years respectively. The Bürgerschule would then parallel the duration of the lower level (Unterstufe) of the college preparatory schools. It was a simple rationalization of a needlessly complex system that fulfilled a precondition for introducing more flexibility into the Unterstufe of the Gymnasia and Realschule to allow students to transfer from Bürgerschule to college preparatory schools should they discover talents or interests between the ages of ten and fourteen not served by their current schools. The conservatives indicated their willingness to support reform by backing this measure because the alternative of transferring from one school to another between the ages of ten and fourteen was scarcely possible without the basic compatibility of the schools. There was also agreement to make the Realschule a full eight-year middle school by adding another year to the current seven and concluding the course with a comprehensive examination that would entitle graduates to enter technical colleges.

The second major topic of discussion went directly into curriculum and the possibilities for transferring between schools. It offered most of the opportunties for fruitful negotiations despite the serious differences of opinion. The conservatives doubted that higher education was possible for the masses without watering it down, while the socialists charged that the existing system of higher education was a monopoly of the privileged classes that perpetuated an aristocratic social system and prevented the children of workers from rising in society. It was an old struggle, but positive attitudes among many Christian Socials toward democracy and certain liberal values made the difficulties not insurmountable. Hard bargaining went on for several months as the conservatives tried to protect the integrity of a demanding system that produced a limited number of highly qualified graduates while the socialists pressed to open the system to more people regardless of whether they came from families that supported and encouraged a high degree of academic achievement. The net effect in better educated masses would more than offset the decline in academic standards feared by the conservatives. Curriculum and teaching methods needed reform anyway, said the socialists, to reflect the greater importance of science in modern life and to eliminate the drudgery of the Lernschule cordially hated even by defenders of the system.

Differences of opinion with social implications became concrete in the question of making the curricula of the Bürgerschule and the Unterstufe of the secondary schools the same. Identical curricula meant realization of the long-desired Einheitsschule of the socialists in which all children would receive the same basic education for the eight years of compulsory schooling. After that, differentiation would take place according to aptitude and accomplishment. The socialists hoped that homogeneous training of all students going into the ninth grade would weaken the educational monopoly of the propertied class. They wanted to break the vicious circle of ignorance and poverty in many worker's households by putting off the choice of a vocation to an age when the aptitudes of a child had been more thoroughly assessed and the youngster was more capable of resisting the unreflective inertia that kept children following in the footsteps of their parents. The faith of the socialists that social engineering would have beneficial results was nowhere more evident than in the hopes they held for the Einheitsschule.

The Pan-Germans and Christian Social conservatives thought that the goals of compulsory schools were sufficiently different from preparation for work at a university that distinctions in studies should be made beginning with the first year of middle school, that is the fifth grade. The compulsory school, they argued, prepared a youth for practical rather than analytic and scientific work. The aim of gymnasia and now the eight-year Realschule was preparation for college and should be reflected in the curriculum despite the sad fact that a definite decision of vocation had to be made for the child at the age of ten.

As the prospects for a negotiated settlement appeared on the horizon the socialists regretfully realized that the Einheitsschule, or the General Middle School of Glöckel and more recent reformers, could not supplant the Unterstufe of the gymnasia. Reconciling the curricula of the Bürgerschule and the Unterstufe of the gymnasia in consequence became even more sharply focussed on the question of language study, particularly when the study of foreign language should commence, what languages should be taken, and how many class hours per week should be spent at them. Some socialist reformers recognized as early as 1920 that the question of language study was the only problem of real significance in the middle schools.[3] The entrenched university professors had long been unwilling to budge on lowering the language requirements, notably the Latin requirement. Though Latin was the official language of the church, which may have affected the attitudes of some Catholic conservatives, the argument that the place of the church would be eroded yet more appeared seldom if at all. Nationalist professors were quite as adamant as Catholics on maintaining classical standards.

The *Guidelines* of Schmitz, representing the original conservative negotiating position, called for parallel curricula between the Bürgerschule and the Unterstufen of all secondary schools except for foreign languages. As in Glöckel's *Directives* there would be no compulsory foreign language in the Bürgerschule although one or two languages, even Latin, might be taught there as electives in a separate track. In the college-preparatory secondary schools a foreign language became compulsory in the second semester of first year, Latin at the Gymnasium and Realgymnasium, Latin or a modern language at the Realschule. Greek was added in the fourth year of the Gymnasium, a modern language at the Realgymnasium. This was a significant departure from the *Directives*, in which the first foreign language began in the third year, the second in the fifth year. It was more conservative even than Schneider's final plan in which the first foreign language would have started in second year. Schmitz added a weak and artificially stringent concession to potential transfer students by allowing graduates from Bürgerschule to enter college-preparatory schools after taking an entrance examination in the required foreign language and waiting a semester. Furthermore, assignment to the upper track of Bürgerschule would be on the basis of an entrance examination.

The socialists lost no time in jumping on the plan. In actuality it would not allow a child to transfer from one type of school to another because not one but two foreign languages were taken before the end of the first four years. Only the rare student who had taken two foreign languages at the Bürgerschule—and the right ones at that—had any chance of transferring. The parents of such a student would most likely have already sent him to a regular secondary school rather than undergo the uncertainty, not to mention absurdity, of a qualifying examination and a useless waiting period. In short, the plan would effectively keep the doors of the gymnasia and Realgymnasia shut to transfer students and continue the divisions in secondary schools according to social class. Glöckel went further to charge that the prospect of an entrance examination would not open college-preparatory schools to the children of workers but close even the upper track of the Bürgerschule. He proposed instead the *Directives* in their entirety as the negotiating basis of the socialists, winning support as expected from the City School Board, the Zentralverein der Wiener Lehrerschaft, the parents' organizations and the Verein Deutsche Mittelschule.[5]

Schmitz' plans for two other kinds of schools deserve attention. To remedy the deficiencies of spending eight years in a one room rural schoolhouse and to open the Hochschulen to youth from the countryside, he proposed an experimental five-year "Aufbauschule" ending with a *Reifeprüfung*. Girls' schools were likewise included in the plan. The Oberlyzeum would get a curriculum similar to the Realgymnasium with a modern foreign language from the second semester of first year onward and Latin starting with the fifth year. A Frauenoberschule was designed as a high school for women who did not intend to pursue further studies with a curriculum like that of the Oberlyzeum for the first four years and more emphasis on practical homemaking thereafter. There was no dispute in principle about the equality of women's schools though there were reservations about co-education among conservatives.[6]

The solid grounds for conducting negotiations over rationalizing and reorganizing a course of studies for ten to fourteen year olds did not extend to religion. Schmitz' *Guidelines* contained a paragraph of fourteen lines dealing with the goal of education in the middle schools. It was an expanded version of the preamble to the elementary school curriculum that said the goal of the school was to educate in a social, patriotic, national and moral-religious spirit. The socialists objected that it was a sneaky way of inserting the goal of moral-religious education that had never been explicitly stated for the secondary schools as it had been for the elementary schools. It was a step backward from secularization to which they were categorically opposed. The Christian Socials responded that under the law religion was a compulsory subject for all eight years of compulsory schooling, including the ages ten to fourteen, regardless of the school in which this obligation was fulfilled. If the socialists wanted to reconcile differences between Bürgerschule and college-preparatory schools they would have to agree to that principle. Karl Renner had tried in 1919 to distinguish between compulsory and non-compulsory schools, arguing that because gymnasia, for example, were not compulsory schools religious exercises at least should not be compulsory.[7] The argument might be extended to religious instruction as well, and it was to block this potential loophole that the preamble was inserted. No one quarreled with the existing provision that fourteen year olds could decide for themselves whether to continue religious instruction. The form of a preamble, which seemed acceptable to both sides in the grade school curriculum, also seemed to be the best way to handle the problem for middle schools. But no one was quite sure how many vague statements of principle the socialists might suffer in return for concrete reforms, especially when stating such principles was an innovation.

III

Though the parliamentary crisis over the schools had passed when the new budget came up in December 1926 there was still material enough to make the debates rancorous. Partly in consequence of the events of the previous summer the Nationalrat became the scene of an especially bitter debate over the confessional school system of Burgenland. This small province of only 100,000 on the eastern edge of Austria had been part of Hungary until a plebiscite after World War I. It had escaped the liberal Kulturkampf after the *Ausgleich* when the Austrian half of the Dual Monarchy underwent many administrative changes, which left it with the system of church sponsored elementary schools confirmed by law in 1868. School legislation was taken over intact along with the other Hungarian laws of the province when it became part of Austria except for the introduction of Provincial and District School Boards and the eight-year term of compulsory education.[8] In several respects the system was like that of Alsace which kept its confessional schools when the province rejoined France in 1918. Edouard Herriot, the French Minister of Education, who as Premier had tried unsuccessfully to change the system two years earlier, made a point of spending a week in Vienna in early 1927 to study Glöckel's reforms and lavish praise on the school system of Vienna.[9]

Unfortunately, the schools of Burgenland had evaded reform along with unpleasant turmoil. All the evils of neglect, poor pay for teachers and subordination of education to the ministry of the sacraments continued as before. Teachers were still sextons, organists, choirmasters and sacristans, but the outnumbered liberals could do little to change the system. After 1919, however, the socialists captured control of the Provincial Diet and started to exert pressure on the church. Cardinal Piffl had special interests in Burgenland because he was named Apostolic Administrator until the diocese of Eisenstadt could be set up.

The controversy about extending Austrian school legislation to Burgenland had been simmering for a number of years. In 1924 the Social Democrats in the Nationalrat tried to win approval of a law passed by the socialist Provincial Diet that assumed financial responsibility for the schools by diverting funds away from the church into the province treasury. The church protested, and the law did not even reach the Finance Committee of the Nationalrat.[10] The socialists tried the Constitutional Court next, but in March 1925 the question of financial control was laid aside until an "authentic translation" of the Hungarian law was available. Nearly two years later the court had still not reached a decision.

The key to the question of state control still seemed to be finances. Glöckel was elected to the Finance Committee in October 1925 therefore to represent the Social Democrats. In that year the Pan-Germans joined the Christian Socials on the Finance Committee to reject state financing

of the schools in Burgenland, but it was impossible to prevent the socialists from embarrassing the Pan-Germans by raising the issue on the floor
of the Nationalrat. The liberal traditions of the Pan-Germans prevented
them from opposing state control of the schools in principle, but in
answer to accusations that they were traitors to their ideals they protested that it was impossible to extend the Elementary School Law to
Burgenland without a national law for financing the schools. They put
off the problem for another year, therefore, by sponsoring a successful
motion that the Constitutional Committee take up the question of reconciling Hungarian and Austrian school legislation.[11]

Things were different in 1926. The Pan-German constituencies had
been aroused more than the politicians by the snub they had suffered
in summer, which moved the deputies to action. Pan-German teachers
demanded the abolition of confessional schools in Burgenland at their
congress during the summer. The Constitutional Committee had so far
gotten nowhere with the legal question. Carefully calculating the results,
the Pan-Germans decided to vote with the Social Democrats on the Finance Committee in reallocating funds to extend the Elementary School
Law to Burgenland. It was a face-saving device at best because the combination of Pan-Germans and Social Democrats on the Finance Committee could muster only a tie vote (12-12). The section was not included
in the budget approved by the committee therefore and could be introduced in the Nationalrat only as a minority motion. Passage in the full
assembly would then be only in the form of a resolution that did not
bind the government in any way.

The Christian Socials were quiet during the session on December 23,
1926 when the Pan-Germans broke ranks with their coalition partners
and voted openly with the Social Democrats to extend the Elementary
School Law to Burgenland. Both the coalition parties were embarrassed
at the need to break ranks over a cultural issue, but it was just retribution
for Christian Social violation of the coalition agreement on consulting
the Pan-Germans as equals in cultural questions. Though it did not force
the government to do anything, the resolution was more than a symbolic victory because it made less likely the possibility that the Catholics
would use the confessional system of Burgenland as a model for the rest
of the country, as Glöckel often feared aloud. Perhaps it was just as well
Glöckel was reassured because Piffl had no such intention—the Holland

solution was quite different—but the Cardinal still felt it his duty as Apostolic Administrator to issue a pastoral letter in January against the resolution.

Schmitz found a way to continue the delaying tactics even when he was forced by the provincial government of Burgenland at least to clarify whether existing confessional schools should be supported from provincial or local tax revenues. He asked the Hungarian government for authentic copies of the applicable Hungarian laws, decrees and regulations to determine whether they were applied consistently in the past and to find out which schools were supported by state and which by local government. There followed dozens of requests for the decrees authorizing individual schools that went on into November 1928, and it was with relief that Schmitz learned that the practice of state or local support for confessional schools had been consistent.[12]

IV

Partisan bickering was also marked during the evaluation of the *Guidelines* prior to drafting bills and entering negotiations. A notable incident occurred on January 12, 1927 when Josef Pohl, a government expert who had explained the details of the *Guidelines* to the Nationalrat, issued a gag order to stifle criticism originating in the Education Ministry. Schmitz had decided that the socialists would not be allowed to undermine his efforts from within, unlike Breisky who allowed members of the Reform Department to take exception in public to one of his decrees. The order forbade officials to take a position publicly in meetings or in writing to directives or proclamations of the Education Ministry without explicit approval of the Education Minister.[13] Schmitz cited a similar action of Glöckel as a precedent. The socialists quickly decided to test the order. Hans Fischl of the Reform Department asked Pohl if one of his letters fell under the ban, and when Pohl replied that it did, Fischl asked for the opinion in writing. Pohl refused. Fischl then asked permission to deliver a lecture on the status of classical languages in the *Guidelines*.[14] When Pohl again refused he took the case to court.

Fischl's case made its way with unusual speed to the Constitutional Court. In his argument, Fischl claimed that his right of free speech had been abridged. Glöckel's order had not been as blatant as that of Schmitz;

furthermore, it referred to an actual decree of the Education Ministry rather than mere guidelines for discussion. The government contended that the *Guidelines* were cast in the form of a general decree; in addition, the *Service Manual* recognized "official silence" (Amtsverschwiegenheit) as part of professional ethics.[15] The Constitutional Court decided that written opinions but not lectures could be regulated by the *Service Manual*. It expressed little sympathy for Fischl, however, saying, "An official must submit to certain limitations on the right of free speech which, if he acts to the contrary, make him subject to disciplinary procedures."[16]

While the court case was going on, the evaluations of the *Guidelines* came in. Of the one hundred and twelve opinions submitted by individuals and groups, seventy five approved entirely or with minor modifications. All the Hochschulen and all provincial school offices with the exception of Vienna were among the groups. There were seven unconditional rejections coming from the City School Board and groups of liberal and socialist teachers. Seven more criticisms could not be counted as approving the *Guidelines* though they did not expressly reject them. The remaining opinions dealt with individual questions without touching the main points, and the German commentators restricted their reservations to the number of hours per subject rather than the subjects taken.[17] The experience gained by school authorities in the past six years of experimentation on the basis of Glöckel's *Directives* made the comments perceptive and well-informed so that bills could be drafted quickly and negotiations could begin in earnest.

Developments in education took place against a background of increasing violence and alienation in Austria. In late January, the most serious confrontation to date between paramilitary formations of right and left ended in the deaths of two persons, one a boy, at the village of Schattendorf in Burgenland. The sensational trial of the rightists involved in the shooting kept the story on page one for the next six months until the riots of July 15. In March the government invaded a socialist stronghold and confiscated a store of rifle parts that could have been assembled in the event of an uprising. A few days later antisemitic riots took place at one of the Hochschulen. Similar riots in June led by the Nazis closed the University of Vienna for a time. Not even enthusiasm over Lindbergh's flight across the Atlantic could lift the pall descending upon the country.

For a variety of reasons the Christian Socials sought new elections in Spring. The Social Democrats agreed on the condition that the elections would not interfere with passage of a law on unemployment compensation. The coalition parties then tried a new campaign strategy by offering a unified list of candidates. Unfortunately, one professed Nazi was included in the list. The voting on April 24 ended with a sharp setback for the so-called Unity Front; the Nazi was an especially bad liability. From a combined 57.8% of the vote in 1923, the coalition fell to 48.2% and the Christian Socials and Pan-Germans no longer had a working majority. Seipel rose to the challenge by bringing the Peasants Party (Landbund) into a coalition of all bourgeois parties through the simple expedient of adding some agrarian planks to the platform. In this way the socialists were denied representation in the government, and the victorious cries that the tide of history was with them died away again in bitterness. On the bourgeois side, the exultation that Marxism had been turned back once again sounded more hollow than ever.

Seipel's fifth declaration of policy made more room for education than usual with him because the government introduced the texts of the laws reorganizing the middle schools in the same session. He urged that they be passed quickly because the school year was drawing to a close. Glöckel, chosen by the Social Democrats to answer Seipel, could respond to the bills only that the party would scrutinize them while continuing to press for the *Einheitsschule* for all children from the ages of six to fourteen. Most of his speech was given to an extraordinarily sharp denunciation of the bourgeois coalition that forced the socialists onto the defensive more than ever. He attacked Schmitz by name, calling him a minister for ongoing provocation.[18]

The proposals for reforming the middle schools were contained in two bills, one an amendment to the Elementary School Law and the other a new law dealing with reorganization of the middle schools.[19] Two laws were needed because the legal history of the elementary and middle schools contained distinct lines of development that had to be accommodated separately.

The so-called Bürgerschule Amendment to the Elementary School Law rationalized the education system and made it possible for pupils finishing the upper of two tracks to receive further academic education instead of permitting only technical training. The school would be four years long starting after the fourth grade of Volksschule, so it would correspond in time and duration with the first four years of the established middle schools. All the pupils in the second track could expect to enter apprenticeships or vocational schools, but those in the first track could take the foreign language that would allow them to attend the next highest class of middle school without any interruption as long as they maintained the equivalent of a "B" average. Determination of a track was left to the discretion of teachers based on earlier report cards and the extensive "pupil description" introduced by Glöckel. The government therefore dropped two unpopular parts of the *Guidelines* before negotiations began, namely, the entrance examination for the Bürgerschule to determine which of the two tracks would be suitable for the child, and the final examination for pupils of the first track entitling them to transfer to a middle school. Significantly, the school finally became integrated with higher education instead of being a dead end followed only by technical training.

This statement corresponded to most of the ideas of the Social Democrats on the General Middle School. By the end of June, the only differences between the parties were the matter of a name other than the liberal-sounding Bürgerschule, and a question about locations for future Bürgerschulen. Despite the brave rhetoric, the socialists were willing to give up on a unified junior high school system for all children ten to fourteen years of age. The government proposed only to upgrade the Bürgerschule, not to abolish the Unterstufe of the middle schools.

The prospects for agreement on a middle school law were not as bright. The government did not withdraw the fourteen line paragraph in the preamble containing the goal of moral-religious education, for one thing, perhaps expecting it to be one concession they would have to make during the bargaining. In matters of curriculum, the conservatives tried to reaffirm the distinction between the Bürgerschule and the middle schools by setting down in the law which subjects were required and which were elective. There was little doubt that some foreign language would be obligatory in the middle schools in contrast to the Bürgerschule where it would be elective. Otherwise the sides agreed that the curriculum could be the same at all lower middle schools and Bürgerschulen.[20] The main objective of the socialists, therefore, was to limit the extent of disruption in the unity of Bürgerschulen and lower middle schools caused by differences in language study. The government proposed that the first foreign language should begin in the second semester of first year. Latin at the Gymnasium and Realgymnasium, Latin or a modern language at the Realschule. Greek would be obligatory in the fourth year of the gymnasium, a modern language at the Realgymnasium. These marked no change from the *Guidelines.* There were other differences of a less serious nature over coeducation, tuition and girls' schools, open to revision once the bargaining position of the coalition parties had been established.

The bills received a first reading in the Nationalrat on May 25, 1927 and moved to the Education Committee. The committee elected a subcommittee under Leopold Kunschak that met fourteen times between June 8 and July 4 to discuss the texts. By June 27 agreement had gone far enough to pass portions of both bills, and on July 8 the full Education Committee approved both texts with the exception of disputed points which were handed to the parties for further negotiations.[21] When the negotiators submitted their conclusions on August 1 as the term was ending, the Education Committee approved the final drafts for submission to the Nationalrat the next day.

Differences over the Bürgerschule were slight. The socialists objected to continued use of the name because it was the German equivalent of "bourgeois," though it also meant "citizen." Fortunately, there was an old and honored name from the time of Joseph II available for substitution; the negotiators agreed that the school would henceforth be called the Hauptschule.[22] The liberal press protested weakly, but Catholics had no objections of substance.[23]

Differences on the middle schools could not be resolved as easily, but once the parties agreed on the path of compromise, the usual bluster of the Social Democrats lost much of its force.[24] The eight areas of difference reported to Schmitz were: 1) religious-moral education, 2) tuition, 3) the number of foreign languages at the Realschule, 4) the time of beginning the first foreign language, 5) the time of starting the second foreign language, 6) special schools for girls, 7) coeducation, and 8) the Aufbauschule.[25]

Regarding the preamble on the goal of the schools, the socialists wanted to delete the entire paragraph that included the phrase "moral-religious." The Christian Socials refused; they thought they had made a concession already to the Pan-Germans by leaving the phrase as "moral-religious" rather than "religious-moral" as they preferred. The socialists succeeded only in having the paragraph shortened to match the preamble to the curriculum for the Volksschule. They recorded a minority motion to eliminate the whole paragraph in the final debate.[26]

The socialists conceded also on the matter of tuition. Their traditional desire for free education to eliminate the disadvantage to the poor had to bow to precarious finances that made any large-scale redirection of national resources unrealistic at the moment.[27]

The problem of foreign languages was the heart of the matter. It soon became clear that if the socialists insisted on making all foreign languages elective on the Unterstufe of college-preparatory schools no law would be possible. The conservatives dug in and resisted the final step that would have effectively created a nationwide General Middle School. The socialists therefore registered their principle in another minority motion and concentrated on changing individual parts of the law. They succeeded in having Latin dropped as an alternative obligatory language at the Realschule but had to agree that a living foreign language would be compulsory.[28] The original bill called for starting the first foreign language in the second semester of first year; this was moved back to the first semester of second year. It was in reality no concession whatsoever by the conservatives because children would come to the middle schools a year earlier when the Volksschule became a four-year rather than a five-year school. Foreign languages would begin when they always had. The socialists in effect prevented only expansion of emphasis on foreign languages. A minority motion proposed that they start in the first semester of the third year as electives.

The socialists fought bitterly to stop any obligatory second foreign language on the Unterstufe of all middle schools, but to no avail. More than any other part of the law, this destroyed the unity of the curriculum for ten to fourteen year olds. It made transfer from the fourth year of Hauptschule to the Gymnasium impossible because no pupils at the Hauptschule took two foreign languages, least of all Greek which became the obligatory second foreign language at the Gymnasium. The doors of the Realgymnasium remained open a crack when the socialists succeeded in having the second foreign language there restricted to the Oberstufe.

The proposals on girls' schools received a number of changes. They carried the names Oberlyzeum and Frauenoberschule in the bill, but since the curriculum of the Oberlyzeum was similar to that of the Real-gymnasium, the socialists insisted that the name was unacceptable and should be dropped. The bourgeois parties agreed after protracted negotiations, and henceforth the Oberlyzea were called by one of the three traditional names for boys' schools. There was substantial agreement on the distinctive qualities of the Frauenoberschule, but compulsory foreign languages were dropped from the bill.[29]

The problem of coeducation was thorny, touching as it did the widely differing attitudes toward sex among the parties. The government bill said, "If girls are admitted to boys' schools as an exception, they are to be kept together in their own classes when possible by the formation of parallel classes."[30] The socialists were able only to have the phrase "as an exception" dropped. A statement on the equality of girls and boys went through unchanged.

The original proposal for an Aufbauschule to enable rural youth to pursue higher studies was rewritten considerably. The concept survived in the form of an experimental school.

To the relief of the government, Glöckel was among the negotiators who became acutely aware in the course of discussions that legislation was needed more than they had thought. Glöckel was startled to find that the whole organization of the middle schools was, strictly speaking, unconstitutional, not in the sense that the schools were not formally organized according to the Constitution of 1920, but more fundamentally that the system had escaped the regulation proper to the *Rechtsstaat.*[31] Shortly after negotiations were concluded he said in the Nationalrat, "We have no legal regulation of the middle schools, and it is therefore not only a matter of order, but a question of security that we finally go about establishing that which should have been done long ago from a legal standpoint."[32] Any government, he said, had to fear school cases coming before the Constitutional Court. Despite the admission, few people adverted to the fact that Ramek had been correct the year before when he suspended the party agreements which had in effect circumvented the legislative process. It was only when the Constitutional Court reluctantly stepped in to mediate disputes over religion in the schools that the politicians realized that any agreement among the parties could be set aside with alacrity on the complaint of a single aggrieved party. The parliamentary absolutism of the Constitution was being challenged in practice by the Constitutional Court after the Nationalrat proved it could not act in the case of religious education for children. The court even showed it could act with speed in the case of the gag order by Schmitz. It was not ambitious—quite the contrary; decisions in the two cases just mentioned were compromises—but with rising tensions it was becoming intolerable to have a gap in the Constitution that could be exploited to apologize for chaos on the most fundamental level of constitutional government. Regarding church-state relations, the parties would have to compromise or submit to de facto legislation by the courts, much as it was alien to the European legal tradition. Allowing a small group of men, however bound in theory by existing laws, to choose which of conflicting statutes would be enforced, raised the specter of arbitrary government rather than government by law through the representatives of the people. It conceivably meant a return to feudal personal government which all politicians with republican sympathies wanted to avoid.

Another encouraging sign that the impasse might be broken began to appear among Christian Socials in refined distinctions between conservative and religious values in education. The occasion appeared in the form of whispered discussions among bishops and in the innermost circles of the party that an alternative solution to problems of church and state might be found in a new concordat with the Holy See. The unlikelihood of getting socialist support for a concordat may have helped the Christian Socials identify the many areas that would not be touched by a concordat in any case. Successful compromises in these areas might serve to restrict the scope of a treaty with the Vatican and make it more acceptable to the proponents of complete separation of church and state. On the Catholic side, it would not be easy to convince the integral wing that state control over supervision and curriculum was desirable, so the idea of a negotiated concordat did not meet with universal approval within the Christian Social camp. Hence the utter secrecy of discussions about the matter.[33]

V

As the final negotiations on the school laws proceeded, the tensions in the country erupted into violent rebellion.[34] The outburst changed basic attitudes on both sides, the Social Democrats to become more moderate, the Christian Socials more radical. On July 14, the jury that had been deliberating over the Schattendorf incident returned a verdict of not guilty. The next day, perhaps spurred by an editorial in the *Arbeiter-Zeitung*, a mob converged on the inner city. Repulsed by the police at the parliament building, it moved to the Palace of Justice and set it afire. Eighty-five demonstrators were killed and more than a thousand injured in the ensuing armed clash with police. The shock was greatest among the Social Democratic leadership which had informed the police that nothing special was planned and nothing out of the ordinary would occur. The *Arbeiter-Zeitung* had not intended to incite a rebellion; it was practicing the customary "policy of the radical phrase," but the spontaneous actions of the crowd made politicians realize that the rhetoric they used as a substitute for action was having an unintended effect on the masses. The party then began a long, slow move away from the dialectics of revolution toward a willingness to work for social change from within the framework of the state.

One especially bad feature of the worsening political climate was the involvement of school children in demonstrations. The chief of police, Johannes Schober wrote a letter to the Education Ministry shortly after the riots decrying the involvement of children in party politics and suggesting that all parties unite to forbid it. He cited a prohibition on such activities in Czechoslovakia based on the School Code of 1905 which was still valid in Austria. It was not until July 1928, however, that school children were formally prohibited from participating in party meetings and demonstrations.[35]

The school bills came before the Nationalrat in the depressed weeks after July 15. The debate did not avoid sensitive issues, but the mood was markedly different. All sides praised the Hauptschule Amendment as a great piece of legislation. The Middle School Law drew criticisms that were expressed most effectively by Glöckel. Differences on religion brought vociferous interruptions of the session to show that the controversy would survive any compromises on school organization and curriculum, but the debate was anticlimactic because the parties had reached agreement.[36]

There remained one final bit of business—to make everything constitutional. The Nationalrat passed a brief constitutional law exempting the two school laws from the stipulations of the Constitution and the Transitional Law that they be passed in the same form by each of the provincial legislatures.[37] The laws then became constitutional in the strictest sense of the term, not as legislation derived from principles embodied in the Constitution of 1920, but in a peculiar and roundabout way as part of the Constitution itself.

The schools were not blessed with peace, however. The question of religion remained open, for one thing, and the socialists were unhappy as well with any compromise that did not establish the Einheitsschule. The unified school for ten to fourteen year olds remains an ideal of the socialists to the time of this writing, but with parallelism in the curricula and opportunities for transferring to different kinds of schools two of the goals of the reformers were reached. Distinctions remained in the school system—the socialists claimed they were class distinctions, the conservatives said they were differences between academic and practical training—but the compromise solution provided at least some measure of satisfaction for a country which found itself unable to reach a consensus on a single way to modernize the middle school system.

Chapter 9

FALL OF THE REPUBLIC AND THE
CONCORDAT OF 1934

I

The major work of school reform and reorganization was complete with the Haupt- and Mittelschule laws of 1927, and the major parties discovered in the process that the differences between them on questions of pedagogy, curriculum and school organization were, if not minor, at least reconcilable. Not that the socialists could afford to be less vigilant; indeed, Schmitz tried almost immediately to cripple the provision for transferring from the Hauptschule to the more exclusive middle schools, but the socialists beat back the feeble attempt with ease. The chief differences between the parties continued to be based in their world views. Compromises on a few educational issues, disguised for public view anyway by the need to present them as the triumph of some principle, scarcely began to overcome the ideological differences in Austria which by 1927 had polarized the country.

There remained several areas relating to church, state and education left open by the laws which contributed to the tensions leading to civil war in 1934. They included fundamental constitutional relations between church and state, reform of teacher training, the status of teacher-training institutes with church affiliations, the place of religion in the elementary schools which involved both the Glöckel Decree on religious exercises and a new socialist push to dispense children from religion class, and finally, interpretations and enforcement of the laws that might be modified by the courts on appeal from the party currently out of power.

As relations between the Christian Socials and the Social Democrats worsened the church and the Christian Social party continued to drift apart. When the bishops saw the party at the mercy of the Constitution and the courts, set upon by the socialists and lacking support from the Pan-Germans in matters of religion, they decided to answer the call of Pius XI to become more directly engaged in social life through a comprehensive network of Vereine sponsored by the church independently of the state or party. The movement, known as Catholic Action, eventually became a paradoxical threat to the authoritarian state set up by Dollfuss to advance specifically Catholic values in the country. The church furthermore saw no reason to acquiesce in the growing civil strife—after all, most people with socialist sympathies were baptized, if not practicing, Catholics—so at the same time that the Christian Socials were increasing their tolerance of violent right-wing paramilitary groups the church began to reconsider the wisdom of having clergymen in elective office. When the bishops in 1933 withdrew clerics from secular politics it was not merely to reassert the prophetic role of the church as a political and social critic, it was also to reassure politicians that the church had no intention of becoming a totalitarian institution despite its network of social organizations. The bishops had seen the detrimental effects of political involvement by the School Organization, and once the Catholic activists had been firmly disciplined, they began to investigate the possibility of concluding a new concordat with Rome as a way around the problems plaguing relations between church and party as well as church and state.

These changes did not prevent the triumphant cooperation between church and party to settle two outstanding matters. Shortly after Dollfuss suspended parliament, the Glöckel Decree was withdrawn and religious exercises made obligatory once again. In addition, when the authoritarian government was firmly in place, the courts re-defined what a "change of religion" meant to exclude the atheistic or agnostic *Weltanschauung* as a *terminus ad quem*.

Though consistently opposed by socialists on principle, a concordat appealed to the Christian Socials as the best means of regulating unsolved problems of church and state. Socialist opposition to breaking the impasse in church-state relations with a concordat may well have been one of the most important reasons Dollfuss suspended parliament. Even without assurances that it would be ratified by the reconstituted Nationalrat, the government raced with Hitler to conclude a concordat with the Vatican in the Spring of 1933. But the same suspension of parliament that eliminated the opposition prevented its final ratification until a new constitution had been written. The seeming hesitation to ratify a signed document annoyed the Vatican, but it also gave Rome an opportunity to extract further concessions from the Austrian government after its bad experience with the German concordat and after the Social Democratic Party was outlawed in February 1934. The Papal Secretary of State Eugenio Pacelli played the game as much as anybody in the fluid politics of conservative revolution. That the concordat survived the Nazi debacle to be ratified in modified form by the Second Republic testifies to the wisdom of the solution as well as to its status as an acceptable compromise for exhausted and humiliated Kulturkämpfer on both sides.

II

Despite the legal reform of pedagogy, curriculum and school organization, it soon became apparent that the laws did not represent a working consensus in education. Early in 1928 Schmitz proposed revisions to the regulatory decrees governing the Hauptschule to coincide more closely with the legislation from which the regulations were derived. Glöckel objected that an old law left implementation to the provinces.[1] He was right as long as the Hauptschule was not considered part of the middle school system, but with the possibility of transferring to middle school Schmitz also had solid legal grounds. He went ahead and finished a new set of regulations by early June.

The School Board was shocked and angered to find that the new decrees toughened the criteria for transferring to a middle school. Children from the first track of Hauptschule could transfer to a middle school with the same foreign languages only if they had a mark of "good" in the elective foreign languages or a "sufficient" balanced by a "very good" in German or arithmetic. The government of Vienna responded without delay with an appeal to the Constitutional Court, saying that the regulation was contrary to the new law which said only that performance in the foreign language should be "successful." "Sufficient" was successful, claimed Vienna, as the court gave the city a date in October to present its case. Schmitz used the intervening summer to prolong the war of nerves but finally backed down in September by agreeing that a grade of "sufficient" would be enough.[2] The episode showed clearly that cooperation had not replaced confrontation.

The most obvious problem left untouched by the legislation of 1927 was the state of teacher training, or more specifically, the question of reforming teacher training while deciding on the fate of church-related training institutes. The role of the church in the full professional education of teachers was also at stake for even if existing schools retained their church-related character after reform, the additional years of training at the college level desired by everyone would dispense with church influence unless specific provision was made to preserve it. Schmitz began in December 1927 by repeating the proven method of issuing a set of guidelines for reform and distributing them for evaluation.[3] There was agreement on the need for college preparation of teachers, but there were problems associated with granting graduates of teacher training institutes the right to attend Hochschulen with less than adequate training in foreign languages.

The bishops provided almost no leadership at this point on solving the problem of religion. From being the expert on school affairs in the Bishops Conference, Gföllner practically washed his hands of the matter by writing to Schmitz that diocesan officials of Linz were not competent to judge the merits of the proposals, but that they wanted to support the concept of a vocational school for teachers with the demand that religion be made obligatory in the fifth and sixth, that is, college-level years.[4] Gföllner was in effect demanding more religious influence in teachers' colleges than existed even in state-sponsored middle schools, to say nothing of the secularized Hochschulen. His simplistic answer did little for the Catholic cause because it avoided the complicated question of how church influence could be extended to teachers' colleges and how an acceptable legal compromise could be wrung from the socialists.

Glöckel as expected reiterated the socialist demand that teacher training institutes should become regular middle schools followed by a two-year "college-type" (hochschulähnlich) course. He added the twist that such pedagogical institutes should be sponsored only by governments with a territorial base like provinces and municipalities.[5] It was clear with his demand that professional education of teachers be given to the state exclusively that for the time being no systematic reform was possible. Anyway, the universities were dragging their feet with reservations about setting up pedagogical institutes under their auspices.[6]

Nowhere was it more clear that religion was still the major divisive force in education than in continued disagreement over the place of religious exercises and instruction in the elementary schools. There was little new in the matter of religious exercises; school boards and principals made use of the Glöckel Decree as it suited them, with little anyone could do to change policy one way or the other. Glöckel felt quite as frustrated as the bishops, with perhaps greater cause since academic religious instruction remained everywhere in the schools. He decided on a new tack, therefore, to follow the successful precedent set by Albert Sever in granting dispensations for remarriage to divorced persons though it was against the law. He started granting individual dispensations from religious instructions in response to letters from parents. Slowly at first, and then in a flood, the parents of Vienna petitioned the School Board for exemptions from obligatory religious instruction. The requests were invariably granted despite the outrage of the federal government and the church. At first the Education Ministry had reason to deny that form letters were being used, but when the petitions started arriving by the hundreds with the same wording, opinion quickly changed and a three-year struggle to enforce the law began.[7] Eventually the weary Glöckel decided to give up the fight and wrote sadly to the principals that they should inform parents it was legally impossible to free their children from mandatory religion class.[8]

Seipel resigned as Chancellor for the second and last time in May 1929. The "Chancellor without pity," who was blamed unfairly for the deaths in 1927, was unlikely to extract concessions from the socialists on planned constitutional reforms, but he also had a deep personal reason to leave found in thousands of defections from the church that seemed traceable to his involvement in politics. Johannes Schober, who as chief of police in 1927 in fact bore more responsibility for the tragedy than Seipel, became Chancellor once again as a suitable compromise candidate. He seemed likely to win agreement from the socialists for changes in the

Constitution to increase the authority of the executive. Schmitz left along with Seipel, to be replaced by Emerich Czermak, a middle school professor like Schneider who had refused the post during the stormy days of 1926. This began Czermak's tenure of office through five different governments with the exception of one year (October 16, 1929-September 26, 1930) when the noted historian Heinrich Srbik held the office.

Dissension over the schools was only one of the factors that led the Schober government to propose amendments to the Constitution shortly after Seipel's resignation. It had been clear to Seipel and the government parties at least since 1923 that the Constitution did not give sufficient power to the federal president or the executive. In localities where ideological differences led to regulations that contradicted those of the central government, federal authorities were powerless to enforce their will. The defiance of the School Board in Vienna on various occasions was a case in point. The socialists, fearing a right wing coup d'etat by the fascist Heimwehr or at least violence and extraconstitutional activities by ultraconservatives, agreed to some adjustments.

The Christian Socials took the opportunity to make demands on the socialists incompatible with the continued existence of democracy in Austria. Among the changes was a series of proposals to make Vienna a city administered directly by the federal government like Washington D.C. rather than remain a combination of federal province, district and local government that concentrated power in the hands of a few. The socialists immediately noted the obvious fact that it was unrealistic to deny one-third of the population of Austria rights of subsidiary self-government enjoyed by the rest and hope to preserve democracy. It was quite unlikely that two-thirds of the Nationalrat would agree to such a change. Rather, the government was probably using the scheme to demonstrate the strength of feeling among conservatives that held the socialists responsible both for the parliamentary absolutism contained in the Constitution of 1920 and for the progressively disruptive refusal to cooperate with federal authorities. The socialists opposed the change absolutely, of course, and when Schober indicated to the Heimwehr that he intended to respect constitutional procedures the threat to Vienna subsided. Only the name of the city was changed from the Province of Vienna (Land Wien) to the Federal Capital of Vienna (Bundeshauptstadt Wien) without altering the authority of the City Council.

The socialists likewise turned back a move to strip the School Board of its rank as a Provincial School Board with supervisory authority over elementary and secondary schools; it was to remain only a District School Board with authority over Volks- and Hauptschulen.[9] In the end its change was insignificant. With the change of name for Vienna the School Board could no longer be called a Provincial School Board (Landesschulrat) but had to be named explicitly in parentheses wherever reference was made to Provincial School Boards.[10] The functions of the School Board were in fact confirmed by being included explicitly in the constitutional articles as they finally appeared. The constitutional reform also restated the old law that all bills affecting the schools had to be passed in identical form by the Provincial Diets (City Council of Vienna) and the National-rat.[11] The laws of 1927 on the Haupt- and Mittelschule were also re-affirmed in their entirety.

The Education Ministry did not come up empty-handed. It won an important clarification of its authority to direct subordinate school bureaus including elected, collegial bodies like the School Board of Vienna. The constitutional amendment prevented Glöckel from repeating his defiance of 1926 in the case of dispensing children from mandatory religious instruction and gave the Education Ministry new leverage in enforcing the law which it had lacked before. Subordinate offices were ordered to follow the directives of higher bureaus. If they refused, the government could take them as far as the Constitutional Court.[12]

III

The controversies of the past decade were as much an education for the bishops as they were for the parties. From the misguided attempt to address the entire social question with a letter on the schools in 1920, the bishops gradually became aware of the complexity of modern social and educational questions as well as the inadequacy of their appeals to Catholics phrased in the old religious language of dedication and defer-ence. Slowly, too, differences began to emerge between their interests and those of their staunch and outwardly respectful allies, the Christian Socials. They tried to meet the challenge first by issuing a pastoral letter on the social question itself in 1923 and then by taking firmer control of their own deliberations in the Bishops Conference to tighten up their collegial identity. In the meantime they were cast about by conflicting opinions on education from the party and the School Organization to be left with no more answers than before to the problem of how effectively to educate baptized Catholics in the faith.

The bishops continued to put their house in order in the years after 1927 by curbing the political ambitions of Ressiguier and Rotter while they explored the possibilities of a comprehensive negotiated settlement that would take into account the prescriptions of Canon Law and eventuate in a suitable compromise that avoided the extremes of re-establishing religion or separating church and state entirely. The issue of civil divorce and remarriage was the most powerful goad driving the bishops toward a concordat. Compared with the challenge of civil dispensations to remarry passed out by the thousands, relations between church and school were secondary.

The bishops as a body were notably ineffective throughout the negotiations leading to the Haupt- and Mittelschule Laws. At times they were a step behind events, it seemed, but in fact they were thinking ahead to a concordat. Because of the need for secrecy they were unable to provide leadership for the Catholic lobbying effort or give concrete direction to the Christian Socials though the party had on numerous occasions asked for such direction. In the fall of 1926, most of the bishops approved an extensive questionnaire drawn up by the School Organization to be submitted to 250 Catholic educators throughout the country. A united effort was stymied, however, when Gföllner balked. He allowed only Josef Pfeneberger, by then an outspoken opponent of the School Organization, to answer for the Catholics of Linz. The results of the inquiry came in too late for discussion at the annual meeting of the Bishops Conference in November, so a special session was called for after Richard Schmitz published his *Guidelines* in December and sent them out for evaluation. The party easily had enough support among the bishops to cripple efforts to maintain an independent Catholic school lobby.

Behind at times, the bishops were ahead of both the party and the School Organization in thinking about the benefits of a new concordat. They did not want to commit themselves publicly to conclusions based on the questionnaire because they had already informally agreed that the best solution to the school question lay in another concordat with Rome. They might have saved the School Organization a great deal of fruitless work had it been possible to inform the active members about their hopes for a concordat, but Ressiguier at least was somewhat informed. He urged the bishops to keep Seipel up to date on opinion about a concordat even as he stressed the need for secrecy to avoid the inevitable storm of protest from the socialists.[13]

Taking no part in the negotiations did not prevent the bishops from objecting to the result. Again a step too late, they addressed a letter to Schmitz in November 1927 with their reservations on the new school laws. They received the curt reply that there was little the Education Ministry could do since the laws had already been promulgated.[14]

The bishops turned in 1928 with greater vigor to defining the roles of various Catholic organizations in the school question. They had been hurt not only by dissension between the party and the School Organization, but by the complexities of the jurisdictional struggle between rival trade unions for the membership of Catholic teachers. Gföllner had lost the desire to imitate the charismatic Rudigier in school matters and passed the torch to Piffl and Sigismund Waitz of Innsbruck. Waitz gave a report on the status of Catholic private education to the bishops in 1928 and made suggestions on the content of a new concordat. Piffl presented another study on organizations that concluded with the feasibility of combining the Katholischer Schulverein, the original militant organization from the 1880's that now concentrated on raising money to support Catholic private schools, with the Education and School Organization of Ressiguier that had carried the banner in the 1920's. His suggestion was accepted unanimously, and the organizations were united.[15] Ressiguier remained president, but Franz Jungmann, a Jesuit priest, became general director of the whole organization. It meant stricter supervision of political activities than before, and Rotter complained that he was no longer allowed to carry on the political struggle.[16] Undoubtedly the bishops wanted to do just that because Rotter had become an embarrassment despite his great dedication and capacity for work. The Frohe Kindheit with its day care centers remained independent to preserve the fruits of its battle with Rotter and the School Organization.

A slight setback for the bishops came from the Constitutional Court in February 1928. Expected since the early days of the Republic, the decision finally came down that the Amendment of 1883 to the Elementary

School Law which restricted the office of principal to approved catechists was unconstitutional. Lest the extent of their decision be misunderstood, the justices expressly avoided deciding upon the constitutionality of the "moral-religious education" provision of the Elementary School Law and its relation to Article 14 on freedom of conscience in the Constitution of 1867 still in effect.[17]

IV

The idea of a concordat grew steadily in select church and government circles after 1927 despite the possibility of vigorous socialist opposition. The chief reason lay in widespread refusal among Catholics to change marriage legislation to allow civil divorce and remarriage unless the Vatican approved and the Austrian laws were compatible with Canon Law. Chancellor Otto Ender, a moderate Christian Social, was so impressed by the need for a concordat to regulate marriages that he was inclined to minimize the school issue as another set of problems badly in need of a negotiated settlement.[18] The thousands of illegal remarriages occuring "by way of exception" in socialist strongholds did not discourage Catholics from continuing the struggle. This fact finally led the Pan-Germans to drop their opposition to a concordat. Reform of marriage legislation would almost certainly include approval of civil divorce and remarriage; socialists and Pan-Germans both could be confident of that as they faced the prospect. The matter of religious influence in the schools might require the socialists to make concessions, which meant that the schools presented a bigger obstacle to getting socialist agreement than marriage legislation. It was possible, however, that the same fears among socialists of mounting conservative reaction and potential undermining of parliamentary institutions that led to the constitutional reforms of 1929 could be used to extract concessions on the schools.

The Christian Socials interested in a concordat had opponents closer to home than the socialists. The radical or so-called "integral" Catholics had reason to fear that the party would relinquish the precarious place of religion in the schools through negotiations. Piux XI gave them ammunition in 1929 when he wrote in an encyclical that interconfessional schools could not be considered the norm for Catholics and instructed states on their duty to help families provide for the Christian education of their children. He even appeared to hold up the Holland solution as a model for church-state relations in the schools.[19] Ressiguier suggested in a report to the Bishops Conference in 1931 that the school problem could be solved only on condition that the dangers to the faith of children in interdenominational public schools were removed, that a "sufficient" number of publicly supported Catholic schools were erected and that Catholic private schools were financially supported by the state on a par with the public schools.[20] These conditions found their way into a government memorandum with the addition that Catholic teacher training institutes be maintained.[21]

The major opponent of a concordat was still the Social Democratic Party. Glöckel expressed the opposition in a speech to the Kinderfreunde in April 1931, and throughout the negotiations, the possible dissent of the socialists made all conclusions tentative.[22] Socialist criticism of negotiations with the Vatican was somewhat cautious at first because it was clear that the first order of business was concessions on the matter of divorce and remarriage. Memories of the Concordat of 1855, kept alive by constantly raising the specter of a "Concordatschule," were strong enough, though, that it was unlikely that the socialists would support extensive aid to Catholic education even if it meant ongoing chaos over marriage. The fait accompli of daily dispensations for civil remarriage appeared to give them the upper hand because moderate Christian Socials wanted to provide a legal base for civil remarriage out of concern for the Rechtsstaat while the socialists felt no need to make similar concessions on the schools. Erosion of respect for the law on the right that accompanied their intransigence, and the possibility of an antiparliamentary reaction among Catholics had only recently made an impression on them.

As socialists became aware of the threat to the Republic contained in the cultural struggle, Catholics were also learning from the events of the recent past. Max Hussarek, the former government minister and historian of the first concordat, proposed modest goals for a new concordat in a speech before Catholic leaders in May 1931. The old concordat, though a majestic structure, had lasted only nineteen years; a new concordat should be merely a useful construction to help solve the concrete problems that could be solved.[23] Pius XI agreed; informed by Sigismund Waitz on opinion in Austria, he said that a concordat was a dialogue rather than a monologue, and therefore an agreement between two parties.[24]

Waitz was in Rome to tell the pope about two conferences held in Austria on the concordat, one a meeting of diocesan delegates and another a special session of the Bishops Conference. There was general agreement at both conferences that a concordat would have to include articles on the schools but that Catholics could realistically hope only for subventions for Catholic private schools. As a result of Waitz's mission, negotiations were officially opened in late May 1931 but information that reached the public during the next six months dealt almost exclusively with marriage legislation.

The Austrian official responsible for conducting negotiations until January 1932 was the Pan-German Minister of Justice. At that time, when the party could no longer demand the post for itself after electoral losses to the National Socialists it went to Kurt Schuschnigg, a Christian Social from the Tyrol.[25] In contrast with the Pan-Germans who merely tolerated the notion of a concordat, Schuschnigg regarded it as a work of reconciliation. He agreed with Max Hussarek that Catholics could no longer think in terms of a counterattack to regain Austria for Catholicism; he wanted instead a settlement that would ease the consciences of Catholics by lessening the tensions between the demands of their religion and the realities of a pluralistic society. Schuschnigg was in charge of negotiations to their completion along with Egon Loebenstein, Section Chief for religion in the Education Ministry. Both favored special caution on the schools lest the concordat fail to be ratified. Schuschnigg tried to impress on Pacelli that many wishes of the Vatican on Christian education were already anchored in Austrian law and that it would be useless to have an international treaty as long as Austria lacked a basis in constitutional law for regulating relations between church and state on the schools.[26]

Despite the good will, negotiations dragged throughout most of 1932. The Depression hit Austria with devastating force, a planned tariff union with Germany was set aside by the International Court, and the deaths of Seipel and Piffl in August removed two active participants from the scene. The bishops expressed concern about the delay in their November meeting and sent a note to the government encouraging it to resume negotiations as soon as possible.[27] Pacelli also exerted pressure on the new Chancellor Engelbert Dollfuss. Pacelli answered reports from the Austrian ambassador that the bishops were intent on getting a commitment to confessional schools into the concordat by saying that he was content to reaffirm the status quo because he gathered from the opposition press that the obstacles to a concordat were otherwise insurmountable.[28] The new Education Minister was Anton Rintelen, back after seven years and still cordially detested by the socialists. He had the backing of the far right, but over his complaints Schuschnigg and Loebenstein succeeded in freezing him out of inner dealings on the concordat.[29]

The negotiations were not without tension between the bishops and the government once they were resumed. The bishops wanted one of their number represented, but the expert among them was the monarchist Sigismund Waitz who was out of favor with officials like Loebenstein.[30] To the dismay of Waitz, the bishops and the government settled on Franz Kamprath, an auxiliary bishop of Vienna who as a monsignor in 1926 had been a member of the delegation that protested the school agreement between Glöckel and Schneider.[31] The Catholics had in him a man who, if he was no longer in sympathy with the integralist aims of radicals, had good credentials with them and an interest in keeping the good will of the school activists. During the negotiations he confided to Loebenstein that he could not offend the School Organization or the bishops who wanted publicly supported confessional schools even though he realized that the socialists would never approve.[32] With Kamprath apologizing for Catholic hard liners, the government expected no difficulty over articles on the schools.

The scope of this work precludes a thorough reassessment of Engelbert Dollfuss and his regime. Nevertheless, the picture conveyed until the present is the distorted one of a man blindly reacting to Hitler's designs on Austria or planning in a sinister fashion the extermination of democratic institutions in response to antiparliamentary pressures from the Heimwehr. In both cases politics dominate the interpretation. He has been given little credit for constructive programs of his own; neither the corporatist economy nor the Constitution of 1934 based on the principles of *Quadragesimo Anno* rate as realistic political programs due to the fact that Austria did not have the means to register a political consensus once Dollfuss prevented the Nationalrat from reconvening in March of 1933. He has been roundly condemned for authoritarian practices as a "clerical fascist," with scant reflection on the conceptual content of the modifier in that phrase and linked ideologically with the dictators around him. If his programs might have transcended partisan politics and educated Austrians on the dangers of associating with the colossus to the north, he was given little time to implement them, leaving historians only with his coup d'etat and short-lived attempt to restructure Austrian political life on which to judge him.

The previous pages of this book have been an attempt to demonstrate both the importance and the divisiveness of the cultural issue. The gap in the Constitution on church-state relations was clear evidence that democracy had not worked in the previous fifteen years. The *Rechtsstaat*, or rule of law rather than persons, was more highly prized than democratic institutions themselves, and yet it had to be suspended where cherished cultural positions were concerned. In no area of public life was compromise lacking more than regarding world views, and Seipel's efforts to subordinate ideology to politics ultimately failed. In pursuit of his twin goals of preserving Austrian independence and transcending party politics Dollfuss was caught in a dilemma. He saw the possibility of preserving Austrian independence by reconciling domestic differences in the face of a foreign threat just as he saw the impossibility of bridging ideological gaps in the country using fear of Germany. The history of the Anschluss movement shows what little fear the German Austrians had over incorporation into the Reich. Not only were democratic institutions weak, Austrian patriotism was also weak, eroded by a poor economy, by German nationalism affronted at the loss of status as a great power and by ideological divisions that created three closed cultural camps.

Under the circumstances Dollfuss looked to Italy both to preserve Austrian independence and to overcome domestic strife. The instrument of the one was to be close diplomatic relations with Mussolini and of the other a concordat. Discussion of relations with Mussolini have been covered amply elsewhere, but the history of negotiations over the Concordat and its meaning in Austrian domestic life remain to be explored in depth.

The political interpretation of Dollfuss' actions has clouded as well the last stages of negotiations over the Austrian Concordat. The reason is that Dollfuss was engaged in a race with Hitler to conclude a concordat in order to keep the sympathies of Austrian Catholics. The political purpose behind the haste to win propaganda points in the Spring of 1933 obscures the fact that negotiations had been going on for some time and that wide segments of Austrian public life had concluded long before that a concordat was the best answer to problems of church and state. Hitler, by contrast, entered negotiations with haste to undercut Catholic opposition at home and to win international recognition for his government. He also had an eye on the loyalties of Austrian Catholics despite his intention to ignore any obligations under the terms of the treaty. The Austrian desire for a concordat was therefore sincere and had a preliminary history that demonstrated the utility of such an agreement while the Nazi desire was cynical and insincere.

Much as the question of potential opposition to a concordat was in Dollfuss' mind, there is no evidence that competition with Hitler contributed to the suspension of the Nationalrat after March 4, 1933. Hitler had stated his intention to abide by the concordats between the Vatican and the various German states in his opening declaration of policy in January, but as late as the time of the Enabling Act of March 23, there was no discussion about a concordat for the entire Reich.[33] Only when Hitler possessed full power to conclude international agreements did he turn to the potential benefits of a concordat. On the other hand, after Dollfuss suspended parliament he had no intention of ignoring the socialists when a concordat came up for ratification. The need to consult the socialists was self-serving because it allowed the Austrian government to claim it could not make as many concessions on the schools as Pacelli wanted.

It was primarily to neutralize the effects of a visit by Papen and Goering and to enlist Italian aid in protecting Austrian sovereignty that Dollfuss traveled to Rome in early April 1933, but he used the opportunity to meet with Vatican officials. Discussions with Cardinal Pacelli on the concordat were friendly but general because Dollfuss was not well-informed about the particulars under consideration. Final negotiations were conducted by Schuschnigg and Loebenstein, who went to Rome shortly after Dollfuss returned to Austria.[34]

The school issue proved to be more thorny than Schuschnigg expected. On the basis of reports from Ambassador Rudolph Kohlruss he had understood that the Vatican would accept the status quo on the schools, but in the meantime Pacelli had changed his mind.[35] Now he wanted some statement on subsidies for Catholic private schools. The government negotiators were relieved to find that Pacelli doubted an entire confessional school system was possible under the circumstances. He was perhaps striking a compromise between the government and the Catholic

school interests that Kamprath felt obliged to represent. Schuschnigg
gladly agreed in the name of Dollfuss and the Council of Ministers.[36]
The negotiators settled on an article confirming the obligatory character
of religious instruction and religious exercises "to the usual extent"
("im bisherigen Ausmass"), as well as the authority of the local bishop
over religious education. In a roundabout statement which tied the question of state support to economic factors, they included support for
Catholic private schools where the existence of such schools relieved
the taxpayers of a financial burden. This first version of the Concordat
signed on June 5, 1933 contained no mention of confessional schools.[37]

Before the formal signing, Kamprath submitted the text to the bishops.
Waitz was upset that confessional schools were nowhere to be found
and made his feelings known, but there was little the bishops could do as
long as the government wanted to win the approval of the socialists
in parliament. As it was, the *Arbeiter-Zeitung* published a strong article
against the concordat. It did little good to argue that the Concordat
between Germany and the Holy See included confessional schools because
they had existed in Germany since 1926.[38]

Pacelli soon had reason to become annoyed with the Austrians. He had
accommodated their wishes to finish the Austrian Concordat before that
of Germany (July 20, 1933), but once signed, it languished until work
on the new Constitution was finished. When Dollfuss used the delay
in finishing the Constitution as an excuse to put off new elections, Pacelli
began to wonder if the concordat was not a convenient public relations
gimmick to support a shaky dictatorship. It was clear by that time that
Hitler had used the Reichskonkordat for that reason. If Dollfuss intended to
maintain a dictatorship all along, Pacelli felt he could have supported
Kamprath to demand confessional schools without fear of socialist opposition in parliament.

Pacelli found his opening after the civil war of February 12-15, 1934.
The socialist revolt was crushed quickly and the Social Democratic Party
outlawed. Parliament would not have to depend on socialist votes to
ratify the Concordat after all. Prompted by German violations of their
concordat, Pius XI and Pacelli decided to seek further guarantees from
the Austrian government on Catholic schools. From the Roman point
of view little but economic factors now appeared to stand in the way
of an entire Catholic confessional system. Kohlruss reported to Dollfuss
as early as February 26, 1934 that Pacelli had raised the question of

"improving" the concordat to make it a "model." When Dollfuss replied by insisting that the present article best protected the interests of Catholics, Pacelli concluded that Christian corporatism was less religious than it pretended.[39] Dollfuss had been using fear of the socialists to support the status quo for reasons having little to do with religion. Like Seipel, Dollfuss was strong on statements of principle but weak on commitment to Catholic education. Kohlruss telegraphed Loebenstein that the answer came as a "very unpleasant surprise" to Pacelli.[40]

Egon Loebenstein found himself stuck with the task of traveling to Rome to confront Pacelli with the difficulties involved in changing a document that had been signed by Vatican plenipotentiaries. Pacelli compromised by agreeing not to demand a confessional system. Rather a statement appended to Article VI moved the question to a future time: "Through these measures, the Catholic school system in Austria ought to be improved (gefördert) and the conditions thereby established for the development of a public, Catholic-confessional school."[41] Another statement added that children would be taught according to Catholic principles. The wording, which injected a moral note of doubtful utility into an otherwise pragmatic document, was a victory of sorts for Dollfuss, but it was a setback for the Roman Curia only insofar as the Vatican entertained illusions about the state of public education in Austria. The concordat was ratified in this form by the signature of Federal President Wilhelm Miklas as his first act of state shortly after midnight on May 1, 1934, the day the new constitution went into effect. From being unregulated under the Constitution of 1920, church-state relations were the first concern of the authoritarian government.

Pacelli may have nursed a grudge over the matter till the end of his pontificate as Pius XII. When the Catholics of Austria succeeded after World War II in salvaging the concordat against the resurgent socialists, he refused to commit the Vatican and left it to his successor John XXIII to confirm a concordat with the Austrians.

V

Perhaps Pacelli had simply gotten his hopes too high because there was clear evidence that the Dollfuss government was actively engaged in changing education to favor the church. A month after parliament was suspended the Education Minister Anton Rintelen formally rescinded the Glöckel Decree. He had what Loebenstein regarded as almost a mono-mania on the topic.[42] Out of fear that Gföllner might do something rash, he prepared for the move by contacting the new Archbishop of Vienna, Theodore Innitzer, and asking that he urge caution upon Gföllner. Innitzer sent Kamprath to Linz in an effort to enlist support for a letter to the clergy counseling forbearance in reestablishing mandatory religious exercises. Gföllner refused, but Rintelen went ahead anyway and withdrew the decree on April 10, 1933.[43] The date chosen contained a tawdry gesture of triumphalism, as it was fourteen years to the day after the decree was published. The government backed Rintelen by successfully prosecuting the *Arbeiter-Zeitung* for a strong article it published against him on April 16.[44] The government of Vienna then turned to the courts with a suit challenging the legality of withdrawing the decree, but it languished on the docket with all other socialist protests against the Dollfuss government until after the civil war. Then Richard Schmitz as new mayor of Vienna withdrew the complaint.[45]

The bishops took a bold step in December 1933 toward withdrawing the church from secular politics. Against a tradition as old as representative institutions in Austria they ordered all clerics out of elected office. This meant that the phenomenon of Ignaz Seipel would not reoccur. It was a giant step toward reconciliation with the advocates of separation between church and state that proved effective after World War II when the bishops abided by their decision.

The church gained far less from the civil war than the political conservatives, even with the revisions to the Concordat. The Concordat contained only promises of state support for Catholic schools, which in any case held only 4% of the students in Austria, and an eventual Catholic public school system. On the other hand, successful suppression of the revolt left conservative school politicians free to implement their reactionary programs without fear of opposition. The result was the destruction not only of the compromise of 1927 but also the reform of 1908 that created the Reformrealgymnasium.[46] The changes dictated on March 23, 1934 reinstated the old system of separation between the middle schools and the Hauptschule. The first track of the Hauptschule was abolished "for financial reasons," though the school remained a four-year institution.[47] The government pointed out with some slight justification that the opportunities for transferring between Hauptschule and middle schools had never been used to any notable degree. Latin became compulsory once again for all eight years of middle school, Greek for six at the Gymnasium. This confirmed the impossibility of transferring from the Hauptschule to a college-preparatory school. In addition, a third foreign language became mandatory for students at all middle schools except the Realschule. Even the Christian Social Ludwig Battista, who had represented the party in the Reform Department of the Education Ministry throughout the First Republic, later found the decrees regrettable. They represented a return to the Lernschule based on authoritarian principles of social conduct and hierarchical notions of social stratification.[48] The decrees appeared over the signature of Kurt Schuschnigg, who had added the portfolio of Education Minister to that of the Minister of Justice. Named Chancellor by Dollfuss as he lay dying at the hands of a Nazi assassin, Schuschnigg's government from 1934 to 1938 was not marked entirely by reactionary policies. He made an attempt to reform teacher education and upgrade it to the college level in 1936, but at the time of the Anschluss the plan had not been implemented.

Another old score was settled in 1936 when the Federal Court reversed the earlier decisions of the Constitutional Court on whether a change of status regarding religion that involved no new religion (Konfessionslosigkeit) could be legally considered a "change of religion." If a person who had no religion assumed one, or if a person who had a religion simply dropped it, he or she would not fall under the laws governing those who changed their religion. This applied as well for children under the age of seven.[49]

In the ashes of defeat Otto Glöckel saw his own death approaching. He ignored a warning from the police and went to his office as usual on February 13, 1934 while bullets were flying in the city. There he was arrested, and when he emerged from a concentration camp in October his health was shattered. He lived nine months more until a heart attack claimed his life on July 23, 1935 at the age of sixty-one. His contributions to education remain inestimable even though his involvement in the politics of church and state contributed much to domestic turmoil during the First Republic.

In many ways the history of the First Republic is the story of attempts to prevent the kinds of reaction that followed revolution during the previous century in Austria. The socialists tried hard to protect the Constitution of 1920 which corresponded in substance to their conception of a good government for Austria. But essential flaws in the Constitution, remedied too late regarding executive authority and not at all regarding church-state relations, weakened respect for it as an instrument of government. By the time the threat from Hitlerian Germany overshadowed all others the Christian Socials were willing to abandon the Constitution of 1920. It had not proven adequate to prevent the socialists from pursuing a cultural revolution in defiance of existing though antiquated laws, and the courts were too unsure of their status to interpret the Constitution of 1867 and subsequent laws in an authoritative manner. The inability to agree in 1920 on matters of church, state and the schools bore bitter fruit throughout the decade to suggest in the end that Austria did not yet possess the essential elements of a democracy. Inability to compromise manifested itself in many forms throughout the period, ending as it had begun with a decree regarding mandatory religious exercises for children in grade schools. The brackets formed by Glöckel's decree of 1919 and Rintelen's of 1933 contain items of perhaps greater substance such as the "dispensation marriages" that led to the Concordat of 1934, but the conflict over education was clearly symptomatic of the entire malaise of the First Republic.

EPILOGUE

The Nazi domination formed a hiatus between the bitter struggles of the First Republic and the relative objectivity and willingness to compromise that has characterized the Second Republic. Besides exhaustion and defeat, the experience of unimaginable brutality and humiliation over their own role in it contributed to the spirit of reconciliation among the parties. Great portions of all party programs had fallen into disrepute—the Anschluss of the Pan-Germans, the revolutionary opposition of the Social Democrats and the close association of church and party of the Christian Socials—leaving the parties chastened and ready to act together. Austrians no longer questioned the value of an independent Austria with its own traditions and civil ideals. Problems of reconstruction and economic backwardness were shouldered with magnanimity and hope for the future by all in spite of Allied occupation.

The parties made an important break with the past in school affairs by taking up discussions about problems willingly. Oftentimes during the First Republic such questions could not even be raised. The Social Democrats and the administration, consisting mostly of old Christian Socialist, formulated two school programs in 1948. The texts showed how far the parties had to go to build a language of understanding because there were as yet no categories available other than the old ones of the cultural struggle. The proposals brought to life the old ideological formulations, making it unrealistic to presume that a compromise could be reached without extensive negotiations as well as preparation of public opinion for conciliatory gestures among party leaders. There was basic

187

agreement on keeping religious education in the public schools, but there were differences on the status of Catholic schools and on state support for denominational schools. Both sides thought there should be nine years of compulsory education rather than eight, but they could not agree on the content of the extra year.

Important progress was made on distributing some responsibilities between the federal government and the provinces, in contrast with earlier times. A constitutional law was passed on April 21, 1948 to regulate relations between the Bund and the Länder regarding conditions of supervisory and teaching service. The federal government would exercise immediate supervision over the administration and faculty of the universities, the middle schools and all other schools supported by the central government. The provinces would supervise personnel at Volks- and Hauptschulen as well as at vocational and specific schools. The right to legislate in financial and disciplinary affairs for all teachers at public schools was reserved to the federal government.[1]

Another conflict was laid to rest when the sides agreed on another law in July 1949 regulating attendance at religious instruction. It went beyond the compromise decision of the Constitutional Court in 1927 which said that a child who had started religious instruction could not withdraw until the age of fourteen. Parents now had the right to take a child out of religious instruction at any time up to the age of fourteen. Thereafter the child had the customary right to do so himself. School prayer had been introduced by executive order on June 24, 1946 "in those classes of the compulsory schools in which the majority of the pupils are registered for religious instruction in the Christian confessions."[2]

Despite such auspicious beginnings, the process of reconciliation took longer than advocates anticipated. In 1952 an attempt was made simply to reinstate the old legislation with some changes, but after two meetings the parties abandoned the attempt. One of the biggest problems was state support for private confessional schools which had started under the terms of the Concordat. Other problems survived as well: organizing the middle schools, the eight-year Einheits- or Gesamtschule of the socialists, the question of the goal of education, and reform of teacher training.[3] A renewed attempt to find a solution in the autumn of 1958 after Austria had regained its statehood had to be dropped as well.

Other points of division were eliminated one by one, however. An old dispute about financial responsibility for the schools was obviated by a

law of July 13, 1955. The financial affairs of the middle schools in their
entirety (not just teachers' salaries) became the business of the federal
government. Basic premises dealing with the finances of the compulsory
schools became the jurisdiction of the federal government, but the provinces received jurisdiction over laws implementing general policies. This
law also wiped out the last vestige of the school patronage system that
still survived in the province of Salzburg.[4]

Proponents of a comprehensive agreement between the parties did
not lose hope despite the lack of success. In 1961 the parties formed
another negotiating committee. It identified ten areas of difference with
an eleventh, the Concordat, as an overarching concern whose settlement
constituted a precondition for agreeing on other points. The socialists
raised the usual questions about the relation of the Hauptschule to the
Mittelschule since they still proposed a unified school for the first eight
years. Three areas touched the church directly; private schools, religious
instruction and teacher training. Other matters like school administration,
supervision and a new code of conduct for teachers contained some
points where the church was involved to a lesser degree.

Eventually the negotiators decided that it was safe to handle the
questions of school organization without involving the church. These
issues had more to do with differences between conservative and progressive views of education and academic or practical emphasis rather
than with religion.

The task of the negotiators was only half done when they reached
a compromise in May 1961. They then had to convince their own parties
that the results were acceptable. Battles that had found peaceful solu-
tions among the negotiators were renewed over and over again within
party ranks. Max Neugebauer, who led the socialist delegation, commented that the word "treason" came easily to the lips of party members.[5]

Internal struggles on both sides eventually subsided enough to pass the
laws, but the kernel of mistrust remained in the form of a separate law
that restated the rule of a two-thirds majority in the Nationalrat for
any school law. Passed on July 18, 1962 a week before the other laws,
it said:

> The Nationalrat can pass federal laws concerning the affairs of
> school offices in the provinces and political districts, as well as in

matters of obligatory school attendance, school organization, private schools, and relations between school and church (religious associations) including religious instruction in the schools, only in the presence of at least half of the members of the Nationalrat and with a majority of two-thirds of the votes. The affairs of the Hochschulen and Academies of Art are excluded from these provisions.[6]

The Constitution of the Second Republic, therefore, requires a law with the status of a constitutional amendment for any changes in the nature of the school system or relations between church and school.

The other laws represent a great work of national reconciliation. The problem of stating the goal of education was finally solved. The Elementary School Law of 1869 had said simply that the goal was moral-religious education with the assumption that knowledge and other forms of personal growth were included. These were now made explicit:

The Volksschule has the task to educate children morally and religiously, to develop their intellectual activities, to provide them with the necessary knowledge and skills for further training for life, and to lay the foundation for the education of able persons and members of the community.[7]

Possibilities for transferring between different types of schools were reestablished by reorganizing the curriculum. The old differences between Haupt- and Untermittelschule were kept, however, which meant that the laws of 1927 were still as close as Austrians could come to a consensus on the kinds of schools that were politically possible. The socialists preserved their goal of the Gesamtschule, as they do at this writing, but like the confessional school system of the Catholics, it remains an unfulfilled dream.[8]

Agreement to keep the Concordat was the most important contribution to civil peace in Austria. As approved by the Austrians, it preserved religious instruction and religious exercises in the public schools along with state support for Catholic schools. The matter of church-run teacher training academies was handled separately. Negotiations with

Rome dragged because Pius XII nursed a grudge over Austrian reluctance to modify the first version of the Concordat in 1934. He was not satisfied with a proposal merely to recognize the validity of the Concordat without adding the somewhat insulting specification that the Austrian government intended to abide by the articles, as for example in the matter of state subventions for Catholic schools.[9] After he died, John XXIII expedited matters. The final agreement confirmed the particulars of the Concordat with a modification regarding the freedom of parents to withdraw their children from religious instruction. Otherwise the state agreed to support Catholic private schools. Religious exercises in the schools continued as before, and religious instruction kept the place accorded it. Even the statement about the eventual formation of a Catholic confessional school system remained, though some older socialists objected strenuously. The school system of Burgenland became public in exchange for a sum of money earmarked for Catholic private schools. The Concordat was approved as a state treaty on July 9, 1962, two weeks before the Nationalrat passed the school laws, and became part of the Austrian constitution along with them.[10]

Many old-timers on both sides remembered the sacrifices they had made and were disappointed in the concessions, but in the new atmosphere there was no point in continuing the old struggles. By contrast, many younger Austrians consider the country an isle of the blessed, made possible in no small part by the resolution of the conflict between church and state.

Called a politicum by Maria Theresa in the 1760's, the schools in the 1960's still testified to the concern for education in government circles. But church claims that the schools were an ecclesiasticum, supported by the experience of centuries before Maria Theresa, modified her claim during the intervening two centuries. In the course of the confrontations, many exaggerated claims to authority on both sides were made. The church in the process realized more and more clearly that religious values could not, indeed should not, be imposed on society as they were during the Counterreformation. The secularizers, if they still held hopes of separating church and school, became aware that the church considered education close to the heart of its religious mission. A mutual understanding of interests, though conflicting, goes a long way toward realizing the democratic ideal of unity in diversity for which modern Austria strives.

NOTES

Notes to Chapter One

1. The Queen wrote, "School affairs are and remain always a "politicum" (Das Schulwesen aber ist und bleibt allzeit ein politicum. . ." Quoted in Johann Schmidt, *Entwicklung der katholischen Schule in Österreich* (Vienna, 1958), 4.

2. The ramifications of this fact are covered in Edith Saurer, *Die Politische Aspekte der Österreichischen Bischofsernennungen 1867-1903,* (Vienna, 1968).

3. In 1847 there were 4143 Trivialschulen, 60 Hauptschulen and 66 girls' schools in the lands that make up present day Austria. In 1935-36 there were 4,582 Volksschulen in the Republic of Austria. Cf. Hermann Zeissl and Ludwig Battista, *100 Jahre Unterrichtsministerium* (Vienna, 1948), 141, 159, 172.

4. The bishops asked for and received an account of the various funds run by the government. There is no indication of the way this was done nor whether the bishops had any of their own financial experts examine the report. Cf. *Actenstücke, die Bischöfliche Versammlung zu Wien* (Wien, 1850).

5. Fifteen years later the Education Ministry was still complaining about instructional materials and pedagogical methods used in the secondary schools. A decree of March 24, 1865 tried to remedy the situation

by directing that teachers were to give yearly reports to the principal. Little was done when Cardinal Schwarzenberg of Prague objected that the state was interfering in church affairs. Cf. correspondence in *Friedrich Cardinal Schwarzenberg* Vol. II by Cölestin Wolfsgruber (Vienna, 1916), 572-573.

6. For a discussion of the Concordat cf. Erika Weinzierl, *Die österreichische Konkordate von 1855 und 1933* (München, 1960).

7. The law governing financial responsibility was passed on March 5, 1862 (*Reichsgesetzblatt,* 1862 No. 18 Art. V). The judgment on improvements in the schools is that of Gustav Strakosch-Grassmann *Geschichte des österreichischen Unterrichtswesens* (Wien, 1905), 245.

8. He said, "We are also convinced that neither a law nor a treaty can irrevocably relinquish for all time to come rights which according to the contemporary development of civil life belong to the essential, sovereign rights of the state." Quoted in Max Hussarek, *Die Krise und die Lösung des Konkordates von 18 August 1855,* (Vienna, 1932), 234-235.

9. For relations with the Holy See cf. Erika Weinzierl, 107-108. For parliamentary developments cf. Gustav Kolmer, *Parlament und Verfassung in Österreich* Vol. 1 (Graz, 1972), 306.

10. Kolmer, 304.

11. Reichsgesetzblatt 1867 No. 141 Para. 11, h.

12. Reichsgesetzblatt 1867 No. 141 Para. 11, i.

13. Edouard Herbst said as early as 1862, "For us, the autonomy of the local community is a major political principle which we will maintain under all circumstances, even in view of the danger that perhaps here and there our nationality can be put in danger or even temporarily placed at a disadvantage." Quoted in Strakosch-Grassmann, 244.

14. Reichsgesetzblatt 1867 No. 142.

15. Hussarek, 248, 250-251.

16. Johann Schmidt, 100-101.

17. Strakosch-Grassmann, 257.

18. Reichsgesetzblatt 1868 No. 48 Para. 6.

19. Cf. Cölestin Wolfsgruber, *Josef Othmar Kardinal Rauscher* (Freiburg, 1888), 234.

20. Rauscher and Schwarzenberg were among a minority of bishops who opposed the definition of papal infallibility at the First Vatican Council. They left the gathering rather than vote against it.

21.　Pius IX wrote, "You see, honorable brothers, how reprehensible and damnable are the laws passed by the Austrian government which violate in the extreme the rights of the Catholic Church. We declare these laws to be completely void now and for all time to come." Quoted in Schmidt, 100.

22.　Schmidt, 112; Wolfsgruber *Schwarzenberg*, III, 102. Wolfsgruber, *Rauscher*, 238, is misleading when it neglects to say that the final decision was up to the bishops.

23.　Kolmer, I, 368, 372; II, 42. The moves were blocked first by the Emperor and then in legal action taken by Rudigier himself.

24.　Strakosch-Grassmann, 308.

25.　The text of the bishops' resolution is found in Wolfsgruber, *Schwarzenberg*, III, 105-108.

26.　Reichsgesetzblatt 1869, No. 62. For details of the debate, see *Die grossen Parlamentsreden über das Reichsvolksschulgesetz* (Wien, 1909). Also Kolmer, I, 375-378. The reports of the parliamentary commissions are contained in Otto Glöckel, *Zur Fünfzigjahrfeier des RVG* (Wien, 1919).

27.　Reichsgesetzblatt, 1883, No. 53.

28.　Strakosch-Grassmann, 273.

29.　Other Austrian Germans reproached the Tyrolers for their "Auchdeutschtum." Cf. Kolmer II, 31-32.

30.　Wolfsgruber, *Rauscher,* 251-252. Rauscher called a meeting for April 30-May 5, 1872 to solicit support for his new direction but only 19 bishops attended.

31.　Criticism by the Education Ministry fell on deaf ears before 1867. Cf. Wolfsgruber, *Schwarzenberg* III, 703. After that time the bishops actively protested. Cf. Ibid., 274.

32.　Leo Schedlbauer, *Handbuch der Reichsgesetze und der Ministerialverordnungen über das Volksschulwesen* Vol. I (Vienna, 1911), 701-702.

33.　Cölestin Wolfsgruber, *Kirchengeschichte Österreich-Ungarns* (Wien, 1909), 96. For the entire speech of Stremayr cf. Hugo von Kremer-Auenrode, *Aktenstücke zur Geschichte des Verhältnisses zwischen Staat und Kirche im 19 Jahrhundert* (Leipzig, 1873), F, IV 155-179.

34.　Wolfsgruber, *Schwarzenberg*, III, 555.

35. Leo Thun gave credit to Rauscher for the idea of the congress. Cf. *Verhandlungen des allgemeinen österreichischen Katholikentages für die gesammte Monarchie* (Wien, 1877), 152.

36. Between 1867 and 1879 nine conferences were held to deal with specific issues: of these, two dealt exclusively with the schools and two others had the issue as their main topic. For a summary cf. Peter Leisching, *Die Bischofskonferenz* (Vienna, 1963), 250-251. As yet the Bishops Conference had not been formally organized.

37. He wrote, "As a result, in my opinion the salvation of the Christian school as well as the entire Christian order, on the basis of which the existence of Austria depends, cannot be won through the Reichsrat but only through its fall." Quoted in Wolfsgruber *Schwarzenberg*, III 579-580.

38. Ibid., 580.

39. William A. Jenks, *Austria Under the Iron Ring* (Charlottesville, Virginia, 1965, 56-57.

40. Ibid., 55-56.

41. This is one of Jenks' major themes. E.g., p. 235-236.

42. Gustav Kolmer, III, 164. The two motions were voted down on February 24, 1881. Eduard Suess, a liberal deputy, expressed liberal objections when he argued that neither monks nor aristocrats were fit to educate youth because they were hard and unjust judges whose love for the church extinguished their love for mankind. Ibid., 174.

43. With Austrian diplomatic finesse, Rudigier discreetly asked Schwarzenberg about the advisability of joining the school boards and Schwarzenberg with delicacy replied that he did not wish to be the cause of not heeding the weighty voices suggesting that Rudigier join the school administration. Wolfsgruber, *Schwarzenberg* III, 721.

44. The motive of Schönborn remains mysterious. Jenks suggests that Schönborn wanted to prevent Taafe from courting the liberals, an element of devious cleverness otherwise missing from the dealings of Schönborn. Jenks, 235.

45. Ibid., 234-235.

46. Friedrich Funder, *Vom Gestern ins Heute* (Vienna, 1952), 51.

47. *Bericht über den III all. ös. Katholikentag* (Wels, 1892), 371-373.

48. Funder, 103.

49. Funder, 129.

50. Ibid., 198-201.

51. Lueger tried to keep liberal and Catholic teachers, the majority, from going over to the Social Democrats by organizing the Verein der Lehrer und Schulfreunde. Eventually it included most of the teachers in Vienna. Catholics complained that it had no specifically Christian program.

52. The school question was demoted from first on the agenda as in all previous Katholikentage, to third. For matters dealing with the schools cf. *Bericht über den IV allg. ös. Katholikentag* (Salzburg, 1896) 219-223.

53. Funder, 198-201. According to Funder, Dipauli first approached him and he carried the message to Opitz.

54. Between 1905 and 1913 only 2,200 people changed their religion in Vienna. E. Weinzierl, *Die österreichische Konkordate,* 142.

55. Quoted in Hugo Hantsch, *Geschichte Österreichs* (Graz, 1968), 428-429.

56. In 1898 The Vienna Party Congress resolved, "Social Democracy fights most decidedly—with due respect for its principle "Religion is a private matter"—the representatives of all religious organizations with all appropriate means when and wherever they calumniate our party and its members, as well as whenever their doctrines oppose the struggle for the liberation of the proletariat." But in 1901 at the Vienna Congress the view was expressed that nine-tenths of the population were believers and the other tenth questionable. E. Weinzierl, 134-135.

57. Oskar Achs and Albert Krassnigg, *Drillschule-Lernschule-Arbeitschule: Otto Glöckel und die ös. Schulreform in der Ersten Republik* (Wien, 1974), 52.

58. Cf. Helmut Engelbrecht, "Die Diskussion um die Einheitsschule zwischen 1897 und 1919: ein Beitrag zum Verständnis des Schulreformkonzeptes Otto Glöckel's" in *Österreich in Geschichte und Literatur* 1971, 15, 2: 73-87.

59. Achs, 26. Public Bürgerschulen contained 4.2% and private Bürgerschulen .7% of the students.

Notes to Chapter Two

1. The spokesman was Josef Schraffl, Landeshauptmann of Tyrol. Quoted in Alfred Diamant, *Austrian Catholics and the First Republic* (Princeton, 1960), 81. Also Britta Skottsberg, *Der österreichische Parlamentarismus* (Göteborg, 1940), 147.

2. Quoted by Diamant, 116-117, from a pastoral letter of the Austrian bishops of August 4, 1918.

3. He justified his stand by saying that the Emperor himself had given authority to the people to form a government and cited Leo XIII's encyclical Immortale Dei which said that Catholicism is not bound to any particular form of state government. Diamant, 117.

4. Klemens von Klemperer, *Ignaz Seipel* (Princeton, 1972), 102. The cautious approval of Piffl was more characteristic of feeling in the episcopate than the diffidence of Sigismund Waitz, monarchist bishop of Tyrol.

5. Klemens von Klemperer, 124, quoting the *Neue Freie Press,* October 11, 1919 morning.

6. Address of Cardinal Piffl published in *Die Wartburg,* 14 Jg. No. 4, January 22, 1915, 32, quoted in Maximillian Liebmann, *Die Rolle Kardinal Piffls in der österreichischen Kirchenpolitik seiner Zeit* (unpublished dissertation University of Graz, 1960), 70.

7. Diamant, 118.

8. Protokoll of the Conference of Austrian Bishops on 22-23 November, 1921 in Bishops Conference Archive, 1919-1923. He used the example of Christian Social farmers in Lower Austria who did not go to church while their Social Democratic couterparts did.

9. Funder, 602. Due to the unsettled status of South Tyrol and South Styria the actual figures are more complicated.

10. Erika Weinzierl, 136.

11. Vienna, Bishops Conference Archive, Karton 1919-1923. Glöckel set up the council on April 30, 1919 but waited ten months before asking for church representation. Letter of Glöckel to Piffl of February 28, 1920. Piffl Präsidial Akten, 1917-1920.

12. In Tyrol, 98.8% of the votes favored Anschluss. Cf. Charles A. Gulick, *Austria from Habsburg to Hitler* vol. 1 (Berkeley, 1948), 121.

13. They declared the privilege to be extinct on March 3, 1919. A. Kostelecky, "Kirche und Staat" in E. Weinzierl et al. *Kirche in Österreich 1918-1945* Vol. 1 (Wien, 1966), 207.

14. The decree (Z950/U) is published in *Volkserziehung,* 1919, Amtlicher Teil, St. I x.

15. Letter of Renner to Piffl, April 11, 1919. Bishops Conference Archive, Karton 1919-1923.

16. Though he claimed to have resigned on April 11, the resignation was published on April 16 in the *Neue Freie Presse* evening, p. 3.

17. Report in the *Neue Freie Presse,* April 20, 1919, p. 9.

18. Ibid., April 5, 1919 evening, p. 3.

19. Ibid., April 20, 1919, p. 9.

20. A signed copy of the letter of April 22, 1919 is in the Bishops Conference Archive, Karton 1919-1923.

21. *Neue Freie Presse,* April 24, 1919, morning, p. 4.

22. For fuller discussion see Chapter 4.

23. Copy of a speech to the Christian Social Congress March 1, 1920 found in Piffl Präsidial Akten 1917-1920, Paket 2.

24. *Neue Freie Presse,* April 24, 1919, morning, p. 6.

25. Friedrich Funder Archive, Seipel folder No. 165. Letter of Glöckel to Seipel, April 26, 1919.

26. *Neue Freie Presse,* April 28, afternoon, p. 5-6.

27. Letter of Renner to Piffl, May 4, 1919. Bishops Conference Archive, 1919-1923.

28. Bishops Conference Archive, 1919 Z 115/Pr. Information in letter of Piffl to the other Austrian bishops of June 20, 1919.

29. "Hiemit ist die bezügliche Aktion zum vorläufigen Stillstand gelangt und es ist zu hoffen, dass wenigstens für die allernächste Zeit neue Vorstosse auf diesem Gebiet von Seite der Regierung umso weniger unternommen werden dürften, als die Abgeordneten der chrstlsoz. Partei nunmehr für eine mehr grundsätzliche Politik und energischere Taktik sich einzusetzen scheinen." Ibid.

30. Cf. Chapter 1, note 32.

31. In May 1927, when it was too late to settle anything, the Constitutional Court (Z.B389/26) timidly applied the treaty to children whose parents changed or dropped their religion between their children's baptism and the age of seven when compulsory schooling began. Once in

school, though, children could not follow their parents in changing or dropping their religion, at least insofar as religious education was concerned. They had to attend religion classes and religious exercises because, the court said, the Treaty of St. Germain had not changed paragraph 1 of the Elementary School Law. Cf. *Neue Freie Presse,* May 25, 1927, evening p. 2-3.

32. The agreements were published in both the *Reichspost* and the *Arbeiter-Zeitung* of October 18, 1919.

33. Seipel's authorship is identified on the copy in the archive but the supposition that the other outline is by Hussarek rests on Piffl's letter to the committee members which mentions that an outline by Hussarek accompanied the letter. Another letter to Hussarek thanks him for his outline. Letters of Piffl, January 24 and 25, 1920. Piffl Archive, 1920.

34. Robert Prantner, *Kath. Kirche und christliche Parteipolitik in Österreich im Spiegel der Kath. Presse der Erzdiözese Wien* . . . (unpublished dissertation, University of Vienna), 21. Also Protokoll of the First Conference of the Austrian Bishops in Vienna on November 9 and 10, 1920, p. 3. ". . . auch nehmen chrisliche Parteiführer beständing Fühlung mit Sr. Eminenz Kardinal in Wien."

35. Kelsen was neokantian in separating ethics from metaphysics. He rejected natural law because it was not grounded in the autonomy of man. For analysis and criticism from the natural law standpoint cf. Johannes Messner, *Das Naturrecht* (Innsbruck, 1950), 180-181, 210, 244-245.

36. Kelsen later succumbed to the temptation to associate the rational-empirical world view with democracy as its political expression. The mythico-religious world view, he said, finds its political expression in autocracy. *Staatsform und Weltanschauung,* (Tübingen, 1933).

37. Friedrich Funder, *Vom Gestern ins Heute* (Wien, 1952), 641-642.

38. "Heraus mit der Verfassung": in Ignaz Seipel, *Der Kampf um die ös. Verfassung* (Wien, 1930), 83-86. Michael Mayr was invited to the conferences in February and April 1920 in a personal capacity as the author of a constitutional outline.

39. Oskar Achs and Albert Krassnigg, *Drillschule-Lernschule-Arbeitschule* (Wien, 1974), 84-91. Short summaries of each are provided.

40. Article 14 of the new constitution read laconically, "In the area of schools, education and people's training, the sphere of activity of the

federal government and the provinces will be regulated by a special constitutional law." Bundesgesetzblatt No. 1. For discussion of the legalities
involved, see Hermann Zeissl, "Die Rechstsorganization des Pflichtschulwesens . . ." in *100 Jahre Unterrichtsministerium,* Egon Loebenstein,
ed. (Wien, 1948), 188-189.

41. In 1926 the parties thought it would be a relatively simple matter
to close a loophole in earlier legislation by way of agreement among the
Provinces and the Nationalrat. The law did not specify whether children
reaching their fourteenth birthdays could leave school immediately or
should finish out the year of school they had begun. A bill to make
pupils finish the year passed the Nationalrat in July 1928, but to name
the most extreme example of foot dragging, the province of Salzburg
had to be forced to accept the law in 1938. Cf. Chapter 6, footnote 40.

Notes to Chapter Three

1. On January 6, 1920, Seipel publicly expressed disillusionment
with the coalition and predicted gains for the Christian Socials in the next
elections. Friedrich Funder, *Vom Gestern ins Heute,* 70.

2. Figures from Britta Skottsberg, 242. Cf. note 24 for bib. data.

3. "The Christian Social Party . . . has included the school reform
in its party program. Next to safeguarding the moral-religious education
of youth, which is a pillar of the Christian Social school program, the
education of youth to increased self-activity, joy in work and thus efficiency for the economy are the chief points of its school reform, which
ought to serve not party politics but the rebuilding of the state." Maria
Maresch, "Schule und Wiederaufbau" in *Reichspost* Oct. 30, 1920, 1-2.

4. Point No. 8 of Gföllner's suggestions to the Bishops Conference
meeting of November 1921 demanded proportional representation of
Christian Socials in the Reform Department. Minutes of the Conference
of the Austrian Bishops on 22 and 23 November 1921 in Vienna. Bishops
Conference Archive, Vienna. "Um die offenkundig religionsfeindlichen
Schulreformbestrebungen der politischen Gegner wirksam bekämpfen
zu können, muss in der sogenannten Schulreform-Abteilung des Unter-
richtsamtes der Christlichsozialen Partei jene ziffernmässige Vertretung
zugestanden werden, die ihr gebührt."

5. In Autumn 1923 the Reform Department was renamed the Department for School Science (Schulwissenschaftliche Abteilung). Hans Fischl says the name change hardly affected the work of the department at all. Hans Fischl, *Sieben Jahre Schulreform*, 28.

6. Ibid., 124, 126, 132, 81-82, 136.

7. Ibid., 114, 107-108, 94.

8. Prof. Dr. Rudolph Peerz "Outline for reform of Rural Schools" Allgemeines Verwaltungsarchiv Fasz 4159 z 5700. Minutes of School Inspectors' meeting at Traiskirchen AVA Fasz 142 z 16531.

9. E. Wienzierl, *Die Ös. Konkordate*, 140-141.

10. Glöckel also criticized the liberals and Pan-Germans on many occasions for the same reason. Cf. O. Glöckel, *Die ös Schulreform: Einige Feststellungen im Kampfe gegen die Schulverderber* (Vienna, 1923), 50.

11. As reported in the *Arbeiter-Zeitung* (Oct. 21, 1924, p. 7) Glöckel said, "A child belongs to its parents, it belongs to the totality of the parents, the state, and we will not tolerate an outsider getting between parents and children without being asked."

12. Seipel answered Glöckel by saying dryly that parents meant to him not a party or the state but the parents. *Neue Freie Presse*, Oct. 22, 1924 morning, p. 6.

13. April 15, 1921 evening, p. 1.

14. April 14, morning, p. 4.

15. For the text of the law erecting the City School Board cf. *50 Jahre Stadtschulrat für Wien* ed. by Dr. Hermann Schnell (Vienna, 1972), 22-43.

16. AVA Fasz 4203 z 5959/II and 120698/III

17. June 21 morning, p. 5.

18. June 22, 1921, p. 1.

19. *Neue Freie Presse*, June 23, 1921 morning, p. 8.

20. Prof. W. A. Hammer, *Neue Freie Presse* June 24, 1921 morning, p. 3, said the motto of the socialists seemed to be not "Bahn frei dem Tüchtigen" but "Bahn frei dem Parteigenossen."

21. Ibid., "We ought not, as we have cause to fear from the social democratic school reform, destroy the ideals of youth which are a most important moral support of mankind in the struggle for existence."

22. NFP, June 25, 1921, p. 10. Also AVA Fasz 4023 z 14615/III-8.

23. This echoed the Renner-Beneš agreement of 1920 but went considerably further in areas of trade relations.

24. Britta Skottsberg, "Der ös. Parlamentarismus," in *Göteborgs Kungl. Vetenskaps-och Vitterhets Samhälles Handlingar* (Göteborg, 1940), 296.

25. An example of the kind of harrassment the church objected to came in February of 1922 when the School Board decided to require religion teachers to take part in school inspections, from which they had been free heretofore, because of a cutback in teachers. (Glöckel to BMU 23 Jan, 1922 z 13542/22 Fastz 4674). The bishops answered that a decree from 1906 exempted catechists from such work, and when Glöckel replied that such a decree was not to be found in the official register of 1906 Breisky stepped in to say that the law required only that the church provide religious instruction. Any other duties should not be imposed. (Z3315/III-9 10 April 1922) Glöckel answered with a lengthy legal defense saying such duties were not exceptional and cited letters from 1906. Finally in exasperation, the Education Ministry declared that there was no doubt that the duties of religion teachers could not be expanded and admonished Glöckel that a lower office had no right to change the interpretation of a higher office (Z 13542 Fasz 4674 BMU to StSR). There was more harrassment over using retired teachers as religion instructors. Since the School Board would not allow it, there were no religion teachers at some schools (Z 11926, May 29, 1922).

26. Rieder was absent for this meeting but sent a representative.

27. Minutes of the Conference of the Austrian Bishops on 22 and 23 November 1921 in Vienna. Bishops Conference Archive 1919-1923.

28. Gföllner's nine point program is an instructive document. The substance of the points follows:

1. The school is an educational institute. Education is possible only on a purely religious-moral foundation.
2. The bishops fundamentally endorse confessional schools.
3. Religious-moral education requires compulsory religion class and religious exercises.
4. Repeal the Glöckel Decree as illegal.
5. The church claims the right to supervise religious-moral education.

6. The church claims representation under the law.
7. The bishops oppose the present school reform insofar as the socialist school is used as an ideal.
8. Proportional representation of Christian Socials in the Reform Department.
9. The bishops expect that the Christian Social party will represent church principles with unbending firmness (unbeugsamer Festigkeit). "The school is an ecclesiasticum, not just a politicum."

29. Piffl was recorded as saying "The purely materialistic tendency in politics has hurt so much else that a person has to cover with the term "Christian" a lot that is no longer Christian." Minutes p. 4.

30. Ibid.

31. There was some confusion among the bishops about the Breisky decree. Gföllner though it might have referred to the Glöckel Decree and visited Breisky to inquire about a "counterdecree" (Gegenerlass). Disabused that anything of the sort had come from Breisky's office, Gföllner wrote to Piffl to clear up the matter. Letter Gföllner to Piffl, Nov. 27, 1921, Bishops Conference Archive.

32. Max Liebmann, op cit., cites a letter from Hefter to Piffl of April 13, 1920 in which he suggests a complete breach rather than tolerate a worsening of the school and church question. p. 108.

33. Published in the Reichspost February 26, 1922.

34. The bishops habitually reversed the priorities of the liberals to make the phrase "religious-moral education" rather than the other way around.

35. Found in Bishops Conference Archive 1919-1923.

Notes to Chapter Four

1. Otto Glöckel, Selbstbiographie (Zurich, 1939), 227 pp. Pages 13-67 contain his autobiography up to 1918; the rest is filled in by editors.

2. Ibid., 29. He also tried to inject new life into another liberal organization called "Volksschule" but failed. Together with Seitz he founded the militant periodical Freie Lehrerstimme.

3. For example, in 1926 as he accused Seipel of making religion a business he said he held religion as "zu fein und über alle Diskussion gestellt." *Neue Freie Presse*, May 28, 1926, morning, 5.

4. Hans Fischl, *Sieben Jahre Schulrefrom in Österreich* (Vienna, 1926), 7, 9-10, 21, 24. This turned out to be an embarrassment on at least one occasion when 80% of the upper middle school students in Vienna petitioned Glöckel to keep religion as a required subject. Hans Kriegl, "Kirche und Schule" in *Kirche in Österreich 1918-1965* (Vienna, 1966), 304.

5. Glöckel put down these goals in a pamphlet put out in January 1917 called *Das Tor der Zukunft* (The Portal of the Future). For a fuller discussion cf. Oskar Achs, *Drillschule-Lernschule-Arbeitsschule* (Vienna, 1974), 60-65.

6. Karl Bühler's developmental psychology, for example, had little room for the influence of institutions on children.

7. Hans Kelsen's later attempt in *Staatsform und Weltanschauung* (Tübingen, 1933) to associate religion and myth with autocratic government implicitly united the papacy and Nazi Germany in a spiritual partnership. It corresponded neither to the Catholic universalism of the past nor to Catholic condemnation of nationalistic excesses. The national history of Austria in the 1920's is one of the best examples of a political struggle between science and religion.

8. Glöckel regularly used the word "Kindesgemässheit" (adaption to the child) to describe this combination of principles.

9. Cf. May H. Siegl, *Reform of Elementary Education in Austria* (New York, 1933), 108-110.

10. Achs, *Drillschule-Lernschule-Arbeitsschule*, 84-91, gives short summaries of each.

11. Cf. Viktor Fadrus, "Österreichs Schulbücher im Wandel zweier Jahrhunderte" in *100 Jahre Unterrichtsministerium* ed. by Egon Loebenstein (Vienna, 1948), 203-221.

12. Fischl, op.cit., 30-31.

13. Viktor Fadrus, *Die österreichischen Bundeserziehungsanstalten* (Vienna, 1924).

14. The only possibility was to fall back a year or more in school.

15. Fischl, 51.

16. Glöckel, *Selbstbiographie*, 200-201. Georg Gimpl was especially complimentary on the Federal Educational Institutes.

17. Leuthner's attack came on April 29, 1920. Maximillian Liebmann, *Die Rolle Kardinal Piffls in der österreichischen Kirchenpolitik
seiner Zeit* (Unpublished dissertation, U. of Graz, 1960), 83. He said,
"Instruction must be purely secular; that means it must be built up solely
on the results of science." The association of science and secularism is
striking.

18. Ibid. A copy of the speech is found in Piffl Präsidial Akten,
1917-1920, Diocesan Archives in Vienna.

19. For Catholic criticism cf. Johann Schmidt, *Entwickling der
katholischen Schule in Österreich* (Vienna, 1958), 140.

20. In 1915 Piffl wrote, "After the monstrous and gigantic struggle
of the nations a new war will break out, a Kulturkampf worse than that
of 1871." Quoted in Max. Liebmann, *op. cit.*, 70.

21. Minutes of the Conference of Austrian Bishops on November
22-23, 1921 in Bishops Conference Archive, 1919-1923. Price gouging
by farmers during the famine of 1919-1920 gave rise to criticism among
church leaders.

22. This was confirmed by a constitutional law of January 25, 1921
(Bundesgesetzblatt No. 85).

23. There are striking similarities between Burgenland and Alsace
which returned to France in 1918 with its Concordat with the Vatican
intact. Efforts to extend the secular school legislation of France made
by Edouard Herriot met similar resistance and failure.

24. Hermann Zeissl, "Die Rechtsorganization des Pflichtschulwesens"
in *100 Jahre Unterrichtsministerium,* 190.

25. Minutes of the First Conference of the Austrian Bishops in Vienna on November 9-10, 1920 in Bishops Conference Archive, 1919-1923.
Seipel was most concerned with the economy and said it afforded the
best opportunity for cooperation among the parties.

26. Seipel said it would be unfavorable to raise the school question,
but as the minutes record, "If it must come to that, it would in fact be
possible to set up the confessional school with the Social Democrats.
But confessional school means something different from earlier. The
free school must also be considered a confessional school." Ibid.

27. Piffl Archive, 1920.

Notes to Chapter Five

1. This was the reason Seipel originally gave for his resignation. Skottsberg, *op.cit.,* 316.

2. Cf. Walter Goldinger, "Der geschichtliche Ablauf der Ereignisse in Ös. von 1918 bis 1945" in Heinrich Benedikt, ed., *Geschichte der Republik Österreich* (Munich, 1954), 134-135 and Klemens v. Klemperer, *Ignaz Seipel* (Princeton, 1972), 244-246.

3. Minutes of the Austrian Bishops Conference meeting of Nov. 22-23, 1921, p. 12 Bishops Conference Archive, Vienna.

4. Klemperer (*op. cit.,* p. 176) found in the minutes of the Christian Social party caucus that Seipel had first made the demand there. He cites material from the Schmitz Archive Karton VIII. Karton VIII was missing when I examined the Schmitz Archive.

5. *Arbeiter-Zeitung,* May 31, 1922, p. 1.

6. The socialist experiment on separating the offices of Education and Public Worship had already been given up and the offices reunited administratively.

7. Hans Fischl, *Sieben Jahre Schulreform in Ös.,* p. 28 says that the department was renamed but that the work suffered not at all.

8. Ibid., 77. Fischl counted 552 lectures delivered between 1920 and 1924.

9. Ibid., 54.

10. Glöckel, too, had to recognize the state of affairs although he disliked releasing teachers. In September, 1924 he closed 350 to 400 classes in Vienna. In response to urgent meetings called by parents he gave explanations and assurances that received comparatively little adverse comment from the Catholics. *Reichspost* Sept., 25, 1924, p. 5 and Sept. 26, 1924, p. 5.

11. Fischl, Ibid., 52-53.

12. Charles Gulick, *Austria from Habsburg to Hitler* Vol. 1 (Berkeley, 1948), p. 601.

13. There was a vast number of organizations formed by the socialists to preserve the integrity of the workers' movement by isolating them from contact with people of different opinions. There were, for example, Marxist rabbit breeders' associations, Socialist Friends of Animals, associations of socialist Esperanto students and socialist mandolin players

in addition to gymnastics and sporting groups, burial associations and many more. Cf. Gulick, 644-682.

14. *Reichspost,* August 23, 1922, morning p. 3.

15. *Reichspost,* August 24, 1922, morning p. 3. According to M. Liebmann, Ibid., 97, Glöckel claimed that Piffl had stopped the decree. This ignores the broader base of the reaction among Catholic laymen. Letter of Erzbischöfliche Ordinariat to Bundesministerium f. Unterricht, 25 Aug. 1922. Allgemeines Verwaltungsarchiv, F 4668 8/25/22.

16. Weinzierl, *Die ös. Konkordate,* 141.

17. Ibid., 142. The socialist compaign of 1923 led 22,888 Catholics to change their religion in that year, up from 9,268 the year before. The number of those dropping religion entirely as opposed to changing religion rose from 4,723 in 1922 to 20,403 in 1923. Statistics from Statistisches Amt der Gemeinde Wien found in Nachlass Ernst Hefel, Karton 15. Allgemeines Verwaltungsarchiv, Vienna.

18. The experience of the Social Democratic Party in Germany was perhaps too far removed in time to benefit Bauer at this point. Radical voices prevailed at the time the party was founded in 1869 at Eisenach. In 1872 August Bebel, founder and leader of the party until 1913, said in the Reichstag, "If we bury heaven and its authority, then earthly authority soon collapses, and the consequences will be republicanism in politics, socialism in economics, atheism in religion." The phrase "religion is a man's private concern" entered with the Gotha Program of 1875; the formula helped unite the Lassallean and Marxist wings of the party, but Bebel and his followers interpreted it as meaning that religion should be eradicated from public life. By 1890 the atmosphere had changed. Wilhelm Liebknecht said at the Halle Congress that once the class state fell, the church would fall with it. He added, "Those among us who declare war on religion . . . do but strengthen the enemy." Bebel was unmoved, but motions against religion in party congresses kept dying for lack of support. Before the end of the century two Protestant pastors joined the party, creating a sensation, and in 1905 Rosa Luxemburg published a pseudonymous dissertation entitled *Socialism and the Churches* in which she said no one has the right to attack the religion of another. She criticized the churches for being unfaithful to the Gospel, that is, for being irreligious rather than religious. Cf. Owen Chadwick, *The Secularization of the European Mind in the 19th Century* (Cambridge, 1975), 80-85.

19. Letter of Rotter to Piffl, July 23, 1923. Piffl Archive "Schulsachen."

20. Other complaints coming in 1924 included not promoting religion teachers, refusing school rooms to children assembling for religious exercises, and sex education at too early an age as well as ongoing complaints about inconsiderate transfers and not filling vacant positions. *Reichspost* April 28, 1924, p. 4.

21. The changes in parliamentary strength become complicated because the number of seats in the Nationalrat was reduced from 183 to 165 between the elections of 1920 and 1923. Accordingly, the Christian Socials dropped from eighty five to eighty two seats, the Social Democrats from sixty nine to sixty eight and the Pan-Germans from twenty eight all told to ten. The Social Democrats went from 37.7% of the seats to 41.3%. the scope of their victory seems to be rather the work of analysts. Cf. Gulick, 689-691.

22. The words "in the true sense of the word" (im wahrhaften Sinne des Wortes) are in the interpretation of the *Neue Freie Presse* (Nov. 22, 1923, morning, p. 1) rather than in the speech itself. It was clear he meant this, and within a few years he began using the term "true democracy" in contrast with the reality of the Republic.

23. For an analysis and critique from the standpoint of the free market cf. C.O. Hardy, *The Housing Program of the City of Vienna* (Washington, D.C., 1934). For a socialist view see Gulick, 407-504.

24. Ludwig Rotter, *Das Ringen um die Schule der Freien Elternwahl* (Klagenfurt, 1958), 39-40.

25. Entwurf zur Reform der ös. Schulgesetzgebung found in Bishops Conference Archive, 1919-1923. The preamble makes clear that the School Organization sponsored the discussion at the Katholikentag.

26. Rotter, 42-45.

27. Eventually the School Organization established 172 Catholic parents' organizations for the Vienna public schools. Ibid., 42.

28. Ibid.

29. *Arbeiter-Zeitung* October 19, 1924, morning p. 1. The paper said such a system would enable every small town to insist on four different schools, a public school and one each for the three major religions.

30. I am telescoping matters a bit. In March 1923 Gföllner wrote to Piffl about a proposed letter concerning lifting of the decree. He was

double checking on a report from Pfeneberger that Piffl wanted to put off sending the letter until after the national elections. He agreed with the suggestion, one reason being that Dr. Schneider did not appear to have the necessary energy to pursue repeal of the decree. Letter Gföllner to Piffl, March 10, 1923. Bishops Conference Archive, 1919-1923. This corroborates socialist opinion about the listlessness of Schneider.

31. The Breisky decree of June 1921 had interpreted the earlier decree in the light of existing laws, but perhaps the bishops were unaware of it or considered it insufficient.

32. Copy of letter dated January 14, 1924 in Bishops Conference Archive, 1924-25.

33. Letter Schwimmer to Piffl, January 6, 1924. Bishops Conference Archive, 1924-25.

34. The letter was dated January 20, 1924. Bishops Conference Archive, 1924-25.

35. Letter Schwimmer to Piffl, January 22, 1924. Letter Gföllner to Piffl, February 1, 1924. Bishops Conference Archive, 1924-25.

36. *Reichspost,* April 28, 1924, p. 4. Piffl was informed ahead of time about Christian Social intentions in Vienna and apparently approved. Letter of Rotter to Piffl, May 7, 1924. "Bei unserer Besprechung, die wir anlässlich der Vorberatung über die Beschlüsse des Wiener Christlichsozialen Parteitag bei Eurer Eminenz hatten . . ."

37. Much of the letter is published in Rotter, 48-49.

38. Seipel's speech to the national party congress in November contained much the same wording. Cf. Hans Kriegel, "Kirche und Schule" in *Kirche in Österreich 1918-1965,* 305-306.

39. Letter Seipel to Piffl, October 18, 1924. Bishops Conference Archive, 1924-25.

40. *Neue Freie Presse* October 19, 1924, morning, p. 8, and October 20, pp. 1-2.

41. *Arbeiter-Zeitung,* October 19, 1924, morning, p. 1.

41A. Rotter, 66-67, 133.

42. *Arbeiter-Zeitung,* October 21, 1924, p. 7.

43. Stenographisches Protokoll, 59 Sitzung des Nationalrates; II Gesetzgebungsperiode, p. 1652.

44. *Neue Freie Presse,* October 22, 1924 morning, 6. This contradicted a pessimistic appraisal contained in his letter to Piffl of October

18 in which he said, "It is naturally another matter in a country in which the struggle over the school appears already to be lost for good. . ." Bishops Conference Archive, 1924-25.

45. The *Neue Freie Presse* put the size of the crowd at 6,000, the *Arbeiter-Zeitung* at 8,000 and the *Reichspost* at 2,000. The *Reichspost* estimate drew caustic comment from the *AZ* the next day even as its was quietly revising its own estimate down to between 6,000 and 7,000.

46. Rotter, 55.

47. Rotter, 56. Further information on this meeting is lacking. The Christian Socials did not abandon Rotter altogether. When Glöckel fired Rotter shortly thereafter from his job at the Pedagogical Institute of Vienna the new Chancellor Ramek interceded and had him kept on. Rotter resigned not long afterwards to devote himself full time to the School Organization. Glöckel was probably justified in objecting to his massive moonlighting.

48. Schmidt, *op. cit.,* 152-153. Substantial quotation from the speech on pp. 209-210.

49. Neue Politische Akten 275 No. 381, 390, 392. Haus, Hof and Staatsarchiv, Vienna.

50. Official minutes of the meeting appear to be lacking. None are contained in the Bishops Conference Archive, Piffl Archive or Archive in St. Pölten. Rössler took notes which are preserved in the Archive in St. Pölten. The proceedings on the school question are patched together from Weinzierl, *Kirche in Osterreich,* 30 and Rotter. In the light of objections about the proceedings of the Bishops Conference that came up after this meeting it is not surprising that no official minutes were kept. It had happened before.

51. Rössler Karton 5, Diozesanarchiv St. Pölten.

52. Rotter, 66.

53. Weinzierl, 30.

54. Rotter, 72.

55. He said, "Even though my words about a spiritual regeneration, a regeneration of souls have been ridiculed so often, I adhere to them strongly. . ." *Neue Freie Presse,* November 21, 1924.

56. Weinzierl, 31. A copy of the suggestions signed by Rössler is in the Diozesanarchiv, St. Pölten, Rössler Karton 5.

57. Letter of Schneider to Piffl, November 21, 1924. Bishops Conference Archive 1924-25.

Notes to Chapter Six

1. *Neue Freie Presse* November 21, 1924 morning p. 3. Also Skottsberg 313-315.

2. This occurred on July 29-30, 1925.

3. Cf. Hans Kelsen, *Österreichisches Staatsrecht* (Tübingen, 1923), 209-214. The Constitutional Court could direct the legislature to change the law, but the Nationalrat could change the Constitution, including the parts dealing with the power of judicial review, except for the Treaty of St. Germain.

4. *Neue Freie Press,* October 19, 1925, evening p. 5.

5. Adam Miterlehner case, published October 22, 1925, *Neue Freie Presse,* October 22, 1925, evening, p. 2.

6. Max Hussarek, "Die kirchenpolitische Gesetzgebung der Republik Österreich," in Alois Hudal, *Katholizismus in Österreich* (Innsbruck, 1931) 36.

7. Minutes, p. 12-13. Bishops Conference Archive.

8. I presume the existence of the protest from a letter of Gföllner to Piffl of January 11, 1926 thanking him for a copy of the letter. Bishops Conference Archive, 1926-27.

9. Cf. Ch. 2 p. 32.

10. *Neue Freie Presse,* May 17, 1927, morning, p. 7. A law of April 9, 1870 regulated the status of children who did not have a religion in most particulars, but left the question of religious instruction unsettled. Cf. Karl Umlauf." Religiöse Schulprobleme in Österreich," in Alois Hudal, 107.

11. Hussarek, Ibid., 34.

12. Deixler case Z. A346/4. Hussarek, ibid., 34.

13. Josef Pfeneberger echoed the government in a letter to Piffl when he wrote, "Regarding the question about how *Konfessionslosigkeit* should be judged legally, I think the following should be considered: until now *Konfessionslosigkeit* did not have legal status as a *Konfession.*

It is not at all certain despite the judgment of the Administrative Court of January 18, 1924 that this interpretation has become untenable through the Treaty of St. Germain." Letter Pfeneberger to Piffl November 18, 1925. Bishops Conference Archive, 1925.

14. Hussarek, 29, describes the decision as a "Versuch das Getriebe amerikanischen Sektenunwesens auf unsere Heimaterde zu verpflanzen."

15. Glöckel speech to Nationalrat, *Neue Freie Presse,* May 28, 1926, morning, p. 5.

16. *Neue Freie Presse,* March 30, 1927, morning, p. 5.

17. Ibid., May 17, 1927, morning, p. 7.

18. Z. B389/26.

19. *Neue Freie Presse,* May 25, 1927, evening p. 2-3.

20. Karl Umlauf, Ibid., 108.

21. Paul Dengler, editor of the English edition of Robert Dottrens, *The New Education in Austria* (New York, 1930), 198, comments, "It can therefore not be denied that unfortunately those parents' communities sometimes become an outspoken political instrument in the hands of the leading party in Vienna." One example of pressure was to favor applicants with socialist sympathies for municipal apartments where low rents were charged and long waiting lists the rule.

22. For Seipel's views on dictatorship cf. Klemperer, *Ignaz Seipel,* 288.

23. Cyrill Fischer to Piffl, January 6, 1925, Piffl Archive, 1925.

24. Rotter, Ibid., 59-60.

25. Rotter wrote much later with ill-disguised satisfaction. "After the Second World War the Frohe Kindheit had disappeared." Ibid., 60.

26. Cyrill Fisher predicted this move in his letter of resignation to underscore the antagonism between the Christian Social Party and the School Organization.

27. Minutes of the meeting in Piffl Archive "Schulsachen."

28. The Germans reached agreement on interconfessional and confessional schools in July, 1927. A resolution of the German Katholikentag in August 1926 supported a new law based on parents' rights and freedom of conscience. Cf. *Neue Freie Presse* August 24, 1926 and July 14, 1927, evening, p. 3.

29. Rotter, 70-71. There is no other source for this contention.

30. Letters of December 7 and 15, Pfeneberger to Bishops Conference, Rössler, Karton 5 Diocesan Archive St. Pölten.

31. Letter Pfeneberger to Piffl, February 15, 1926 Bishops Conference Archive, 1926-27.

32. The *Reichspost* objected only that the number of schools was too high. July 24, 1925, p. 6.

33. Differences between the Reformrealgymnasium and the Realgymnasium (an extra year of Latin in the latter) seem to have been disappearing rapidly.

34. Glöckel could act with greater freedom in the case of Realschulen because they were financed and administered by the provinces rather than the federal government, as in the case of the Gymnasia. In spite of the need to upgrade the Realschulen and even the support of Schneider, the change in status faced a battle because it had to be fitted into a comprehensive scheme of middle school reform.

35. Letter Glöckel to Education Ministry March 20, 1925. Allgemeine Verwaltungsarchiv Fasz 142. Josef Pohl replied for the Education Ministry that no one else had a say in the agenda when Glöckel was Undersecretary for Education.

36. Oskar Achs, *Drillschule*, 106.

37. *Reichspost* July 19, 1925, p. 10.

38. Fifty-four percent of all middle school students lived in Vienna. Hans Fischl, *Sieben Jahre Schulreform,*, 79.

39. May H. Siegl, *Reform of Elementary Education in Austria* (New York, 1933), 113, provides the information. It is hard to agree with her conclusion that the advantages far outweigh the disadvantages.

40. Hard as it was to get a two-thirds majority in the Nationalrat for a school law, the way of paktiert legislation was much more difficult. The parties though they could use paktiert legislation (identical bills passed by the Nationalrat and each of the provincial Landtage) in the case of closing a loophole that was being used by children to leave school on their 14th birthdays rather than wait until the end of the school year. Seitz agreed with Schneider as early as May 30, 1926 that a simple amendment to the law could be done through paktiert legislation, but the provinces balked. The law passed the Nationalrat on July 7, 1928, but in March 1930 when Carinthia passed the bill it still had not been adopted by several other provinces Allgemeines Verwaltungsarchiv Fasz 4203 Z 3510, 10384/4, 18286, 21864 and Fasz 4205 Z 10993. The Province of Salzburg was finally forced to accept the law in 1938: AVA Fasz 4162 Z 23795.

41. *Neue Freie Presse*, October 22, 1924, morning p. 6. Stenographisches Protokoll, October 21, 1925, p. 1650. Also Letter of Glöckel to Education Ministry June 13, 1925, Allgemeines Verwaltungsarchiv, Fasz 4674 Z. 14673-II.

42. Allgemeines Verwaltungsarchiv Fasz 4668 Z 14673-II/8 as part of packet Z 2382/4.

43. Packet Z 2382/4.

44. Amtserrinerung March 3, 1926 signed by Johann Egger. Ibid.

45. Letter Schneider to Glöckel of January 30, 1926. Ibid.

46. *Neue Freie Presse* February 22, 1926, evening p. 3. This report corroborates Rotter's account in enough particulars to conclude that Rotter's figure of 40,000 may not be exaggerated. Rotter, 83-84.

47. Letter Schneider to Seitz and Glöckel, May 22, 1926. Allgemeines Verwaltungsarchiv Fasz 4668 Z13948/16. He published a report in *Volkserziehung* (Amt. Teil, St. II, 1926) and wrote to all the Provincial School Boards that might be affected.

48. Letter Seipel to Heinrich Mataja (Foreign Minister) May 29, 1926. Carbon of Letter in Funder Archive "Seipel" folder.

49. *Neue Freie Presse*, May 28, 1926, morning, p. 5.

50. Ibid.

Notes to Chapter Seven

1. On March 17, 1925, Schneider announced this intention in a speech to the Nationalrat. *Neue Freie Presse,* March 18, 1925, morning p. 6.

2. The difference in the arithmetic was accounted for by teacher training academies and experimental schools of various sorts. Report of Glöckel's speech in *Arbeiter-Zeitung,* June 12, 1926, p.2.

3. Ibid., June 1, 1926, p. 7.

4. *Arbeiter-Zeitung,* June 18, 1926, p. 3.

5. June 2, morning, p. 7.

6. June 6, 1926.

7. June 8, p. 2; June 11, p. 5.

8. June 8, morning, p. 6.

9. *Neue Freie Presse,* June 10, evening, p. 3 and June 11, morning, p. 18.

10. *Arbeiter-Zeitung,* June 12, p. 2.

11. Ibid.

12. June 16, morning, p. 2.

13. June 13, p. 6. The caption read, "Volksschule Lerhplan im Auftrag des Erzbishchofs erlassen, damit ich weiter Minister Bleiben darf."

14. Ludwig Rotter, *op. cit.,* 100.

15. *Reichspost,* June 13, 1926. The *Arbeiter-Zeitung* quoted the *Reichspost* as writing, "If the present Education Minister cannot dissolve the fateful compromise with Glöckel himself, he ought to leave it to a successor immediately." June 14, p. 1.

16. June 14, p. 1.

17. *Arbeiter-Zeitung,* June 15, p. 1.

18. *Neue Freie Presse,* June 15, 1926, evening, p. 1.

19. *Stenographisches Protokoll,* December 22, 1926, p. 4219.

20. *Arbeiter-Zeitung,* June 16, 1926, pp. 1-2.

21. The *Neue Freie Presse* reported that Glöckel said, "We do not want to be school masters, but masters of the school." The *Arbeiter-Zeitung* had a somewhat qualified version of the same statement. June 16, 1926, p. 6.

22. Ibid., p. 7.

23. *Schulreform, Demokratie und Österreich,* (Vienna, 1950), 58. The report of the *Reichspost* said that Schneider on his own initiative had decided already during the trip home from Cologne to resign. June 16.

24. *Sten. Protokoll,* December 22, 1926, p. 4219.

25. Haus, Hof- und Staatsarchiv, Neue Politische Akten, Fasz. 275 No. 475-478. Report of Ambassador Ludwig Pastor, June 18, 1926.

26. This was the judgment of the *Neue Freie Presse* which criticized Ramek. Funder apparently agreed at least partially. The *Arbeiter-Zeitung* cited him as saying that Ramek had gone to Geneva with the conviction that on June 7 the final reform of the curriculum would appear. June 16, 1926, p. 6.

27. The *Arbeiter-Zeitung,* June 18, p. 4, said, "But then Zelenka went wild." The *Sten. Protokoll* puts things matter-of-factly. "The Social Democratic deputies pound on their desks.—Great clamor.—Rushing up to the bench of Gürtler, Witzany snatches the manuscript from a stenographer

and shouts; Nothing doing! No speaking here! (Das gibt es nicht, dass hier geredet wird!)—A brawl ensues between Deputy Witzany and other Social Democratic deputies on the one side, and several Christian Social deputies on the other. June 17, 1926, p. 3630.

28. June 18, p. 3.

29. *Arbeiter-Zeitung,* June 19, p. 3. The demonstration had as another purpose to mobilize the workers in favor of the socialist Free Trade Unions in the elections set for June 26. It wholly succeeded in this objective. The Free Trade Unions in Vienna got 95,000 votes (87.6%) among the industrial workers (Arbeiter) to 6.5% for Kunschak's Christian Trade Unions and 4.16% for the Communists. Among the service employees (Angestellter), the socialists captured 38,000 votes (72.2%) to 13.2% for the Christians. *Arbeiter-Zeitung,* June 27, p. 1.

30. *Arbeiter-Zeitung,* June 24, p. 6-7. Also June 23, p. 5.

31. *Arbeiter-Zeitung,* June 21, p. 4 and *Neue Freie Presse,* July 20, morning, p. 8.

32. *Reichspost,* June 22, p. 3.

33. *Arbeiter-Zeitung,* June 23, p. 1. "Keine Illusionen, Herr Dr. Ramek!"

34. The proceedings are in the *Sten. Protokoll,* June 30, 1926, pp. 3641-3664. Richard Schmitz said the Social Democrats had to bear responsibility for the malfunctioning of the parliamentary system in Austria (p. 3657).

35. *Arbeiter-Zeitung,* June 25, p. 3. Official text found in AVA Fasz 4668 Z 11406/33.

36. By June 23 the *AZ* was becoming vague on what constituted repration of the breach of faith. It wrote, "The shameful breach of faith must be completely repaired, the threat of the clerical curriculum must be withdrawn from our schools—otherwise there will be no calm and no peace in parliament and outside parliament!" (p. 2). By July 9 the socialists were giving the government a clear option." If the resumption of normal parliamentary relations is a goal, then either the agreements must be implemented in their entirety or the decree of the Education Minister, which was the reason for these negotiations, must be abolished." *Arbeiter-Zeitung,* July 9, p. 3.

37. *Arbeiter-Zeitung* June 18, p. 1; July 15, p. 1, and *Neue Freie Presse* July 30, evening, p. 1.

38. July 3, 1926, p. 1045.

39. June 15, morning, p. 2.

40. Reported in *Der öesterreichische Volkswirt,* June 19, 1045.

41. *Neue Freie Presse,* July 1, evening.

42. AVA Fasz 4203 Z 19764/26.

43. The phrases "moral-religious education-by-doing," and "moral-religious educational methods," for example, received headlines in connection with the prosecution of clerics for sexual offenses. *Arbeiter-Zeitung,* June 25, p. 6; July 23, p. 10; March 14, 1927.

44. *Arbeiter-Zeitung,* July 31, p. 1.

45. *Neue Freie Presse,* August 1, 1926, p. 10, for agreements.

46. July 30, evening, p. 1-2.

47. Covered in the *Arbeiter-Zeitung,* August 10, 1926, p. 8. "Verbrüderungsfeste zwischen Land- und Stadtproletariat."

48. *Arbeiter-Zeitung,* August 8, 1926, p. 3.

49. Ibid., September 19, p. 3.

50. Ibid.

51. Cf. ch. 6 sec. III pp. 106-112.

52. *Arbeiter-Zeitung,* September 17, p. 6.

Notes to Chapter Eight

1. The party offered him the job back, but the Social Democrats felt so strongly about the nomination that they resorted to obstruction tactics in the Styrian Landtag to block his election. The Christian Socials then withdrew his candidacy. *Arbeiter-Zeitung* October 14, 1926, p. 3. At about the same time there were brawls in the Lower Austrian Landtag, indicating the poor health of the Austrian parliamentary system. *Arbeiter-Zeitung,* October 21.

2. Britta Skottsberg, 325-326.

3. Viktor Fadrus report to meeting of school supervisors at Traiskirchen. Allgemeine Verwaltungsarchiv Unterricht Fasz 142, Z 16531.

4. *Arbeiter-Zeitung,* December 24, 1926, p. 7.

5. *Arbeiter-Zeitung,* January 7, 1927, p. 6; January 8, p. 7; *Neue Freie Presse,* January 29, morning, p. 5.

6.   Both in its initial and final form the law spoke of the "fundamental protection of equality" (grundsätzlicher Wahrung der Gleichwertigkeit) with boys' schools.

7.   "I can firmly establish at the start that at *middle* teaching institutions the school youth...cannot be compelled to participate in church services because these schools are not compulsory schools." Letter Renner to Piffl May 4, 1919 Bishops Conference Archive 1919. Underlining his.

8.   These actions happened on July 22, 1921 and July 19, 1923 respectively. Hermann Zeissl in *100 Jahre Unterrichtsministerium*, p. 190.

9.   *Neue Freie Press,* March 27, p. 8; April 3, p. 8. For a fine account of the education controversy in France cf. John E. Talbott, *The Politics of Educational Reform in France, 1918-1940,* (Princeton, 1969).

10.   *Arbeiter-Zeitung,* December 21, 1926, p. 1. A provincial regulatory decree of August 24, 1924 attempted to implement the law, but without success.

11.   *Stenographisches Protokoll,* December 11, 1925, pp. 2923-2944 for the debate.

12.   Haus- Hof- und Staatsarchiv, NPA Fasz 409 No. 363 ff.

13.   Reported by the school reformer Karl Furtmüller in *Arbeiter-Zeitung,* January 13, 1927.

14.   *Arbeiter-Zeitung,* January 21, p. 5.

15.   Paragraph 24 of the *Service Manual* said, "Private opinions of a professional nature (Private Sachverständigengutachten) may not be given without prior permission of the Minister." An article on the background of the decision can be found in the *Neue Freie Presse,* May 17, morning, p. 7.

16.   Quoted in the *Neue Freie Presse,* May 16, 1927, p. 3.

17.   *Neue Freie Presse,* March 19, 1927, evening, p. 2.

18.   *Sten. Protokoll,* May 19, 1927, p. 16. Also Skottsberg, p. 330.

19.   The texts are found as Beilagen No. 1 and No. 2, Nationalrat. III. Gesetzgebungsperiode.

20.   Though the curriculum for the reformed Bürgerschule was not expressly stated as it was for the Gymanasia, Realgymnasia and Realschulen, it was similar by implication in the legal stipulation governing transfer to the next highest class of the middle school without an entrance examination. Paragraph 5 no. 1 of Middle School Law and Paragraph 18B No. 1 in the Hauptschule Law.

21. *Neue Freie Presse,* June 27, evening, p. 3.

22. Much as Glöckel derided the conservatives for quibbling over names the summer before, the socialists did the same themselves. The names Bürgerschule and Oberlyzeum were as offensive to socialists as Deutsche Mittelschule and Allgemeine Mittelschule were to the conservatives. All disappeared from usage.

23. *Neue Freie Presse,* July 29, 1927, evening, p. 7. "Die Aechtung der Bürgerschule."

24. With Karl Leuthner a member of the negotiating team, it could be expected that the meetings would contain a good deal of rhetoric. Wotawa of the Pan-Germans said that it was often heard in the committee "if this or that is not done, then the laws would be unacceptable for the opposition." *Sten. Protokoll,* August 2, 1927, p. 253.

25. Schmitz Archive, Karton XVII.

26. Number 58 der Beilagen. Nationalrat. III Gesetzgebungsperiode. Paragraph 1, No. 2.

27. Ibid.

28. Ibid., Paragraph 5 No. 2.

29. As a result, a statement in the law that the curricula for both kinds of girls' schools were to be the same in the lower four classes had to be dropped. Cf. No. 1 der Beilagen. Nationalrat. III Gesetzbeungsperiode, Paragraph 6, No. 4.

30. Ibid., Paragraph 7, No. 3.

31. The reformers had been vaguely aware at least as early as June 1920, however, that legislation was needed. Viktor Fadrus reportedly told a meeting of school supervisors that the solution to the middle school problem lay not with educators but with the National Assembly. Allgemeines Verwaltungsarchiv Fasz 142 Z 16531.

32. *Sten. Protokoll,* August 2, 1927, p. 246.

33. Seipel is quoted as saying at one time he had to speak with Vicechancellor Hartleb of the Landbund about "an extremely delicate matter" (heisses Eisen). E. Weinzierl, *Die ös. Konkordate,* 182. When Hartleb replied that state support for Catholic private schools would entail a certain amount of supervision and control over curriculum, the proposal did not meet with the approval of the integral wing of the Christian Socials. This information was supplied to E. Weinzierl by a confidant of Hartleb, Dr. Friedrich Jölly.

34. Violent clashes were becoming more frequent. On July 9, when Nazis in full uniform demonstrated in Favoriten, a socialist stronghold of Vienna, they were nearly murdered, and on July 10 beatings took place in Klosterneuburg, a suburb of Vienna. *Neue Freie Presse,* July 11, morning, p. 1. "Jetzt ist's aber genug!"

35. Letter Schober to Education Ministry September 23, 1927. Allgemeines Verwaltungsarchiv Fasz 4204 Z 3671/29 (complete packet on the question). Also Fasz 4204 Z 19889/1928 for order signed by Johann Egger on July 17, 1928.

36. *Sten. Protokoll,* August 2, 1927, p. 249.

37. Number 60 der Beilagen. Nationalrat. III Gesetzgebungsperiode. Artikel I.

Notes to Chapter Nine

1. Allgemeines Verwaltungsarchiv Fasz 4161 Z 1240/1928.
2. Z 16847 I/4.
3. Published in *Volkserziehung,* Päd. Teil St. I January 1, 1928.
4. All. Verwaltungsarchiv, Fasz 4161 Z 1240.1928.
5. Letter Glöckel to BMU February 1, 1928, Fasz 4161.
6. Letter of RectorPöschl of University of Graz to BMU, Fasz 4161.
7. A letter of the Chancery office to BMU of August 9, 1928 received the reply that no forms were being used at that time. The Chancery first complained to the School Board but received no satisfaction. All. Verwaltungsarchiv Fasz 4674.
8. His letter was written on September 21, 1931. All. Verwaltungsarchiv Fasz 4668 Z 5820/31.
9. The original proposal anticipated defiance from the City Council over possible changes in the makeup and functions of the School Board. Until constitutional regulation of relations between the Bund and the Länder on the schools, legislation affecting the School Board would follow the usual "paktiert" model of agreement between the Bund and the Vienna City Council. If the City Council and federal legislature did not agree on a plan to regulate the makeup and function of the School Board under the future constitutional law, the federal government would be

entitled to regulate the School Board directly through federal law. Cf. I.
Seipel, *Der Kampf um die ös. Verfassung*, p. 309.

10. Ibid., 343-344.

11. Ibid., 354.

12. In the case of conflict between the Education Ministry and a
collegial board, the law prescribed the usual system of recourse to the
courts as high as the Administrative Court. Ibid., 343-344.

13. I could find no evidence of communication between the bishops
and Seipel on the matter, however.

14. Minutes of Bishops Conference meeting of November 26-27,
1928. Bishops Conference Archive.

15. Ibid.

16. Rotter, *Das Ringen*, 131.

17. Ibid., 117.

18. E. Weinzierl, *Die ös. Konkordate*, 195. A government memorandum of May 1931, however, put the schools in their proper place
as the second most important question to be regulated. Haus-Hof- und
Staatsarchiv NPA Fasz 317 p. 591.

19. *Rappresentanti in terra*, December 31, 1929, paragraphs 79 and
81.

20. Weinzierl, 196.

21. Haus-Hof- und Staatsarchiv, Fasz 317, p. 591.

22. Weinzierl, 196.

23. Ibid., 199.

24. Ibid., 200-201.

25. Schuschnigg's first encounter with Glöckel was the source of
some amusement in the Nationalrat. In answer to an attack on the state
of morals among school children in Vienna, Glöckel replied that according
to Dr. Schuschnigg, an official from Tyrol, 30% of the school children there
used alcohol. When a voice from the benches objected that he was quoted incorrectly, Glöckel asked who had the audacity (Kühnheit) to accuse
him so. A chorus responded that it was Schuschnigg himself. Glöckel
answered with a smile and that he was delighted to meet Dr. Schuschnigg
in such an extraordinary way; he said he was merely quoting from the
newspapers. *Neue Freie Presse*, May 20, 1927, morning, p. 1.

26. Haus-Hof- und Staatsarchiv, Fasz 317 No. 707.

27. Weinzierl, 208.

28. Haus-Hof- Und Staatsarchiv, Fasz 318 No. 271.

29. Typescript of diaries of Egon Loebenstein in All. Verwaltungs-archiv, Nachlass Ernst Hefel, p. 18. A xerox copy of the Loebenstein diary is in possession of the author through the graces of Fr. Dr. Anna Coreth and Dr. Walter Goldinger at the Staatsarchiv. The Hefel Nachlass has since been transferred to the Verwaltungsarchiv but has not been catalogued. An attempt by the author to locate the Loebenstein diaries in the Verwaltungsarchiv proved unsuccessful in 1982.

30. Loebenstein diaries, 42.

31. *Arbeiter-Zeitung,* June 14, 1926. Technically, Kamprath was a delegate of the Holy See in the negotiations. Loebenstein, p. 24.

32. Loebenstein diary, 27.

33. Cf. Rudolph Morsey, *Das Ende der Parteien,* (Dusseldorf, 1960), 363.

34. Weinzierl, 213, is under the impression that Dollfuss' visit was responsible for the speed of subsequent negotiations. The Loebenstein diary indicates that Pacelli expected Schuschnigg and Loebenstein at the end of March. Loebenstein was chosen to go no later than April 9. Loeben-stein diary, 13-14.

35. Loebenstein, 24.

36. Ibid., 28, "whereupon the matter was taken care of" (worauf die Sache erledigt war).

37. Erika Weinzierl, 228, is aware that the Concordat was renego-tiated but more or less concludes her discussion of the Concordat at this point. With the appearance of the Loebenstein diary the story can be pursued in more detail over the course of the next eleven months.

38. Loebenstein, 43.

39. Haus-Hof- und Staatsarchiv, Fasz 318, No. 397 and 399.

40. Ibid., No. 366, "stark unangenehme Überraschung."

41. Weinzierl, 261. For discussions within the government cf. Loeben-stein, 58, 63.

42. Loebenstein, 16, 18.

43. All. Verwaltungsarchiv, Fasz 4668 Z 11406/33.

44. Ibid.

45. Fasz 4668 Z 38784/34.

46. In this type of school Latin was confined to the last four years.

47. All. Verwaltungsarchiv Fasz 4162 Z 7769/1934.

48. Ludwig Battista, *100 Jahre Unterrichtsministerium,* 163.

49. *Reichspost*, January 21, 1936.

Notes to Epilogue

1. This eliminated differences in conditions of service among the Länder. Celibacy, for example, had been required for female teachers in some provinces.

2. Max Neugebauer, "Schulwesen" in *Österreich, Die Zweite Republik*, ed. by Erika Weinzierl and Kurt Skalnik, vol 2 (Graz, 1972), p. 326.

3. Ibid., 330.

4. The school patron paid the costs of the school and then had a voice in hiring the teacher.

5. Neugebauer, 331.

6. Ibid., 333.

7. Ibid., 336.

8. An article in *Die Presse* of May 22, 1975 indicated the dream was still alive. Under the headline "Gesamtschule schon bis 1985" the paper wrote, "Schnell (School Board President) sees the advantages of the Gesamtschule in genuine equality of opportunity for all pupils; beyond that, the final decision on a vocation would be put off until the age of 14." Little has changed since. Another article in *Die Presse* of December 22, 1981 under the headline "Mock zeigt Härte: Keine SP-Mittelschule" says, "Mock's position on any foreseeable reform of the school for ten to fourteen year olds is adamant: 'Latin is staying. And if anyone believes the 'Middleschool' is coming, he is deceiving himself.'" Alois Mock was head of the People's Party.

9. Erika Weinzierl, "Die katholische Kirche" in *Österreich, Die Zweite Republik*, 289.

10. Ibid., 294.

BIBLIOGRAPHY

Archives

Kardinal Piffl Archiv.

Österreichische Bischofskonferenz Archiv.

Allgemeines Verwaltungsarchiv—Wien.

Friedrich Funder Archiv (Haus- Hof- und Staatsarchiv).

Richard Schmitz Archiv (Haus- Hof- und Staatsarchiv).

Nachlass Ernst Hefel (Haus- Hof- und Staatsarchiv).

Government Documents

Allgemeines Reichs- Gesetz- und Regierungsblatt für das Kaiserthum österreich.

Bundesgesetzblatt der Republik Österreich.

BMU. *Österreichische Vierteljahrshefte für Erziehung und Unterricht.*

Bundesministerium für Unterricht. *Das Reichsvolksschulgesetz einschliesslich des Hauptschulgesetzes.* Wien: 1936.

Die Erfahrungen der Mittelschule mit der Volksschulreform Bundesverlag Wien, 1925.

Jahresberichte des k.k. Ministeriums für Kultus und Unterricht.

Die Mittelschule-Enquete im k.k. Ministerium für Kultus und Unterricht Wien: Holder. 1908.

Unser Staatsprogram: Fuehrerworte. Bundeskomissariat fuer Heimatdienst, Wien, 1935, 158 pp.

Verordnungsblatt des Bundesministerium für Unterricht 1918-1938.

Volkserziehung, Amtlicher Teil.

Newspapers

Arbeiter-Zeitung
Neue Freie Presse
Die Presse
Reichspost
Wiener Zeitung

Periodicals

Die Erziehung
Erziehung und Unterricht
Freie Lehrerstimme
Österreichische Pädagogische Warte
Der österreichische Volkswirt
Die Quelle
Schulreform
Die Schulwacht
Sozialistiche Erziehung
Volkserziehung, Pädagogischer Teil
Wiener Diözesanblatt

Books

Achs, Oskar u. Albert Krassnigg. *Drillschule-Lernschule-Arbeitschule:
Otto Glöckel und die ös. Schulreform in der Ersten Republik.* Wien:
Jugend u. Volk, 1974. 163 pp.

Austrian History Yearbook. Rice University, 1965-

Battista, Ludwig. *Die oesterreichische Volksschule.* Wien: Oes. Bundesverlag, 1937, 1946.

Bauer, Otto. *Die österreichische Revolution.* Wien: Volksbuchhandlung,
1923.

Bauer, Otto. *Schulreform und Klassenkampf.* Wien: Volksbuchhandlung,
1922.

Bauer, Otto. *Sozialdemokratie, Religion und Kirche: ein Beitrag zur Erläuterung des Linzer Programms.* Wien: Wiener Volksbuchhandlung, 1927.

Benda, Oskar. *Die oesterreichische Kulturidee in Staat und Erziehung.* Wien: Saturn Verlag, 1936.

Benedikt, Heinrich, ed. *Geschichte der Republik Österreich.* München: R. Oldenburg, 1954.

Bericht über den III allgemeinen österreichischen Katholikentag. Wels: Pressevereins-Buchdruckerei, 1892.

Bericht über den IV allg. ös. Katholikentag. Salzburg: Selbstverlag des Comités, 1896.

Bischöfliche Versammlung. *Actenstücke.* Wien: Wilhelm Braumiller, 1850.

Boyer, John W. *Political Radicalism in Late Imperial Vienna: Origins of the Christian Social Movement 1848-1897.* Chicago: University of Chicago Press, 1981.

Chadwick, Owen. *The Secularization of the European Mind in the 19th Century.* Cambridge (Eng.): The University Press, 1975.

Diamant, Alfred. *Austrian Catholics and the First Republic: Democracy, Capitalism and the Social Order, 1918-1934.* Princeton, New Jersey: Princeton University, 1960.

Dottrens, Robert. *The New Education in Austria.* Edited by Paul L. Dengler. New York: John Day, 1930.

Egger von Möllwald, A. *Österreichisches Volks- und Mittelschulwesen.* Wien: Holder, 1878.

Ender, Otto. *Die Schule in der Neuen Verfassung.* Wien: Jugend und Volk, 1935.

Engel-Janosi, Friedrich. *Österreich und der Vatikan,* vol. 2 Graz: Styria, 1958.

Engelbrecht, Helmut. "Die Diskussion um die Einheitsschule zwischen 1879 und 1919," *Österreich in Geschichte und Literatur,* 15 (1971), 2, 73-87.

Fadrus, Viktor. *Die österreichischen Bundeserziehungsanstalten.* Wien: Jugend und Volk, 1924.

Fischl, Hans. *Schulreform, Demokratie und Oesterreich, 1918-1950.* Wien: Verlag Jungbrunnen, 1950.

Fischl, Hans. *Sieben Jahre Schulreform in Österreich.* Wien: Jugend und Volk, 1926.

Fischl, Hans. *Wesen und Werden der Schulreform in Oesterreich.* Wien-Leipzig: Jugend und Volk, 1929.

Freie Schule Verein. *Die grossen Parlamentsreden ueber das Reichsvolks-schulgesetz. Zur Feier des vierzigjaehrigen Bestandes des RVG.* Hrsgr. vom Verein "Freie Schule." Wien: Verlag des FS, 1909.

Funder, Friedrich. *Aufbruch zur christlichen Sozialreform.* Wien: Herold, 1953.

Funder, Friedrich. *Vom Gestern ins Heute.* Wien: Herold, 1952.

Funder, Friedrich. *Als Österreich den Sturm Bestand.* Wien: Herold, 1957.

Funder, Friedrich. *Das weiss-blau-goldne Band: "Norica": Fuenfzig Jahre Wiener Katholischen deutschen Farbstudententums.* Innsbruck: Verlagsanstalt Tyrolia, 1933.

Glöckel, Otto. *Drillschule, Lernschule, Arbeitschule.* Wien: Verlag der Organisation Wien der Sozial-demokratischen Partei, 1928.

Glöckel, Otto. *Die Entwicklung des Wiener Schulwesens.* Wien: Jugend und Volk, 1927.

Glöckel, Otto. *Zur Fuenfzigjahrfeier des RVG: Der Motivenbericht Hasners und die parlementarischen Kommissionsberichte mit einem Geleitwort vom Unterstaatssekretaer fuer Unt. Otto Glöckel.* Hrsgr. Deutsches Unterrichtsamt. Wien: Manzsche Verlags und Universitaets Buchhandlung, 1919.

Glöckel, Otto. *Die österreichische Schulreform.* Wien: Volksbuchhandlung, 1923.

Glöckel, Otto. *Schulreform und Volksbildung in der Republik.* Wien: Volksbuchhandlung, I. Brand Co., 1919.

Glöckel, Otto. *Selbstbiographie.* Zurich: Verlag Genossenschaftsdruckerei, 1939.

Gulick, Charles A. *Austria from Habsburg to Hitler.* 2 vol. Berkeley: University of California, 1948.

Hantsch, Hugo. *Die Geschichte Österreichs.* vol. 2. Graz: Styria, 1968.

Hardy, Charles O. *The Housing Program of the City of Vienna.* Washington, D.C.: The Brookings Institution, 1934.

Haulik de Varallya. *Österreich der Konkordatsstaat.* Wien: Braumüller, 1859.

Hesse, K., S. Reicke, ed. *Staatsverfassung und Kirchenordnung:* Festgabe für Rud. Smend. Tübingen: JCB Mohr, 1962.

Hudal, Alois, ed. *Der Katholizismus in Österreich,* Innsbruck, Tyrolia, 1931.

Hussarek von Heinlein, Max Freiherr. *Die Krise und die Lösung des Konkordats vom 18. August 1855.* Wien: Archiv f. ös Geschichte. vol. 112, 1932.

Hussarek von Heinlein, Max. *Leitsätze und kritische Betrachtungen zur Schulreform in Österreich.* Wien, 1920.

Janik, Allan, and Stephan Toulmin. *Wittgenstein's Vienna.* New York: Simon Schuster, 1973.

Jenks, William A. *Austria under the Iron Ring, 1879-1893.* Charlottesville, Virginia: The University Press of Virginia, 1965.

Johnston, William M. *The Austrian Mind.* Berkeley: University of California Press, 1972.

Kann, Robert A. *The Multinational Empire: Nationalism and National Reform in the Habsburg Monarchy 1848-1918.* 2 vol. New York: Octagon Books, 1970.

Kelsen, Hans. *Staatsform und Weltanschauung.* Tübingen: Mohr, 1933.

Kirche und Staat in Österreich. Hrsg. im Auftrag der österr. Bischofskonferenz. Wien: Selbstverlag der Sekretariats, 1955.

Die Kirche und das Staatsproblem in der Gegenwart. Forschungsabteilung des Oekumenischen Rates für Praktisches Christentum. Genf: Furche-Verlag, 1935.

Klemperer, Klemens von. *Ignaz Seipel: Christian Statesman in a Time of Crisis.* Princeton: 1972.

Knoll, August Maria. *Kardinal F. G. Piffl und der österreichische Episkopat zu sozialen und kulturellen Fragen 1913-1932.* Wien: Reinhold-Verlag, 1932.

Knoll, August M. *Das Ringen um die berufsstaendische Ordnung in Österreich.* Wien: Schriftenreihe des Oes. Heimatdienstes, 1933.

Kolmer, Gustav. *Parlament und Verfassung in Österreich.* 8 vol. Wien und Leipzig: C. Fromme, 1902-1914.

Krasser, Robert. *Kathol. Studententum in Österreich.* Wien: Verlag "Albrecht Dürer," 1947.

Krasser, Robert, *Ständestaat und Schule: Grundsätzliches zur ös. Schulerneuerung.* Wien: Schriften des Päd. Institutes der Stadt Wien, 1935.

Kremer-Auenrode, Hugo von, ed. *Aktenstücke zur Geschichte des Verhältnisses zwischen Staat und Kirche im 19. Jahrhundert.* Leipzig: Duncker & Humblot, 1873-1880.

Kunschak, Leopold. *Österreich 1918-1934.* Wien:Typographisches Anstalt, 1935.

Leisching, Peter. *Die Bischofkonferenz.* Wiener Rechtsgeschichtliche Arbeiten Band VII. Wien: Herold, 1963.

Liebmann, Maximillian. *Die Rolle Kardinal Piffls in der österreichischen Kirchenpolitik seiner Zeit.* Unpub. Diss.: University of Graz, 1960.

Loebenstein, Egon, ed. *100 Jahre Unterrichtsministerium 1848-1948.* Wien: Oes. Bundesverlag, 1948.

Maass, Ferdinand, ed. *Der Josephinismus: Quellen zu seiner Geschichte in Österreich 1760-1790.* Wien: Herold, 1951.

Macartney, Carlile A. *Problems of the Danube Basin.* Cambridge: The University Press, 1942.

Macartney, Carlile A. *The Social Revolution in Austria.* Cambridge: The University Press, 1926.

Messner, Johannes. *Das Naturrecht: Handbuch der Gesellschaftsethik, Staatsethik und Wirtschaftsethik.* Innsbruck: Tyrolia, 1950.

Papanek, Ernst. *The Austrian School Reform: Its Bases, Principles and Development–The Twenty Years between the Two World Wars.* New York: F. Fell, 1962.

Patzer, Franz. *Der Wiener Gemeinderat 1918-1934.* Wien: Jugend und Volk, 1961.

Piffl, Rudolph, and A. Simonic. *Geschichte der Erziehung und des Unterrichts, 3rd Edition.* Wien: Ös. Bundesverlag, 1938.

Prantner, Robert. *Katholische Kirche und christliche Parteipolitik in Ös. im Spiegel der Katholischen Presse der Erzdiözese Wien unter der Regierung Kardinal Piffls von der Gründung der Republik Ös. bis zum Tode des Kirchenfürsten (1918-1932).* Unpub. Diss.: University of Vienna, 1955.

Rabinbach, Anson. *The Crisis of Austrian Socialism: From Red Vienna to Civil War, 1927-1934.* Chicago: University of Chicago Press, 1983.

Reimann, Viktor. *Zu Gross für Österreich: Seipel u. Bauer im Kampf um die Erste Republik.* Wien: Molden, 1968.

Reimann, Viktor. *Innitzer, Kardinal zwischen Hitler und Rom.* Wien: Molden, 1967.

Rotter, Ludwig. *Das Ringen um die Schule der freien Elternwahl.* Klagenfurt: Carinthia, 1958.

Rotter, Ludwig. *Zielwege und Irrwege zur neuen Schule.* Wien: Herder. 1952.

Saurer, Edith. *Die Politischen Aspekte der oesterreichischen Bischofsernennungen 1867-1903.* Wien: Herold, 1968.

Schedlbauer, Leo. *Handbuch der Reichsgesetze und der Ministerialverordnungen über das Volksschulwesen.* 2 vol. Wien: Kaiserlich-königlich Schulbücher-Verlage, 1911.

Scheibner, Otto. *Arbeitsschule in Idee und Gestaltung.* Heidelberg: Quelle & Meyer, 1962.

Schmidt, Johann. *Entwicklung der katholischen Schule in Österreich.* Wien: Herder, 1958.

Schnell, Dr. Hermann, ed. *50 Jahre Stadtschulrat für Wien.* Wien: Jugend und Volk, 1972.

Seipel, Dr. Ignaz. *Der Kampf um die österreichische Verfassung.* Wien: Wilhelm Braumiller, 1930.

Shell, Kurt L. *The Transformation of Austrian Socialism.* New York: State University of New York, 1962.

Siegl, May Hollis: *Reform of Elementary Education in Austria.* New York: Columbia, 1933.

Silberbauer, Gerhard. *Kirche und Sozialismus in Österreich, 1918-1938.* Wien: Gerhard Silberbauer, 1961.

Skottsberg, Britta. "Der österreichische Parlamentarismus," *Göteborgs Kungl. Vetenskaps-och Vitterhets Samhälles Handlingar.* Series A vol. 7. Göteborg: Wettergren and Kerber, 1940.

Strakosch-Grassmann, Gustav. *Geschichte des österreichischen Unterrichtswesens.* Wien: A. Pichlers, 1905.

Stur, J. *Mittelschule und Bürgerschule.* Wien: Österreicher Bundesverlag, 1927.

Talbott, John E. *The Politics of Educational Reform in France, 1918-1940.* Princeton, 1969.

Verhandlungen des allgemeinen österreichischen Katholikentages. Wien: Mayer & Co., 1877.

Verhandlungen des II allgemeinen österreichischen Katholikentages. Wien: "St. Norbertus" Buchdruckerei,1889.

Verhandlungen des V allgem. ös. Katholikentages. Wien: Heinrich Kirsch, 1906.

Verhandlungen des VI allg. ös. Katholikentages in Wien. Wien: Ambros Opitz, 1908.

Weinzierl, Erika; Klostermann, Ferdinand; Kriegl, Hans; and Mauer, Otto, eds. *Kirche in Österreich: 1918-1965,* 2 vols. Wien: Herold, 1966-1967.

Weinzierl, Erika, and Skalnik, Kurt, eds. *Österreich: Die Zweite Republik.* 2 vol. Graz: Styria, 1972.

Weinzierl, Erika. *Die österreichischen Konkordate von 1855 und 1933.* München: Oldenbourg, 1960.

Weiss, Anton. *Die Entstehungsgeschichte der Volksschulplanes von 1804.* Graz: Styria, 1904.

Weiss, Anton. *Geschichte der österreichischen Volksschule 1792-1848.* Graz: Styria, 1904.

Wodka, Josef. *Kirche in Österreich: Wegweiser durch ihre Geschichte.* Wien: Herder, 1959.

Wolfsgruber, Cölestin. *Friedrich Kardinal Schwarzenberg.* Vol. I-III. Wien: K.u.K. Hof-Buchdruckerei, Mayer & Company, 1906-1917.

Wolfsgruber, Cölestin. *Joseph Othmar Kardinal Rauscher.* Freiburg: Herder, 1888.

Wolfsgruber, Cölestin. *Kirchengeschichte Oesterreich-Ungarns.* Wien: Heinrich Kirsch, 1909.

INDEX